Introduction

Kenneth Thunderburk

Contents

One

"The source of all things, the luminescence, has more forms than heaven's stars, sure. And one good thought is all it takes to make it shine. But a single mistake can burn down a forest in your heart, hiding all the stars, in all the skies. And while a mistake's still burning, ruined love or lost faith can make you think you're done, and you can't go on. But it's not true. It's never true. No matter what you do, no matter where you're lost, the luminescence never leaves you. Any good thing that dies inside can rise again, if you want it hard enough. The heart doesn't know how to quit, because it doesn't know how to lie.

You lift your eyes from the page, fall into the smile of a perfect stranger, and the searching starts all over again. It's not what it was. It's always different. It's always something else. But the new forest that grows back in a scarred heart is sometimes wilder and stronger than it was before the fire. And if you stay there, in that shine within yourself, that new place for the light, forgiving everything and never giving up, sooner or later you'll always find yourself right back there where love and beauty made the world: at the beginning. The beginning. The beginning." (Gregory David Roberts, "Mountain Shadow")

Two Forward

I remember the exact day I was separated from my immediate family: three sisters, two brothers and my father. I was in the middle of my tenth-grade year in high school in Whittier, California.

The prior year we all lived in San Gabriel in the back shed of my grandparents' house — all seven of us. I went to Gabrielino High School. I was one of only three other students in the whole school that played three sports in a single year. I played football, basketball and baseball. I was always super hyper and would piss off and annoy all my friends and teachers. I always got into fights, often after school. We would meet up behind the Blockbuster Music in the alley to fight — it seemed like the whole school would show up. Even though I was super skinny and short I was fearless and super-fast. I don't ever remember losing a fight, nor ever getting caught. It was like the sports I played made me want to get good grades — well, at least the two-point-three grade point average required to play. Somehow, twice I managed three-point-zero honor roll; I even managed to somehow pull off an award for Most Improved Student of the Year.

I guess cause the year before I was into all types of trouble, I just switched gears on everybody. The most dreaded teacher was Mrs. Krasinski. She taught English. Everyone hated her and she hated everyone likewise. Somehow she adored me and I likewise. I know, it's crazy right? My all-time favorite teacher. Anytime I hear an analogy I think about her cause every day on the dry erase board she would have a new analogy posted so the class could figure it out — no one ever could. But there I was every day with my hand going crazy like, "Over here! Over here!" She would take her sweet ass time then finally call on me like, "OK Kenneth what is it?" I would get it right every single day for reals. I used to look forward to her class — almost as much as I did P.E.

Anyways, as I was saying, we were all up using the restrooms getting ready for school — all 6 of my family, my cousin Beau who is now the lead singer to BLESSTHEFALL, my two other cousins Claire and baby Pascal, plus my aunt Monica and uncle Alex, my aunt's mom and dad—making breakfast and all types of shit. I'm in the restroom usually 'til the last minute trying to plaster down my hair with as much gel and hairspray as possible so it doesn't mess up while I'm at school during the day.

My Dad tells me I am not going to school today, that he's taking me to see my therapist. I was all like, "Hell yeah!" cause my therapist was Mrs. Nino, a short young cutie I loved talking to.

I jumped into my dad's work truck and while sitting in the front seat I noticed my dad putting my favorite Notre Dame Starter jacket in the trunk, which to me was odd. I have always been super perceptive, so I knew something was up. Driving away from my aunt and uncle's house, there was an awkward silence between me and my dad which was super weird cause if you ever met my dad, you would feel the love radiating from him.

Around my father there were never awkward silences. He is a very lively and humble man you automatically feel at ease around. He is a plumber for life as a self-employed plumber. He would take crazy jobs in the craziest places and cities at the oddest hours. He'd usually be in Chinatown, South Central, Los Angeles, even as far as being in the riches of areas such as Beverly Hills sometimes.

Well, quite often he would take me with him no matter the hour. I loved crawling under houses with him at 2am crawling through attics of closed restaurants in Chinatown. It would amaze me at my dad's lack of fear. At times we would pull up to a house with "Beware of Dogs" signs, five or six vicious dogs going crazy, my dad would simply just open the gate and walk up to the door and knock. The homeowner would just look at my dad and be all like, "Sir, my dogs..." My dad would just smile and be all like, "Who, these guys?" The big vicious dog would be laid on its back, feet all up in the air, tail wagging as my dad scratched its belly. Crazy, the whole time I would be outside the gate like, "Hell naw, I ain't going in there!" Even animals sensed the man's pure spirit.

He would often get into trouble with his company 'cause, say he would go to fix a leaky sink — he'd notice other stuff that needed fixing and he would just fix it, no worries, even though he was on company time. It just came natural to him to be a great man. I have yet to come across another man that comes close to his pure love and great heart, with the exception of my uncle Willie — my dad's twin.

I kinda knew the route to my therapist from previous trips and naw this wasn't the way at all. My pops had a somewhat sour look on his face like he was holding something in. He knew I wasn't stupid. My dad knows how clever and insightful his ADHD son was and he knew I knew something was up. It was like he was looking for a way to tell me something. Being honest, my intuition told me what was up: the night before, my uncle Alex hit his breaking point with me, and I knew they were done with me.

The previous day, my dad told me after school I could go to the park to play basketball in the gym and I was really looking forward to it too. My aunt's father usually picked us all up from school — me, my sister Jessica and my cousin Beau; we all went to the same high school, Cal High in Whittier, California.

We got home and I rushed to change and asked my aunt's father for a ride. He said, "No," that I couldn't go! I told him my dad already said that I could go. He said my dad never told him anything. So, I took my cousin's rollerblades and took off anyways.

I got back to the house at like 8pm. My uncle and aunt were home and were pissed. As soon as I walked in my uncle told me to sit at the table and he started to chew me out. I wasn't trying to sit and hear all that, so I got up to go to my room. He put his arm out, blocking me and kinda restraining me and physically pushing me back down.

In my mind I snapped.

I was fifteen. Up until about thirteen I was physically severely beaten by my mother almost every single day. The days I wasn't beat, I watched my older brother Kelly get beat, praying I wouldn't get it next. In all reality, my mother beat the fuck out of me, but my older brother got it way worse. I could only imagine.

My mother swore my older brother was the product of her being raped so she hated him and took it out on him at all possible times, usually for the smallest thing too, so you could imagine. Growing up at the time around my mom was like living in a real life mine field.

We had all kinds of animals: ducks, geese, goats, chickens, dogs, cats.... we had a dog named Kona; he was part wolf. He was the best dog ever. The goat's name was Billy and he was my best friend. I would curl up on the old sofa recliner we kept outside with him like he was a puppy until one day he suddenly disappeared. They thought I didn't know they ate his ass. We also had a goose named Scooter, he was always running down the street with the dogs chasing police cars and eating the neighbor's plants.

The neighborhood we lived in was called "Lomas" which was a barrio: a Mexican neighborhood and gang-related, but real close knit — all families and usually everyone knew each other.

The local gang didn't really shit in their own backyard so it was relatively safe unless the rival gang Sangra from the city of San Gabriel would roll in and do a drive by, which was usually about once a week. But we all learned to look out for the signs and avoid getting shot in the crossfire and stray shots. When those happened, you could hear my dad yell, "Kelly! Kenny!" no matter where we were in the barrio — he was that loud — that meant to get our asses home ASAP, so once it was clear we would run home as fast as we could.

The cops and ghetto bird would scour and patrol the area looking for the suspects. No one I could ever remember was ever caught nor shot due to the drive-bys. All-in-all it was a relatively decent place to live. Don't get it fucked up, all types of twisted shit went down.

For example, me and my older brother Kelly found a dead body that was dumped in a sewer behind my creepy neighbor's house in a place we called "The Warpath".

I can only describe The Warpath as a super huge open area full of trees and chest-high grass and rolling hills that was all the way down Bailey Street at the dead end. It reminds me of "the barrens" out of Stephen King's "IT" — if you have ever seen the movie you would understand. It has a "DO NOT ENTER" sign and a super high gate that was padlocked. We would jump the gate and go exploring — usually me, Kelly, and our two friends Chad and his older brother Snapper.

Anyways, there was this super high hill that was super steep, all dirt, that ran straight up behind our neighbor's house. The back of the house had a rope tied around this sewer entrance that was raised coming out of the ground about four feet high and the circumference of a regular sized manhole you find in the street, like those big heavy circle ones made of steel. We would pull ourselves up the hill using the rope. Once at the top, we had cardboard boxes we would flatten down and sit on like makeshift sleds and zoom hella fast down that hill, weaving through all that super high grass. Looking down onto that grass from the top of the hill, come to think of it, looked like crop circles — all types of flattened grass. We would aim at the fresh grass every time. It was more fun to go through the fresh standing grass 'cause you couldn't see anything — running blind. Once at the bottom, we would jump up and do it all over again, all day.

Everybody had noticed for a few weeks a strange smell in the barrio — no one could place it. My brother and I pulled ourselves to the top of the hill and I was all of a sudden drawn to that concrete encasement like a magnet. It was weird 'cause we had been on that same hill doing what we do for years — never did I ever give it a piece of mind other than to use it for an anchor for our rope.

I tell my bro, "Let's see what's in there."

Then, as if for the first time ever noticing it, he's all like, "Hell yeah."

I say, "How we gonna open it?"

Like a sign, we both see a large piece of rebar just sitting there like, *Here I am!*

I tell Kelly, "Let's use that piece of metal."

My brother picks up the metal rebar and sticks it in the little hole in the lid and pries the lid off halfway off. I help slide the lid 'til it's almost off, but it's heavy so we leave it part way on. Right away the smell is horrible but shit we are curious kids, so that overrides anything else. We both peer over the top into the hole. We notice metal rungs going down the side into the hole. The hole is too deep and dark to see the bottom, plus we are under tree cover so no sun shines down into it. Keeping it real, I was really hoping my bro would chicken out 'cause I didn't really want to go down in that hole — not without a flashlight at least.

So, I was all like, "Let's go get a flashlight fool."

So down the hill we go running top speed until we get to the long ass steep hill — ain't no way we are running all the way up that hill. We finally make it home but it's now about dinner time so shoot, we both forget about going back to the hole. We eat then jump on the Nintendo. Later we fall asleep. It's summertime so ain't no school.

At around lunch time the next day my mom mentions something about the smell which triggers my memory about the sewer, so I tell my brother, "Come on, let's go check this shit out."

We grab two flashlights and our skateboards and high speed all the way down Bailey Street, jump off our boards and slide through the gate. We pull ourselves up the hill.

We go to turn on the flashlights and wouldn't you know it, one of them is dead, the other one is hella low. I know, right?

My brother shines the light down into the hole, but it only goes about halfway so fuck it, I go first, taking the flashlight. I hurry down the stairs, hit the bottom and shine the light around the hole. It opens to about a six-foot room with a gutter cut into the center of the room going into a three-foot hole on each side like a drain. I immediately notice a large pile. I shine my light on it and step closer to see 'cause the dim flashlight ain't doing shit. My brother jumps and lands right behind me. We both see it at the same time — it's a dead body!

I do not even remember climbing back out the hole nor running back up Bailey Street. Next thing I know I am in our kitchen and my older brother is telling our mom. It was a big deal, I guess a dead body always is. To us kids it wasn't really shit, it was just the shock that got us.

Another time, my little sister Jessica and I watched out our room window as the neighbor Howard — from the same house of which the dead body was found — beat on his door to be let into no avail. A couple days later in a nursery they found his body chopped up in some trash bags.

Then a local kid named Andy Landeros who lived on the corner house across from our church was found murdered with "VSGR" Varrio Sangra Gang Rifa cut into his head.

My dad's best friend was a cartel drug dealer. His son Lil Victor who was older than me was my homie. Me, him, my brother Kelly and his brother Memo would play tag football every day in the street under the streetlights.

Oh yeah, and the infamous Night Stalker Richard Ramirez lived right around the corner. His sister Mrs. Ramirez was our school recess monitor. What a trip, huh?

My neighbor Don had these vicious dogs I used to tease all the time. One day during summer break little Don decided he wanted to invite me swimming in his back yard. I was all like, "Naw, hell naw your dog's gonna eat me."

He was like, "Naw they won't fool for reals. Come on let's go."

I was standing in his front room in nothing but my swimming trunks — all 70 pounds of myself — looking out these big glass sliding doors that opened up to his back yard as his big ass dog is growling and going nuts barking and trying to get into the house, pawing the screen door, drooling, and all that shit. I turned to look at his sister Tera and his grandma Mary. As I did that, little Don slid the door open. THE AKITA DIDN'T WASTE NO TIME. He jumped straight through the screen door and attacked me.

The weight of the dog dropped me flat on my back. His front paws were on my shoulders as his snout dug into my throat savagely ripping his head left and right as it had ahold of my throat. I was like a rag doll and the dog was trying to shred me to pieces, literally. I put up absolutely no fight — I was dominated. My eyes were wide open. I was conscious the whole time. All I could see was the fur on its head and I only felt tugs — no pain, just pressure.

No sound. It all happened so fast.

Suddenly the dog released me — the other dog attacked the Akita that was attacking me. For a second the two dogs fought, then the Akita turned back on me, biting the top of my head.

Somehow the savage attack was over, and the dog was off me. Someone closed the glass sliding door so it couldn't get at me anymore, pretty much saving my life 'cause for reals, it was not looking good me at that point.

I remember sitting up, then I stood up, looking around the room. I noticed everyone's faces: Mary the grandmother had her hands covering her mouth as if to cover her scream. Tera was crying. Don's eyes were as wide as saucers.

Still NO sound. All movement was slow motion.

I felt heat on my chest and stomach, so I looked down to see the source. My whole lower body was completely covered in blood — feet and all. When I looked down, I guess I must have pinched the wound in my throat 'cause blood started to spray out of my throat where as before, with no restriction, it simply just flowed out.

I raised my hand to inspect the wound. As I put my right hand up, touching my face, my two fingers — middle and pointer — slid all the way into my mouth! I then put my tongue in cheek and my tongue touched my fingers. The dog literally tore my whole face open. I then passed out, I guess due to blood loss and shock.

I awoke to Mary wrapping my head like a Hindu. They said the paramedics were coming. I told them I couldn't take an ambulance; it was too expensive.

The next thing I know, I'm at the ER. I don't remember how I got there, but I think my parents showed up and my dad took me. Three hundred sixty stitches and plastic surgery. I had to eat with a straw forever. It's funny 'cause even to this day I don't remember getting any of those stitches removed from my face and head, and I remember everything.

Anyways, my bad, I tend to go on one and get side-tracked and start talking about stuff that even though it pertains to my story isn't exactly on the subject I left off on. My bad, where was I?

Oh yeah, I snapped on my uncle Alex. Well, I almost did — he seen the look in my eyes and just moved out of the way.

The rest of my night was uneventful — I said the rest of MY night.

Pops usually showed up late at night and as soon as he stepped in the house, my aunt and uncle were on him. I don't know all what was said and though I can speculate, I won't. All I know is they both said they couldn't take me anymore — they had enough, and I had to go.

My dad had to do something. My dad was clueless as to what to do. I was his son, what could he do? I know the ultimatum they left him with was it was either me, or all of us. For a single father in the process of a heart-breaking divorce with six children that had no choice but to rely on the charity of so-called loved ones, he was mind-fucked and heart-confused.

He called all of us his Army. He meant that. He was a Marine, so it was a term of endearment: "No man left behind." Man, my stupid-ass aunt and uncle were never at all sympathetic to what we all just been put through — all of us, even my dad. They didn't stop to realize we were all fucked-up from severe physical and psychological — as well as emotional — abuse by my mom. My aunt being a psychologist was way off her mark — you would have figured she'd understand the underlying cause to my behavior was from what we all just went through.

The trauma I'm talking about — aside from the years of physical abuse — was in 1993. I was freshly healing from the dog attack. I guess my mom did something that had to do with check fraud with one of my dad's cokehead friends that got her in trouble. The verdict is she got kicked out of California. The first sign of duress was we couldn't take our beloved family dog Kona — he had to be put to sleep. That really fucked us all up. Kona had a special place in every one of our hearts. I swear that he had the same spirit that my father has. For reals. We all loved our neighborhood pets and friends so moving away was super hard.

We relocated to Phoenix, Arizona. My dad made the trip with us to help unload the U-Haul truck and only stayed a couple of weeks, then he had to go back to Cali to finish up a big job that he had. My mom stayed with us six kids — my sister Alyssa was still an infant.

It seems immediately after my dad left, so did my mom.

We were never enrolled in school — if we were, I don't remember. It seems like the only time we would see our mom was when she would come home with some dude named Greg. I'll never forget the night my sister and I laid awake listening to noise coming from my mom's room to me opening the door to see her having sex with Greg. That same night, my dad called. As Greg laid in his bed, my mom sat there telling my dad we were all good and she loved him. I remember that bitch ass fool laughing at my dad!

It seems months passed — no sign of my mom. My younger sister Jessica took charge. I still remember her putting something in the oven like she been doing it her whole life. She held us down — even my older brother listened to her.

I really don't remember too much else, but I know one day, me and my older brother were running around the neighborhood with BB guns and I guess someone called the police and said we had guns. I went in the house and next thing I know is there is knocking on our door. I thought it was my older brother knocking 'cause I locked the door so I opened the door and said something like, "What the fuck you want" with the gun aimed at him, but it wasn't my brother, it was the cops. Dang, I could have been shot dead by the cops right then and there.

I also remember we didn't have no phone — well, we did but my mom would take it when she left so we couldn't tell my dad what was going on. When we did talk to my dad, my mom would troll over us so we couldn't say anything except that we were all doing fine. Well one day my brother Kelly runs in the house with a phone. He plugs it in the jack, next thing I know is he's talking to my grandma — he told her everything! I went to sleep to later be awakened by an officer telling me to get my stuff together, my dad was there to take us. I thought I was dreaming! My mom was home that night and she was going nuts, talking about he couldn't take me or my brother Kelly since he wasn't our real dad. The cop told her straight out, "Lady, he's taking all of them," and he did. He and my uncle Willie did.

Up until that point, though a great man, my father was an alcoholic. I literally watched him quit cold turkey that day and take all six of us kids, put us on his back and never look back: NO MAN LEFT BEHIND.

I know it killed him that he had to leave his wife behind, but what could be do?

My aunt Vivian and uncle Willie took us all in, plus they had two kids of their own: Natalie and Noel. We all got along great; the only thing is we all had to sleep in the front room — they really didn't have any room. We stayed about a year. It was beautiful.

They loved us with no conditions — we all needed that desperately. The whole time, my mom kept playing head games with us all, especially with my dad. We were all messed up in our own ways — I had nervous ticks like I would snap my teeth together or shake my head all day, plus I would fight a lot, not to mention my ADHD. My baby brother Joseph pissed and shit his pants even when a toilet was available. My old brother Kelly was an emotional wreck. My dad stayed in his work and turned to The Word — I guess he was looking for an outlet.

My aunt and uncle were great. My uncle took me outside every day and taught me to play basketball. I know I was his favorite 'cause I took most of his time. When he used to take me to work with him, he would tell people I was his son and I loved it. My aunt was really stern but keeping it real, we needed it. She has always been great people — I love her dearly.

The love they showed us — even the love from my cousins — was drastically needed and is something I turn to even to this day when I'm feeling bad. To be around great people during our most trying of times was a blessing — we all knew we were loved dearly. Every single morning we were fed and sent to school with a lunch made by my aunt Vivian — all eight of us kids. She's crazy but it's something you can't fake or do half-ass. At no point did they ever show any kind of impatience, or that they were tired of us all. We all knew at any point a hug and love was just a touch away.

Thank you, Aunty Vivian and Uncle Willie and Nat, and Noel — you are forever in my heart.

We all wound up moving to the back house at my grandparents' house, which I kinda already told you about — it was a garage converted to a small one room, half bathroom bachelor's house. Super small, but for now it was home. I won't lie, it saddened me to have moved from my aunt's and uncle's house, but we all loved my grandparents so it wasn't so bad.

We started a new school which for me was Gabrielino High School. I was a freshman; ninth grade. We were all still battling our own demons — I was always in trouble in school. I was always super smart but I was just disruptive and always fighting. Drugs were never an issue for any of my family. I had cost my dad a fortune on therapists, but he never once complained. I always had a new glove and cleats for the first game of Little League baseball every year — we all did. I had good friends too, I was just embarrassed to ever bring them to my house 'cause like I said, we lived in a shack, literally. All my friends loved my dad — everyone did and still does.

I played three sports that year in a single year — it was called being a Golden Eagle. Only two other students did that — I was the only one to do it and make the Honor Roll, which is a three-point-zero grade point average or better for a semester. I just hid all the bullshit in my head in my sports. As for the schoolwork and stuff, I didn't even really think I was doing that well 'cause it seemed too easy. Like I said:

"They would say I was abnormal

'Cause I would overcome any task cordial."

-Nas

All my friends had an idea of my situation with my mom, but they all had both their moms and dads, so I never told anyone that I was beat or any of the ordeals I went through, nor did my siblings or I ever talk about it but on our weekly visits to the therapist.

Somehow my aunt and uncle convinced my father it was better that we all move to their house which was way bigger and had more supervision. I don't even know what they were thinking or why my dad decided it was also a better move — we were all happy and doing well and now here we were moving again. Three schools in three years! I honestly believe that was the beginning of the end of my real childhood and happy days 'cause everything since then has been all bullshit. I blame them. I know I could have been a different man if they even gave me half a chance. I wasn't a bad kid, just real hyper and mouthy. I didn't cut school, or get bad grades or do drugs.

Okay, back all the way up.

Me and my dad have been driving about an hour or so by now. I know for sure we ain't going to no therapist, and like I said, I kinda already knew where we were going — my gut told me. But it was like I was scared that if I voiced it, I would make it come real.

Eventually we pull into a Carl's Jr. My dad gives me a twenty and tells me to go get some food, so I go in and order. When I come outside, he is on the phone with someone and I hear him say, "It's okay, I'll see you in a minute."

I go stand next to my dad and wait for him to hang up the phone and I ask my dad, "See who soon?"

Those were the first words spoken the entire trip. He didn't respond.

About thirty minutes later my mom pulls up with her boyfriend Randy all excited like I should be excited to see her.

"What the fuck?"

I look at my dad. He is already in the trunk pulling out my stuff and taking it to my mom's car like he is trying to just get it over with, but at the same time he is hiding his face. I already knew he was hurting in his heart way more than I was.

I started to cry.

I didn't ask why; I already knew the whole play. I knew if I made a scene it would have killed my dad even more — it's like I wanted to spare my dad any more heartache than he already had 'cause I know if I would have pressed the issue he would have jumped out there and took me back and he would have told all us kids to "Pack your shit, we are leaving!" and I didn't want to put my bros and sisters through any more bullshit.

I took it like a soldier.

My dad told me, "I love you son." He was crying full-on. He embraced me in a classic Bill bear hug. I thought he'd never let go but eventually he did. The last thing he told me was, "I'm losing one of my soldiers."

Three

...INTRODUCTION...

This is my "INTRODUCTION". I believe life to be just one big introduction into a sea of circumstance; every day is a different introduction. We don't always make the best first impression on these introductions 'cause we all handle stuff different. These are my impressions on all the introductions of my life.

Four
When thugs cry...

In the car driving to my mom's house my tears dried up. I didn't want to show her how I really felt. I didn't want to show her any emotion. I didn't respond to any of her questions — hers nor Randy's. In my mind I was still trying to put it all together: I was wondering how my dad was feeling, driving all the way home alone.

The whole reason for this book ain't for the masses — it's for my family. I want them to know the missing years between our relationship; what transpired in my life to turn me into the person I am today. I didn't write it to place blame or shame anyone — it's all one hundred percent truth as I remember it to be. No names or places have been changed. This is what happened where I went. My Introduction.

Tenth grade.

My first impression of my mom's house was, "Fuck."

It was a small, two-bedroom apartment in the front by the street. We pulled into the garage. First thing I noticed was the smell of cigarette smoke. We walked in and there were two extremely old elderly people — one man and one woman, Winfield and Irene. Winfield was sitting in an old dirty recliner smoking a pipe with drool hanging down his mouth, all over his shirt and lap; pipe tobacco spilled all over his shirt and pants too. The TV was turned to the History Channel and the volume was blasting super loud. Irene was at the sink with a little black Wizard of Oz-looking dog attached to a leash. She was washing something.

The dog started going nuts.

Irene tells it, "Shut up Toto!" (how ironic, right?)

She says, "Hello."

I don't say shit. I want it to be known I ain't happy to be here and fuck all of you! My mom, she ain't tapping into any of that. She tells me to take my shit out of the trunk and put it in the closet, I sleep on the floor in the front room.

I look at the floor — it's filthy. Full of spilled tobacco with burn spots everywhere and I could only imagine what else.

I will be honest, my aunt's house was extremely clean and this house was super filthy, and I have only seen the front room. I was instantly disgusted by the sight of Winfield — all that drool and shit. I didn't want to touch shit. Ewww, old people koodies.

I went outside 'cause I didn't even want to breathe the air in that house. I was repulsed, literally! Man, I thought, "What the fuck am I gonna do? How can I get away from this? Is this really happening? And for how long?" I got so caught up in my head, the next thing I know it's dark outside and I had to use the restroom.

Holding my breath, I went into the house.

I guess my mom and Irene were in their rooms. Winfield sat in his chair, the TV muted as he read a book. I thought, "Thank God I don't have to hear that TV all night."

The restroom was surprisingly clean — the only thing is it had a high chair toilet seat so I guess Winfield could sit on it and not have to squat down so low. On the sides of it was dried shit. Damn. I held my breath and did my business and got out of there.

I walked back into the living room looking for the cleanest spot to sit. I located a somewhat clean spot in the corner on the floor. I laid down and fell asleep.

I was jarred awake by the TV volume blasting super loud!

"What the fuck?"

I come to find out, during commercial breaks, Winfield mutes the TV to read, then when the show resumes, he unmutes it! It's gonna be a long ass night...

I say, "Fuck it." I get up and take my blanket and sheet and go into the garage and sleep on the floor — literally on the floor — almost under the front of the car. I would rather put up with the smell of gas and oil than be in that dirty ass loud living room.

So passed my first night. Surprisingly, I slept soundly.

I was awakened by a car starting up. My mom's boyfriend Randy was on his way to work. I sat up hella sore from sleeping on the concrete floor. I held my breath and went back into the house.

Winfield was already up and at the breakfast table smoking his pipe and reading the newspaper and drooling everywhere still. Irene was making toast. She still had Toto on his leash sitting next to her. When the dog saw me, he approached me and sniffed me a couple of times. I guess he figured I was cool 'cause he put his paws on my leg like, "Please pet me."

I thought, "What the hell, it ain't the dog's fault," so I scratched him behind his ears.

Irene said, "His name is Toto. I'm Irene. That old man at the table is my husband. His name is Winfield. It's nice to meet you, Kenny."

I was always taught to respect my elders, so even though I was still pissed, I exercised some humility and said, "You too, ma'am."

I really did not have no plan of what to do when I came into the house. Irene asked me if I was hungry. I looked at Winfield drooling all over the table and plate and thought, "I ain't eating shit off anything that fool may have ate off," so I said, "No."

My mom was still asleep, so I went and sat in the front room on an old love seat and just stared at the muted TV.

Finally my mom woke up and told me to get dressed — we had to go enroll me for school. I told her I was ready. She said, "Okay, we'll leave in a minute."

We get to South High School. I get enrolled. I start the next day. Everything goes as planned. My first day of school is uneventful. Down the street from my mom's house is a small park that has a half court basketball hoop. A couple of black guys are playing so I call next. They finish their game. I pick up the losers, toss my new Nike hat — it's a Jordan hat, all black with red letters and a red Jump-man — on the floor.

We win the first game. I notice some skinny black kid has my hat on his head turned backwards like it's his. I think, "What the fuck?"

I go to snatch my hat off his head and he dodges me and starts talking shit.

I tell him, "Shoot my hat back."

He says, "Fuck you whiteboy!"

He starts to run but I catch up to him and push him in his back, so he falls to the floor and I take my hat back.

Everybody in the park is watching all of this go down. They all know dude is in the wrong too, but it seems they are all tripping on me.

I say, *"Fuck it, as long as I got my hat back."*

The kid is talking all types of shit: *I'm gonna do this. I'm gonna do that. Imma go get my big brother.*

Who cares? I think to myself.

I go back to playing basketball. I keep my hat on my head this time.

Next thing I know, I look across the park to see a mob of people walking towards the court. One of the guys playing basketball says, "Damn nigga, you best be ready."

I'm like, *Fuck it.*

An older skinny black kid yells like, "Nigga why you hitting on my lil' brother?"

I simply tell him, "He tried to steal my hat. Plus I didn't hit him, I pushed him. I wasn't trying to hurt him."

The black kid — mind you, there are at least 30 other fools in the park, all of which are black, I'm the only one that ain't — says, "Shit nigga, I'm Bobby Collins, East Side Stroller Boy Crip Gang. I'm finna smash you!"

I don't even hesitate, I take off on his ass before he even has a chance. Next thing I know is he is on the ground and his mouth is bleeding. A black kid I was hooping with says, "You better run nigga!" So I do just that.

They chase me all the way to my doorstep. I had a whole mob right behind me!

I get into the house like, "Fuck! What's next? This is only day two!"

I'm starving but can't bring myself to use the plates or silverware or cups I think Winfield used 'cause I think he may have drooled on them at one point — like I said, *old people koodies.* I notice the entire counter top has those white boxes of Entenmann's pastries donuts and cakes. I find out later they stay stocked up on all those 'cause they get them free. I guess it's commodities. I open a new box 'cause I know it's untouched. I take half a chocolate cake and go eat in the garage 'cause like I said, I was super disgusted. I didn't even want to breathe the air in there; kinda like being in a dirty ass port-a-potty — if you ever been forced to use one, you know the feeling. I can't describe it any better.

For the whole first month, I literally survived off those Entenmann's pastries. I know it sounds hateful and mean the way I felt towards Winfield, but shoot, I was young and didn't know any better. But for reals, I'm grown now and I still think I'd do the same thing!

School ain't shit — it's all mostly blacks. The only class I liked was P.E. My P.E. teacher was fine as fuck, running around in little gym shorts. It was too late to play basketball, so I was like, "Fuck it. Fuck school too."

I went from playing three sports and making the honor roll the year before to not doing shit. The only reason I even went to school wasn't 'cause my mom made me — she didn't give two fucks. It was simply 'cause I didn't want to be at home. For reals, I didn't do no homework, didn't do no tests, I really didn't do shit, just checked out the females and ate the free lunch they provided for me. I couldn't play at the park by my mom's house 'cause I knew they was waiting for me to slip.

At school one day, a pretty girl named Sylvia Estrada — who turns out later to be one of my new homies, Trippy's sister — says, "Will you walk home with me later please?"

I say, "Yes, but where do you live?"

She says, "In the mobile home park behind where you live."

I said, "Huh?"

She says she seen me sitting outside on the curb, which I usually did just to stay out of the house. We walk home and talk. She asks if I would like to come over and chill and maybe go swimming. I say, "Yes, but I don't have no shorts."

She says, "One of my brothers will loan you some."

"Okay."

We get to her house. She gots five brothers, three sisters, like four girl cousins, aunts and uncles, all types of fools up in this house. No one even pays me any attention until some tall ass fool comes out a back room. He is all like, "Who this fool?"

I say, "Sup homie. I'm Kenny."

He says, "Cool. I'm Trippy. Bakers Trece Gang, what's good."

I tell him I'm Sylvia's friend from school. He don't even trip.

We all wind up chillin' later. We all go swimming. Trippy asks where I'm from. I say, "L.A." Mind you, I'm now living in Bakersfield at my mom's.

After we all finish swimming, we all go back inside and eat. It's crazy 'cause it's like right off the jump I was part of the family. To be honest, after that first day, I only remember talking to Sylvia a few more times. It's like she just took me to her house to save me or something, or she knew I was lonely. Instantly, all the brothers — even the mom — took me in. it was almost like the mom had so many kids she didn't know I wasn't one of hers; I just fell right in.

The dad was doing life for murder. All the aunts and uncles were on parole — even the mom — but it somehow worked. I felt I found my new family and in more ways than not, I did.

That night, I went home super late thinking my mom was gonna trip, but naw, she didn't say shit. I took a shower and sat in the front room, laid down then fell asleep, just to be awakened by that TV again. I thought, "Naw, fuck all this."

I waited until the next time Winfield muted the TV, snuck up behind him and took the batteries out of the remote. I laid back down. A few minutes later, Winfield tried to unmute the TV to no avail. *Ha, got 'em!*

Winfield yelled, "WENDY. The remote don't work."

She yelled back, "The batteries are dead and we ain't got no more."

That put a temporary end to all that, LOL.

Winfield usually stayed up all night reading two alternating books at a time and watching The History Channel. That night we had our first conversation. I found out he was ninety-eight years old, played in three World Series' for the Boston Red Sox, and was actually "Winfield Lang III" from a super rich Bostonian family that disowned him for marrying a peasant woman; that woman being Irene. They were married at eighteen so they had been together eighty years — fucking crazy! He also told me he had been smoking a pipe for eighty years with no sickness. He collected matchbook covers from all over the world and time periods.

I guess his son got tired of taking care of them and got them a trailer in Oildale, which is like the Meth Capitol of the USA, and he pretty much just dropped them off and left them to fend for themselves. My mom seen them and in her twisted heart felt some type of way or seen an opportunity and started kinda being their caretaker. She got them to appoint her as their payee and lived for free off of them. I can't honestly say she didn't do her job — she did, even if she was bitching the whole time. At times, I admit, she had to do some fucked up shit like clean Winfield after he shit all over himself, or help him off the toilet, or even wash the bed sheets 'cause he pissed them.

One time, Winfield comes out the bathroom — both hands on his walker, mind you. The man must have been a huge man in his prime — at least six-foot-six and well over two hundred pounds. Old age stooped him over but he was still tall. Anyways, there he is in the doorway with his walker, pants down to his ankles calling, "WENDY, WENDY!" I look up to see what he's tripping on and straight got my eye busted — this fool's dick is swinging well past his knees. I'm like, "God damn." I tell to Irene, "God damn, you took all that dick?"

She looks at it then at me and says, "I thought they were all that size."

She wasn't playing, he's all she has ever known. That shit was hella funny, so I thought I would share it with y'all — like I said, one hundred percent honest.

Time is really the best healer. With time, everything heals. Though I still missed my family, I wasn't so sick anymore; life must go on eventually. I even got over old people koodies. Winfield and Irene weren't too bad at all. I just don't know why Irene kept that dog on his leash. But I guess the dog didn't mind 'cause it loved the shit out of her.

One day, chilling with Trippy and his brothers, they all wanted to go to the park. They told me, "Let's roll."

I said, "Naw fool, I can't go, they waiting on my ass fool."

Trippy said, "Who?"

So, I told him the story and when I was finished, he said, "Let's roll."

All in all, it was ten of us: me, Trippy, his cousin Abel, the homie Gino plus some fools I didn't even know.

We get to the park and old Bobby Collins and all his homies is there, but it was more just like all the neighborhood kids — not really gangbangers. He sees me and starts wolfing, so the homies and I pull up on him.

As I approach him he says, "You ain't shit without your homeboys."

I tell him, "Fool, as I remember, I whooped you heads up, then y'all tried to jump me."

He says, "Shit nigga, you sucker punched me then ran." *Yeah, okay!*

Trippy then says, "Fuck this fool Kenny, run his ass."

I step up to him and tell him, "Let's get down heads up, no bullshit."

He swings a sloppy swimmer-type punch head down. I tee off rapid fire and land about seven shots to the top of his head. He looks up and catches two to the face then he curls up.

It's over.

I attack full-on, he falls, so then I jump on him, striking him all over. One of his people sucker punches me.

That's all it takes.

All my homies jump — so do all the blacks — and now we have an old fashioned race riot. The whole time, I only beat on Bobby Collins. I guess everybody got tired of fighting 'cause everyone stopped. Bobby Collins gets up and still has the nerve to talk shit saying, "Next time I see you I'mma smoke your ass!" Then he walks off.

It's crazy 'cause I really wanted to see if he was 'bout that life, so we hit the park every day for a week.

One day I see the little fool who tried to steal my hat and he has an RIP t-shirt on with a picture on the back. I taunt him like, "Where your bitch-ass brother at?"

He looks at me all serious and says, "Fuck you!"

When he turns to walk away, I see the name and picture clear as day — it's Bobby Collins! I guess he got smoked by some Country Boy Crips, his rivals, a few days back. Shit happens that quick!

Besides the varrio I grew up in, I have never been exposed to the inner workings of gang violence—this was my first-hand INTRODUCTION.

I walked in on my mom hitting the dope pipe — she didn't even hide it. She felt like, "Why should I have to in my own house?"

My INTRODUCTION into drug-abusing parental supervision.

I walked outside shaking my head. I saw this skinny brindle color dog sitting in my favorite seat on the curb. I was looking for company so I went into the house and took a whole Entenmann's cake from the counter and went back outside and shared it with the dog. Even though it was starving, it didn't beg and it took the cake all nice-like. It turned out to be a little girl brindle pit bull, though at the time you wouldn't know it. It sat peacefully by my side the whole time. I got up to go inside. She looked at me all expectantly like, "Could I come inside?"

"Well come on, I'll give it a shot."

Irene and Toto sat in the front room watching whatever Winfield had on the TV. Toto seen the baby pit and acted like they had been lifelong friends and welcomed her in. Winfield looked up and said, "What you got there, Kenny?"

I said, "She was outside and she's nice."

He *hmmmphed* and went back to reading.

I took her in my mom's room and right away my mom took to her. *I guess she's staying.*

My mom named her "Misha". The name fit. She soon put on weight and after her first bath, her coat was a beautiful, tiger-striped color. She was a beautiful dog. Her personality was great too. I took her to Trippy's house a few weeks earlier. All his sisters loved her and most times you would find her snuggled up with one of the many females in his house while I was either outside or in the garage fucking around.

All the homies was in the garage fucking around and smoking and shit. Trippy asked me had I ever done crank. I said, "Naw," I was good on all that, but he spiked my drink, hence my introduction into meth.

The funny thing is it somehow zoned me out; made me feel super focused. I didn't feel all fucked up like I was made to believe. He said, "How do you feel?"

I said, "GOOD!"

I wanted to smoke some so I did and I got lit up. I didn't want to go home 'cause I didn't want my mom knowing I did it (you can totally tell whenever I do any drugs 'cause my eyes are a dead giveaway) so I stayed at Trippy's house.

When I finally came home three days later I thought my mom was gonna trip on me for not coming home. Shit, was I wrong! She was way more upset that I took Misha with me and she was worried about HER. Shit, *I love you too, mom!*

Weeks pass, now we ain't got no dope and we want some but we have no money, so the homie was like, "We need to hit this lick."

We rob a house down the street, sell the shit and buy dope then get high: My introduction to real crime.

It was all too easy too.

That same night a white skinny girl with some big ass tits was walking by the pool area where me and Trippy was and she stops and says she is looking for some dope.

Trippy says, "What do you got??"

She says, "I will blow you for five minutes for a nickle."

Trippy says, "I got a dime. Blow us both."

And just like that, my introduction into sex — all in the same night. Life is that fast. My first sexual experience wasn't what I had in mind but shit, I took it!

The meth easily became an every day thing, so did the petty crime.

Shit got real one day.

Me and Trippy was at the dope man's, just chilling when all of a sudden four masked men ran up in the house and laid everyone down. One began to beat the dope man with the butt of his gun, pistol-whipping him over and over again asking where the dope and the money was. I was thinking, "Shit, even if he wanted to answer, dude couldn't 'cause he was unconscious from being pistol-whipped."

The dude would yell, "Where's the shit?"

When the dope man wouldn't answer, he would hit him again. He must have hit him about thirty times. Then they all ransacked the house. I guess they didn't find shit. The entire time, me and Trippy just sat there until they left. After they left, Trippy said, "Fuck, check to see if he is dead."

I said, "I don't know how. Let's just bounce."

It turns out the dope man died, hence my introduction into murder.

I don't think the cops really tried to find the killers either. It was crazy 'cause later that same day, we were sitting on the back wall that divided my apartment complex from Trippy's mobile home park community and four fools was walking down the road. I swear it was the same dudes minus the masks. Trippy and I looked at each other. We didn't say shit, but we both knew exactly what each other was thinking. It's the same as it was before — the four fools acted like we weren't even there. I guess their drug-induced state gave them tunnel vision or they simply didn't even care.

My first taste of breaking the law wasn't in Bakersfield, but my introduction into the consequences was. When I was younger, I accidentally burned down the back shed connected to my neighbor's house. Like I said, accidentally, one hundred percent.

I lit a match, it burned a piece of paper, then caught an old plastic Christmas tree. I got scared and picked up a can of hair spray to put it out. *Yeah, I know right?*

Well, it turned into an inferno really quick. I tried to put it out but I couldn't, so I ran to my room, slid straight under the blankets and pretended to be asleep. Mind you, it was about 1pm in the Summer.

My older brother came in the room. I smelled straight like smoke — he wasn't fooled. Long story short, fire trucks came to put the fire out. I thought I was cool — nope. It's now about 6pm. My dad comes and gets me, a cop cuffs me, tosses me in the back of his car and pulls off! I won't lie, I'm super scared. I'm crying like a lil' bitch. I guess it was a scare tactic 'cause all the cop did was drive around the block a few times then take me back home. I wish I knew that ahead of time! *Asshole.*

Back to what I was saying about breaking the law while I lived with my dad or up until this point in my life, I was a fairly good kid. Sure, I was mouthy and arrogant, but I never done no serious crimes. Now here I am, full on into it up to my eyes. It didn't really even register though, 'cause like I said, I never seen no consequences from any of it, ya dig?

It never felt like I had to make a transition in my lifestyle from honor student to bad boy; it always felt like it was something that was supposed to happen. I think about it now — I never even called my dad or family. It was as if I blocked all them out — kinda like I did when I got all those three hundred sixty stitches removed from my face. It's not to say I didn't love them, I just kinda got caught up in my own world.

I had been chilling with Trippy and his family every day. I pretty much lived with them fools. They were my new family. The whole family was from the same gang: Varrio Bakers.

One day, Trippy's uncle asks where I was from and I say, "Nowhere."

Next thing I know, Trippy, Abel and Gino are beating the shit out of me. All I am thinking is, *What the fuck did I do?*

Then I hear Trippy asking me, "Are you okay?"

I am hella dazed but I say, "Yeah, I'm good."

He then says, "You're now Kenny from Varrio Bakers, but for reals fool, you need a gang name."

His sister Sylvia is standing there watching the whole time.

She says, "He got a long ass turtle neck, call him "Turtleboy."

The name stuck — I was now Turtle Boy de Varrio Bakers Gang.

The uncle said, "Load up, time to go put in work. Give Turtle the strap and put him in the passenger seat. We gonna go get them Pokie Boys."

"Pokie Boys" being the enemy Okie Bakers that lived on the other side of town. I won't lie, I ain't never held a gun, let alone shot one. I was scared out my ass for reals! I knew what it was though; I grew up watching all this shit go down. I ain't never been no pussy and I wanted to show out in front of the older homies.

Soon as we hit the enemy's block, I jumped on the window seal like a movie and started busting at a crowd of fools in front of a house until the clip was empty. The whole time I was yelling and screaming out the window, "VARRIO BAKERS GANG" over and over!

I knew that I had got off 'cause as we sped all the way back to the hood, everyone was saying so! Once we pulled into the garage, the dope came out. We all got high, all the homies was talking about how I was a nutcase and giving me props! I can say it was almost like I was back at home playing baseball for my high school team hitting the game-winning homerun; these were my new teammates.

I loved these fools. I didn't join my gang out of fear. I didn't do it for protection. I didn't do it for loneliness. It was simply for the fact that these were my boys. I belonged. They made me feel part of something and I knew every one of them would be with me unless the circumstances prevented it!

The next day I got my first tattoo — I got "Bakers" on the back of my neck. It's called "earning your letters". Since I officially put in work, I earned them. I won't lie, that shit hurt like a bitch; even worse 'cause it was stick and poke, which is using just a needle with some thread tied around the tip to absorb the ink and, just like it sounds, you stick and poke until the tattoo is finished. The homie wasn't too good either, plus he was tweaking! I was surprised I didn't get no infection 'cause ain't no part of any of it sterile — I don't even know where we got the needle and ink! But it somehow healed.

After my first drive-by, it's as if I was no longer a child: shit got real.

The fools I busted on found out who it was that done it and in the gang lifestyle, retaliation is a must, so now I had countless, faceless enemies looking for me — not just looking for me, but aiming to kill me on sight!

The older homie let me keep the gun. It's crazy 'cause I could remember not too long ago in the barrio I grew up in, I was just a spectator — now I'm all up in it. That quick. I'm won't lie, I was scared as fuck. My introduction.

Some older homies moved in to the apartments across from my mom's: Kidder and Frosty. The apartments were pretty ghetto so I'm sure they were squatting. Me and the homie used to kick it in my mom's garage a lot.

One day I walk across to Kidder's pad. I see a green Impala sitting at the curb where I used to sit. I tell Frosty and Kidder, "Who's that?"

Frosty shoots the car and they take off, burning rubber.

A few minutes later while we is chilling on Frosty and Kidder's porch, I see that green Impala coming back — them fools have an AK out the window, and even though no one is in front of my house, them lame-ass fools still start to shoot it up! Frosty and Kidder start to let off back. I was just stuck in the middle like a deer in the headlights, that shit went on forever!

The Impala speeds off. Right away, Kidder starts to pick up the spent shells saying, "We need to bounce," but none of us got a car.

I say, "Let's all go in my house." So we do.

My mom comes out her room and sees us all in the living room and tells us all to go hide in her room but I'm all like, "Randy is in there."

She says, "He's asleep."

I think, "Yeah right."

So we all go in her room. Randy is on the bed asleep. I know he's faking though — he's just scared.

My mom takes the guns and opens the back patio where we keep Misha. We keep her food in a five gallon bucket. She sticks both guns in the dog food and closes the door, then lays on the bed.

We all wait for the cops to come but they never do.

Later, we all move to the garage and chill — my mom too. Frosty pulls out the dope pipe. I hit it in front of my mom, then she hits it too, no biggie. That was the first time I ever got high with my mom. It was also the same day I lost all respect for her as a mother. I thought it was cool at the time, but naw, it wasn't. It was just another introduction to how miserable and fucked up life can get.

After losing the little respect I had left for my mother, all my parental structure fell off. I guess that was really my point of no return, with no fear of retribution or consequences for anything I did. I felt I was lawless. I stayed gone for weeks, got as high as I wanted to, brought anyone and everyone to my pad.

One day I steal some checks from Irene and cash them at the local corner store. The lady calls my mom's house about the checks. She says they never gave me no checks. I stole them so the cops are called. I am now on the run, hence my intro into being a fugitive. *I know, right? Stupid.* I stay at Trippy's house instead of going home.

One day Frosty and I are coming down Monitor Street hitting the left turn to put us on the street my mom's apartment is on — Pacheco. We are in his green 5.0 Mustang. I see a long-haired white boy crossing the street about to hit the corner and walk through the open field. I tell Frosty, "That's that lil' bitch Allen."

He says, "Get him!"

I roll down the window and start shooting at him, but he's hella quick and breaks into the open field — it has hills and shit, so as he's pushing up a hill and hits the top, I know I hit him at least twice. I want to finish the job but Frosty don't want to fuck up his car in that field so we leave him! I was pissed! We had been looking for that fool too — he smoked my homie at the cemetery in the hood while he was paying his respects to his dead little brother. Allen shot my homie in the head point blank using a .45. To make matters worse, Allen beat the whole case. But fuck the police, that wasn't what made it worse — it was that after he beat the case, he tatted a big ass ".45" across his chest and "NOT GUILTY" on top of it, clowning that he killed the homie and beat the case. It was also him and his homies in that green Impala with the AK that day. It's even crazier 'cause his whole hood lived right across the street in the Common Court projects, so it was literally a bang on sight thang.

Looking back, maybe I'm glad I didn't kill him 'cause I would most likely be doing a life sentence and this story would be a very different one — GOD works in mysterious ways, huh?

So yeah, here I am, a wanted man for cashing illegal checks. I'm not really tripping 'cause it's a chance my mom is lying — she does that a lot.

Anyways, she and the Langs wind up moving. I don't find out 'til about two years later when I get picked up by my homie John — well, he wasn't my homie. If you weren't from my hood, you didn't mean shit to me!

Like I was saying, he swooped me up in a stolen minivan. He lived across town on the eastside in the Loma — that's another rival gang.

For some reason me and John start beefing. He pulls into a gas station. I tell him, "Take me home."

He says, "Walk."

I'm thinking, "What the fuck?"

He jumps out the car and takes the keys. As he's walking into the store, five Loma Boys run up on him and start stabbing the shit out of him. He's on the floor and shit. I'm tripping 'cause I'm slipping too.

One of them fools says, "You're good, homie, it's personal."

Shit, that's all I need to hear. I pull on back.

Once they are done and leave, I pull up on John. He's looking at me like I'm gonna help him, so I act like I am. Then I slip my hand in his pocket, take the car keys, and turn to bounce.

He says, "You gonna just leave me here? Take me to the hospital please!"

I walk all the way back to him, kneel down and tell him, "You wanna get to the hospital homie, for reals?"

He says, "Yeah, please fool. I'm fucked up bad."

I look at him and yeah, he IS fucked up real bad!

I say, "Yeah, okay fool WALK!"

I jump in the minivan and bounce.

Fuck that fool.

I seen it like this: he knew I was an active gang member. He took me to a rival gang's hood and was about to leave me stranded — a potential death sentence, right? No love, no emotion, he didn't give two fucks about me so shit, I didn't either!

Somewhere in my childhood I watched my heart die and naw, it wasn't just then, it had been dead a long time before — maybe as early as when my dad told me, "I'm losing one of my soldiers!"

I don't know where I am, or even how to drive, I just pull out and stick to the alleys. I wind up on a main street at a four-way stopped at a red light. A cop sees me — sure enough, I am pulled over — the car was stolen. I am then taken to Juvenile Hall.

They ask the usual questions: "Who's your mom and dad?" "Phone number and address."

All I know is their names, nothing else.

I am then taken to a unit. About five of us are told to strip, step into the shower and use the soap.

"If it burns, you got some shit. If not, you're good. Rinse off then get dressed and line up." The officers have no compassion or emotion — all business.

I am then placed in a single man cell with a stainless steel sink and toilet. I never even been in this position — I am tripping for reals!

My first night in that cell is torture. I keep pacing the floor. Every rattle of keys or foot steps, I would run to the door to see if they are coming for me — they never are. Somehow, I fall asleep.

I am woken up by my door being keyed open, so I jump up and shoot straight out my cell.

The guard yells, "What the fuck are you doing, stupid? Get the fuck back in your cell now before I Red Tag your ass!"

I would real soon get to know all about Red Tag!

I go back into my cell.

He finishes unlocking everyone's door and says, "Step out." So I peek out my door to see what everyone else is doing — they are stepping out and standing by their cells, so I do the same thing. I notice all the fools are looking at me — I guess 'cause I am new.

The guard says, "Go sit down."

Everyone sits at a table. It's breakfast time.

Breakfast is served on a small tray with four sections: one main square and three smaller ones. It's a piece of bread, eggs, an apple and some oatmeal with a small carton of milk. I think, *No way, this can't be it,* but it is.

They give us ten minutes to eat, then back to our cells. They don't lock our doors though. The cop then calls out the court list. He calls my name, so I step out my cell.

He says, "That's twice today, stupid. One more time, it's RED TAG.

I snap on him. I say, "I don't know what the fuck to do bitch, you called my name so I stepped out, what the fuck?"

He tells me to get my ass in my cell, so I do. He then puts a red 'X' on my window, and a red '3'—'RED TAG THREE DAYS'.

'Red Tag' is a form of discipline that consists of you being placed in your cell for a duration of time: no school, no rec, no meals outside, or no shower!

The cop takes me to court, which is attached to the juvenile hall. My lawyer reads:

POSSESSION OF A STOLEN VEHICLE, CAMP OWENS

I guess they sending me to Camp Owens, and if I'm good, I can be out in three months. And if not, they can keep me until I'm eighteen. Juvenile court ain't like adult court — it's way faster. I get sentenced that day — off to Camp Owens I go! I don't even know what Camp Owens is!

I get back to my cell and soon experience all about RED TAG. Those three days were the worst days of my memory! Here I was, a super hyper kid trapped in a box for who-knows-how-long. I wasn't equipped with the mental skills to combat what I felt in that cell. I had no books, no paper or a pencil. No games. Just a sheet, a blanket and a paper cup. No way could I sleep — my mind was all over the place. Plus, I could hear all the activity right outside my door. Shit, I wasn't even tall enough to see out my window; I had to roll up my mattress and stand on it to see out. I know for a fact that this is my first introduction into **madness**!

I sat for hours on my concrete floor with my paper cup full of water, dipping my finger in it and drawing on the floor. The floor would absorb the water into the concrete. A cop looked in my cell and seen my floor all wet and the random words scrawled, which was shit mostly like "TURTLE VBKS" or variations of this. He opened up the door, took the cup and said, "No gang shit." That red "3" turned to a red "4".

I died inside!

I went nuts, yelling and screaming and punching the walls, fucking up my knuckles, to no avail. I started to cry, then looked for ways to get out of my cell — it was impossible. I even contemplated suicide. I said to myself, "I'll jump off the sink head-first." I went as far as standing on my sink to actually do it. Just then, the cop looking in my window and rushed in my cell. He grabbed me, but was real nice, like, "Come on kid, you're gonna move somewhere safer, somewhere nicer."

So I'm like, "Okay, hell yeah. That's what's up."

We walk down the hall. When we get to this one door he says, "First you need to change before we go into this unit, so strip out your clothes then step in that room. Get dressed."

So I do.

He then closes the door.

The first thing I notice is all the rubber gray walls with a square drain hole in the corner. The door window has a metal plate blocking my view out, and in the top corner of the room is a camera and the room is super cold!

I knew I was super fucked.

It turns out that room was the SOR room: SAFETY OBSERVATION ROOM. I stayed in that room forever, asshole naked. I don't even remember how I survived it, but I did, and I taught myself from that day, "These fools will never break me!"

When they finally let me out, all the cops is all there standing outside all anxious to see my reaction, like I was a show or something they had been betting on. I simply walk out like nothing had happened. Like I said, same as when my heart died, the same could be said about my mind state: I learned to simply shut it off and repress anything I felt detrimental to my well-being. I had already experienced mental torture, losing my whole family in the blink of an eye. I say "mental" 'cause I know the heart holds no emotions, it's all memory in the mind. Same as with those three hundred sixty stitches — I blocked it out without even trying. I just know after experiencing that SOR room, my whole being was now fully conscious to the nature of being alone. All I remember thinking about was, "I don't even know where my parents are or how to reach them or any of my loved ones — do I even want to?"

This is my introduction to solitude.

Juvenile hall is crazy: a bunch of bad ass kids with no fear of retribution or consequences, with the exception of RED TAG! I literally fight almost every chance that I get: at school, at rec, in the unit — it doesn't matter. I *stay* on RED TAG.

While in my cell, I read like crazy — anything and everything. I write letter after letter too! My letters are never sent, or if they were, it's to some made-up address. It doesn't matter though, it still helps 'cause I would pretend the people I write them to got them and even though I know my letters are phantom letters, every day at mail call I would anxiously await my name being called. And every day, when no letter came, I'd die another slow death. I told you I was slipping into madness!

"Thunderburk, pack your shit. You're leaving."

That's easy, I don't *have* shit. On my way to Camp Owens, finally!

Ten of us pack into a transport van. About an hour later we all pull up to Camp Owens. It's in the mountains, right by Lake Isabella. Camp Owens is just like it sounds — "camp" in the mountains. It has staff living quarters which are cabins. The inmates are housed in two big-ass barracks — one called "D-D", the other called "B-B". It's really like being in summer camp, except for instead of it being willing summer kids, it's all bad ass kids who have been sentenced for various crimes!

It's almost the same rundown as the intake at juvenile hall: the shower and all that, except it don't have any cells. Like I said, it's all open barracks, each one holding about two hundred wards with single bunks on each side of the wall running down the whole barracks.

Being new to camp, to the people who have already been there, they try to fuck with you right off the jump! They test you, gang bang on you, all types of shit. It's easy to fuck off your whole stay literally two minutes upon arrival by saying or doing the wrong thing, or simply by not responding the right way. It's really easy for an ADHD kid like myself to find trouble right off the rip, which I sure did! It's not just a hodgepodge of kids, it's a melting pot of all different gangs: crips, bloods, whiteboys, nazi lowriders, Sureños and Norteños. Anything and everything — if your hood has an enemy, you bet your bottom dollar they are here.

I don't even get to put my shit down and they on me.

"Where you from, esé?"

"Shit," I say, "Turtleboy Varrio Bakers Traviesos!"

Someone else says, "Don't trip, you got some enemies right here!"

Two skinny fools pull up on me:

"Tiny, Flaco Okie Bakers!"

Shit man, fuck!

I ain't never been no victim, so I take off first thang! I get the best of one and his homie pulls off saying, "Don't trip, we'll holla at you later, goon."

'Goon' is a way to diss my hood 'cause we got a big ass cemetery in my hood, hence 'goon'. It's not so much the word, it's more the principle — they are trying to diss the hood, so it's offensive. So I'm like, "Cool, okay 'Pokie Boy!"

A little while later my varrio homies pull up on me: Negro, Beast and Trigger. They give me the rundown — I did the right thing, ain't no one tripping, it's all good. I hear commotion so I turn around to see what's up. I see a white boy I pulled up with. I guess he did some dumb shit. Like I said, literally two minutes in they already giving him the blues. They done took all his shit. Now he is just sitting on his bed and everyone is talking shit.

The rest of my day I just feel the place out. It's not that bad, but I know I got to stay on my toes. They hit the lights at around 10pm. It's bedtime. I fall asleep then my neighbor wakes me up. I'm like, "What's up?"

He says to look at the whiteboy. I look over at him and he is under the covers, head and all, wrapped-up, wadded-up bunches of toilet paper all over his bed and floor-area, like a hundred of them. I was all like, "What is all that?"

The neighbor says, "Nutt rags."

"Huh?"

"Fools jack off into tissue and peg homie with them 'cause he is a bitch."

Crazy. I won't lie, I nut ragged my share of fools too! It's all part of the game.

All the lights turn on at 5am. Everyone has thirty minutes to wash up, get dressed and walk to the super huge mess hall. It's a long ass line and it's all uphill. Once we get to the mess hall, you grab a tray, then you pull up to a bar with loafs of bread and peanut butter mixed with jelly in big tubes. It's all you can eat so shit, I pile on six pieces of bread and three huge globs of mixed peanut butter and jelly. Then we pull into a window and they have eggs and potatoes with oatmeal. I get a whole bunch too!

Once we sit down, I see big metal pitchers of ice cold milk, so right off the jump I pound two glasses of milk like it's going somewhere.

I start to smash my food but man, I'm used to the juvenile hall portions, so my stomach fills up real fast. I can't eat anymore so I go to get up and the cop says, "Naw, clean your plate."

I say, "I can't."

He says, "You will!"

I still have all my oatmeal, 4 pieces of bread and peanut butter.

Fuck!

I'm the last one to finish and be out of the mess hall. I'm so full I don't even want to see no food!

I make it back to the unit just to be told to change 'cause it's gym time! I know ain't none of all that going down, so I go lay down on my bed. The cop says, "If you want to play it that way..."

They come and take all my linens and clothes and leave me on my bed all day in nothing but my underwear!

Just like my juvenile hall days, I fight every day, every chance I get. At the time, I didn't know it but I had a lot of anger. But really, my hyperactivity got on a lot of peoples' nerves too. Plus, I was really just looking for reasons to fight.

To be honest, Camp Owens was really a good place — its whole design. Even though we were incarcerated, it wasn't no step-on-your-neck facility. The whole program was based on points: A good day was 6 points; 42 points, a perfect week; 168 points a month. It was completed when you got to 400 points, so typically in about three months.

You lose points by doing shit like fighting, which then got you a NOMCA: a Notice of Major Corrections Activity which, say for a fight would get you 30 points added to your 400, so about an extra week. For the small shit like not making your bed or talking in class, the staff could take a point or two out of your daily score. If you didn't at least maintain 30 points a week, you failed your week.

You meet with a guidance counselor at the end of each week to discuss your weekly score, to access your needs, and discuss what you need to work on. If you don't maintain a 30 point week, they could put you on "probation" so if you pass the next week, they would honor the previous week, but if you fail that week, you just lost two weeks.

If you 'program', you get a lot of nice privileges and incentives such as late nights, movie nights, popcorn soda and pizza, and being able to play video games. Your family could visit you and have bar-b-ques. They could bring you personal clothes, shoes and hygiene products — even food that you could take back to the unit and put in your personal locker. Shoot, if you have a homie you are cool with, you could even invite him out to share the bar-b-que with you and your family.

At about 200 points, your family can come pick you up and you can leave with them to Lake Isabella all day then come back later that night.

At 300 points, you can go home all Friday through Sunday and be with your family and then come back late Sunday night. The perks are good if you program.

Yeah, I never got any of all that!

What I got was a special program designed just for me and about ten other "wards" or fuck-ups. It's called ORP: Owens Re-entry Program. It's designed as a disciplinary unit to strip us all of our privileges and perks due to our disciplinary behavior. This program is all dead time and it's a mandatory three months of good behavior.

This program consists of fifteen bunks in the back of the D-D dorm where we were still around all the other kids so we could still see all the shit they were able to do that we lost. Mr. Winslow and Mr. Allen — two fat ass, asshole cops — were our guardians.

Owens Re-Entry Program (ORP)

- 5:00am: Rise and shine, everyday, even on the weekends. Absolutely no talking — if you were caught, it's minus one point. Lose three points in a day, you fail your day. Fail two days in a week, you fail your week, it's as simple as that! Shit, Monday morning starts a new week. Thirty minutes after waking up, I'd literally already fail my week! That quick! All that means is I would act like a fool all week. We got ten minutes to all be washed-up, bed made and sitting at the foot of our beds, hands on our laps. Next, we would go outside.

- 5:20am – 6:00am: Calisthenics group workout.

- 6:10am – 6:30am: We would march military-like to the mess hall — no seconds! All bare minimums — back to juvenile hall rations.

- 6:30am – 7:00am: We march to school.

- 7:00am – 12:00pm: We would be in school.

- 12:00pm – 12:30pm: We would march to lunch, eat, then march back to the unit.

- 12:40pm – 4:00pm: We would be doing fire-scaping; hoeing the mountainside to remove all the weeds or unloading hay bales or chicken feed.

- 4:00pm – 5:00pm: Back to the unit, sitting on our bunks facing forward. Count time.

- 5:00pm – 5:30pm: March to chow, eat, march back to the unit.

- 5:30pm – 6:00pm: We would all go sit in a bungalow and they would review our day.

- 6:00pm – 7:00pm: We were able to read books or write letters.

- 7:30pm: Wash up time, brush our teeth, use the restroom.

- 8:00pm: Lights out.

Every day, the exact same thing. It's torture, but it was all brought on by my own behavior — no one but myself to blame!

I was placed in the ORP unit as a trial because I was one of the first fools put into the unit. I was in this unit 'cause I simply refused to stop fighting — it was a last ditch effort to keep me from going "backwards", which means to fail camp, go back to juvenile hall and get resentenced to a more severe facility. They tried to help me, I didn't take the help!

One day while we are hoeing the mountainside, some fool done pisses me off so I hit him with the sharp end of the hoe. I really fuck him up too! He tells, but they didn't see me do it so they take him, not me.

The final straw is one night, Mr. Allen is watching us. It's about 8pm. I already failed my week, so I'm trying to fuck someone else's week off. Mr. Allen tells me to shut up, I tell him to suck my dick! He gets up pissed and yanks me out of bed. I'm like, "What the fuck you put your hands on me?"

He puts his face all up in mines and I hawk a loogie right in his face, almost in his mouth. He spins off, then pepper sprays me and presses his panic button. All the staff come running in. He tells them what happened and they place me in a cell in D-D.

In the morning, Mrs. Minks comes in and next thing I know is I'm on my way back to juvenile hall. I guess I over-extended my stay at Camp Owens!

My welcome back to juvenile hall is cool. It's like I am now an OG since I already know the whole rundown. I know all the cops. Plus, if you "go backwards", it's like an honor — a stripe to us fuck-ups. Plus, I spit on a cop. The cops don't like it, but the wards do. (We ain't inmates, we are wards — wards of the state.)

I am now placed in 200A — the max security unit in Bakersfield juvenile hall. It's a big jump from Camp Owens—it's way more serious, more violent, more racially segregated. It's like prison for kids — no, not "like", it IS prison for kids!

One day at rec, the Blacks want the basketball court but us Mexicans (well, technically I'm Mexican and Indian but I ran with the Sureños: Mexicans! We was cool with the whites too.) The Blacks try to push up on us, so a homie takes off and a riot jumps off. It's hella fun too, I won't lie. No one really gets hurt but it's free violence — a way to get rid of some pent-up aggression. They put the whole juvenile hall on lockdown — everyone is now stuck in their cells.

About a month later, I go back to court. The judge says, "No more Camp Owens, now it's Kern Crossroads" — a new program attached to juvenile hall set up to run like a boot camp.

Since it's attached to the halls, I leave the same day.

I pull up to the unit — I'm in B-wing. I go to my cell — it's just a bunk, but no toilet or sink. I notice a speaker in the wall — I find out all about that speaker soon! A ward named Darnell Pierce — I guess he is a squad leader for B-wing — comes in and shows me how to make my bed, cut corners military style, fold up my clothes and where to put my towel and hygiene items accordingly. I'm given a pair of all-black new shoes that will be used specifically for flag ceremonies and special events — I'll tell you about all that a lil' later. Also, a new pair of dark blue denim jeans and a khaki shirt with buttons. And for gym and rec, we're given another pair of used bubble gum shoes and a small orange pair of shorts.

The day starts at 6am when they unlock the doors. The squad leader calls your name out, then you step out and go use the restroom: wash up, brush your teeth, all that. Then you go fix up your cell. Then you go to breakfast, come back and wait to be called out your cell for flag ceremony.

Darnell calls us out. We exit the cell, and now from this point on, we are being graded on all we do.

We march outside all the way to the basketball courts and face the flagpole, all lined up at "attention". As they present the flag and do all that other shit, the "wing" that does the best all month gets rewarded. Yeah, yeah, I don't give no fucks — all this shit is for the birds.

I somehow make it through my first flag ceremony.

Next, we all go back and change into our school uniform and file to school. The teacher is an older lady that every time she bends over you can see her whole titties — nipple and all. I swear, her ol' ass used to do it on purpose too. Well, she's telling the class that today we are doing sex education. All the jokes come out — everything you can think of, and we don't get in no trouble 'cause she allowed it.

"Well then," she asks. "What's a safe way to practice safe sex?"

Jack off.

Don't bust inside.

Get head.

All that shit.

One fools says, "Condoms."

The teacher says, "Yeah."

Then he says, "They even make flavored ones like cherry and strawberry."

I look up and say, "You would know 'cause your faggot ass be sucking dick!"

He jumps up, we fight.

They take us back to the unit and our cells: 72-hour lockdown. *Damn. I didn't even make it a full day!*

I learned one great thing that day looking out my back cell window: I could see the females! I could look up and across to the other side of the unit to A-wing and see the female 6 woman dorm! I could see titties and talk to them using hand signs. Man, that was a real perk for reals! Also, when they were at rec, they could walk all the way up to my window — all those hood rats in super short gym shorts. I used to look forward to that every day, trust me!

72 hours later, they have a psychologist named Mrs. Anderson pull me out. She is appointed to me for the duration of my stay. I won't lie, I used to enjoy our time together: one, 'cause she was a female and two, 'cause she was cool. I just didn't like that she would bring to surface the memories I was repressing. Blocking out those memories was my only defense. She used to always say that I was a sweet boy 'cause I would be on my best behavior around her — she just couldn't understand that I would fight so much. It was like every week she'd come see me, I would be on lockdown.

After about a year, I not only have the undisputed record for most fights, I also have the fastest time on the facility obstacle course. Besides seeing the females every day, that is the only other thing I look forward too: my outdoor rec alone and hitting that course. For all my fights, they placed me on "administered segregation". Shit, even on that, I still managed to catch fools slipping! I was a real safety issue and I knew the administration was looking for ways to combat that. By law, they couldn't just keep me in my cell like that.

I told you about that speaker right? The one in my cell? Well, as a form of torture, one whole week they left the song "Creep" by Radiohead playing non-stop! Even to this day, if I hear that song, I will flip out.

Somehow I manage to pull off a consecutive month being disciplinary free and they have to let me back into population. All the staff were dreading it, and so were the inmates. I surprise them all — I don't break a single rule.

I excel in the flag ceremony; I am even appointed the position to carry the unit guidon (that's the flag on the stick with our unit banner on it). I have the fastest obstacle course time as well. All the staff are super shocked at my transformation.

One day at breakfast, this weenie named Russell Cash calls me a bitch. I just laugh. Everyone looks at me like I lost my edge. The whole day goes by, I don't do shit to him. Then at nighttime pill line, I am standing behind him. He goes to the counter to get his meds. They make you open your mouth to show you took your pills. Right then, I strike. I swing with all my strength and pop him right in his open mouth — a perfect shot! Oh yeah, he also had braces, so when I hit him the braces cut all the way through his lips and his mouth is stuck open 'cause his braces was all the way through his face! I even fucked up his braces.

I learned from my time in solitude, reading books such as "48 Laws of Power" and "The Art of War", to make every strike the most devastating, so I bid my time and concealed my intentions, then crushed my enemy completely and guarded my reputation all in one move. Back to AD SEG I go. I caught that fool slipping. They acted like putting me by myself was punishment but to me, it wasn't — I used the solitude to hone myself. I even began writing poetry and drawing. I learned a lot about myself in all that — though I am a people person, I seek solitude.

"But then you picked a new direction in the blink of an eye.

My time away just made perfection, did you think I'd die?"

-2Pac, "Why U Turn on Me?"

The next day or so, Mrs. Anderson comes to see me. She's shocked to see me back on lockdown; I was doing so well. She starts saying something about me being so angry at my family is why I fight a lot and why I'm so angry. I'm thinking, "*Wow, did you really find that all out by yourself?"*

I believe there is a flaw in Freudian theory; psychiatrists believe that as soon as you fully remember and understand the childhood traumas that made you into the neurotic person, you can change. They think the key is the hard part, and once you have it, you can open the door in a minute. For me to relive and remember those incidents — the ones I *do* remember — only incite my anger. I don't like thinking about them, so today I don't feel like talking. I actually wanna go back to my cell!

The staff is always on they toes any time I come out my cell. I have at times sat in the bathroom stall until they simply forgot about me and then later popped out on an enemy when they reopened the unit. Even though I get in trouble, so does the staff for forgetting that I was still in there — they put other wards at risk. So just 'cause they been extra careful, I manage to do another couple months disciplinary free in my cell. Once again, they need to put me back into population (I usually know about a week ahead of time I'm coming off lockdown. I don't never tell anyone.

Always say less than necessary.

Conceal your intentions.

These are two of the 48 Laws of Power.

Fools like to run they mouth when you're behind a DOOR but once it opens, they switch all the way up. So I'm trying to catch one of these big mouth fools slipping.

Monday morning, I hear my door open up. Darnell calls my name out.

"Thunderburk, you got ten minutes.

I step out. All of a sudden, fools in a rush to hit they cells. It's funny 'cause I'm hella small causing all this panic in bigger dudes. My day goes by with no incidents.

When we get to school, Mrs. Durham — the teacher always showing them titties — says, "It's good to see you Mr. Thunderburk, welcome back!"

I tell her I missed and you best believe I really did! I bet you can guess why! I never had no issues with any female staff, they all liked me!

About a month of programming, shit starts to get old. Fuck flag ceremony and all that marching. They used to make us "left face," "right face," and "about face" a hundred times without no one fucking up and if they did, we had to start all over again until we all pulled it off. It always cut into our recreation time, so it was annoying as hell. We finally manage to pull off the one hundred consecutive cuts. Staff says, "It's kickball today," so we all rush to the baseball diamond and divide into two teams. I have always been super competitive. I hate losing and I don't ever give up until it's 100% over. Well, we're losing and this white boy named Marty, the pitcher, is talking shit. He pitches the ball, I say, *Fuck this.*

I start to run at him to punch him and he falls to the ground and curls up like a shrimp. I go to football kick his head and miss! I guess I must have popped my hip out of place 'cause I feel the worst pain I've yet to feel in my life. My leg is still in the air, I fall on my right-side hip — the leg I kicked with — and hear a *pop.* I'm fucked up bad and I know it! It's super cold on the wet grass outside. I'm screaming bloody murder. They clear the field. The whole time I'm laying on the ground with my face pressed to the ground. The staff tries to roll me over. I scream, I'm in so much pain. I've been severely hurt before in my life, but this takes the cake!

I must have passed out 'cause now I'm in an ambulance on my way to KMC — Kern Medical Center. We get there, they put me on a gurney and roll me to a room, but first, the cop shackles me to the bed. I'm like, "Damn, really?"

The doctor asks what happened. The staff tells him and he laughs!

I'm thinking, *fuck this Dennis the Menace's dad-looking mutha fucker laughing at me!*

They roll me down the hall for X-rays then roll me back to a room.

About three hours later, Dennis the Menace's dad comes back in and says, "The good news is you broke your hip." And then he starts to laugh.

I sit up real fast-like and tell him, "You find this funny, you bitch-ass fool?"

He gets real serious real fast and then says, "No! I'm sorry, it's just the way you broke it!"

He says my femur popped out of place and when I landed on it, it popped back into place, breaking a piece of the femur bone off — like a chip. He said I needed surgery to remove the bone fragment 'cause it could travel and get in-between the joint — if that were to happen the pain would be unbearable!

The nurse comes in. I could tell she was new. She says I am to be prepped for surgery — no food. When they put in the I-V, I turn my head 'cause I'm scared of needles. If you seen me today, you would laugh 'cause I'm full of tattoos. Anyways, I can tell she is having a hard time 'cause she done already poked me three times. When she finishes, I feel her messing with my sheets and blankets by my right arm. Once the fluid starts going into my arm, I immediately know something ain't right. If feels like my arm is being filled up like under the skin and it hurts! I tell the cop that is watching me to call the nurse and so he does. When she comes in, I tell her. she looks and says, "You're okay, it is just gonna take some time to get used to."

Then she leaves. So I try to chill out, but I know my body, plus my arm starts to swell up like a water balloon. I tell the cop to go get the nurse. He tells me to chill out. I say, "Naw, go get her!"

He says, "She'll be back in a minute."

So I start yelling, "HELP ME, HELP ME, HELP ME," at the top of my lungs!

A nurse passing by looks in my door and I raise my arm and tell her, "Get this thing out of me now!"

She rushes over to me and pulls it out. The original nurse comes in and I hear the new nurse telling her, "It wasn't even in the vain."

The new nurse takes it out and does it right.

Later on, I notice why the original nurse was fooling with my sheets and blankets: there was a huge basketball-size blood splotch all the way through the thick hospital blankets like she severed an artery! *Welcome to KMC!*

I ask the doctor if I really needed surgery. He says, "Your hip is okay, but the fragment should be removed 'cause it could get stuck in the joint."

It was more like a serious precaution. It the fragment didn't travel, I would be fine. It was up to me, so I waited until about 7pm to finally decide I wasn't going to do it! The doctor said I had until about 4pm the next day to decide.

Somehow, the facility contacted my mom 'cause she just showed up all hugs and kisses. *I love you too.* I'm thinking, "*Where the fuck did you come from?"* She can only stay a minute, but I should write to her. She leaves her address. She loves me and hopes I get out soon. *What the fuck was that? REALLY!?*

I tell the nurse I'm not doing the surgery and that I'm starving. They feed me. I keep asking for more food, they keep bringing me more food. I ain't seen no TV for almost two years, so I stay up all night watching TV, getting as much out of this as I possibly can.

The doctor comes in the next day. I give him my decision. He looks relieved, like they don't need to waste any more time on me.

They prescribe me Tylenol 3s and some crutches. I already know what the staff is thinking: *They just gave this psycho a weapon! Hell no!* I figure I'm going back on AD SEG 'cause I almost hit Marty but nope, none of the staff saw it. They think I just got hurt playing. That was a nice surprise!

The next day, Mr. Marcum, the main dude, pulls me into his office.

He says, "Look, we are gonna just release you early. Give is a couple of days to get the paperwork done and please don't hit anyone with your crutches!"

Mind you, Crossroads is on the same kind of point system Camp Owens is on, so I ain't got shit towards going home! I know 100% they were tired of me and deathly afraid I would utilize my crutches as a weapon first chance I got.

I told Mr. Marcum, "Don't be bullshitting me!"

He said, "Son, you're outta here, my word!"

I get back to my unit and yell out, "I'm going home!"

Everybody is all like, "Naw, hell Naw ain't no way!"

Shit, they all watched me leave when it was time to go! I didn't know I was leaving my juvenile days too, 'cause in society's eyes, in about a month or so, I'd turn eighteen.

That's when shit got real.

I WOULD LIKE TO NOTE:

I know I have a big family: five siblings. We all must have seen and remembered different things, such as in the early parts of my book. I was talking to my sister Jessica — "The Memory Bank", I call her. She don't forget shit, and somehow always has pictures of everything. Well, I was telling her I was writing this book about all the missing years I was away from them. I told her some things I must have repressed — one was the removal of my 360 stitches.

She said, "I remember mom did it."

I said, "What?"

She said, "Yeah, she gave you two or three shots of tequila and got to pulling!

I still don't remember!

Another incident which I deem to be the worst: the day my dad took me to my mom's at that Carl's Jr., which actually turned out to be a Jack in the Box.

Jessica says, "I rode in the back seat all the way with you guys. I can tell you exactly what you were wearing and all that. When we left you, it felt like my heart was being ripped out!"

I would have cried if I wasn't in a pod full of men in prison, calling from a prison phone.

The drive-by with that green Impala? Yeah, she was there too that day.

She said, "Yeah fool, you all ran in mom's room, then you made me shave like eight fools' hair to change your identity."

I don't remember any of that!

I started to write this book to show how alone I was. I wanted to fill my family in on what happened to me, but it's crazy 'cause during my most trying of times, my sister Jessica was always there! Like, the real moral to this whole story was to find out she was always there!

I was never truly alone!

Jessica has always been the rock in our family. Even still, later in my book you will see how she still blesses me again.

I know most people wait until the end of their book to give "acknowledgements" and "credits," but I'm not most people, and this ain't most stories!

Truly in my heart, I began telling myself this book is for my family — and it is — but sincerely in my heart, I'm really writing it for my sister Jessica!

THANKS BIG SIS!

Enjoy the rest of the book, undisturbed.

I step out onto the street. I'm wearing the dark blue denim jeans, white t-shirt and all-black flag ceremony shoes. I got my Tylenol 3s in my pocket and my crutches under my arm. The staff gave me my mom's number and address, and sent me on my way.

I go stand at a bus stop 'cause I don't know what else to do. I'm trying to find out how I'm gonna find my mom's house. I see an old lady pushing a basket across the street, so I rush to help her. She is surprised at the help, but she takes it.

We walk towards her car and I help her load her stuff. I ask her if she knows where 720 Irvine Street is.

She says, "Yes. It's all the way across town."

I then ask her how I can catch the bus. I guess that standing there with my crutches under my arm is a pitiful sight, so she says, "Get in and I'll take you there."

She asks me my story, so I tell her the truth. We get in front of my mom's house and she asks me, "Can I pray with you?"

I say, "Okay," just to be polite.

After the prayer, I get out of the car and she leaves.

I knock on the door!

"What the fuck are you doing here?"

"It's okay Mom, they let me out."

My mom's new place was actually a three bedroom house in a somewhat decent area. Winfield, Irene, Toto, Randy, Misha and my mom all stayed there. My mom says I can stay there if I don't start no shit, so I say, "Okay!"

One of the rare times my brother and three sisters came to visit, my mom cooked bacon for dinner. All my siblings got their portion of bacon. Man, there ain't nothing I love more than some bacon, so I piled it on my plate. My mom right away starts bitching. Then Randy says some slick shit. Mind you, I just came from a spot where I didn't take no lip from no one, and here was this lame-ass fool I never really liked, talking slick, and in front of my brothers and sisters.

I tell him something, he says something, next thing I know we're face-to-face about to come to blows. My mom's going nuts. We both pull off. I go to the table. He smarts off again, so I bum-rush him against the fireplace. He hits it then slides down to his ass. He ain't got no fight in him. He's just a drunk.

During the six-mile drive from his job back home, he's already pounded two 40's of "Magnum" malt liquor and is piss drunk.

He used to do some weird ass shit too, like piss in the closet then pass out in his piss. I swear, you could talk to that fool for, say, two hours, and at the end of the conversation realize you didn't talk about shit! He was a washed-up ex-baseball player turned drunk.

Anyways, right in the middle of all this commotion, I guess my mom's case worker shows up, (did I tell you my mom is a mental case?) and the case worker is trying to find out what is going on 'cause she has five different people yelling and shit. In the end it comes down to: either my mom, or I, have to go spend the night in KMC psych ward. If I say, "No," then my mom has to go. Man, all my bros and sisters are there, so I say, "Fuck it, I'll go."

I spend the night there.

I guess the next day shit was fine 'cause my mom comes and picks me up.

My mom says she has multiple personalities. I don't know if she really does or she just thinks or says she does but one thing is fact: she's nuts!

She may have <u>convinced</u> herself she has multiple personalities.

She is a pathological liar, though.

She has a real gift to almost have you second-guessing yourself about shit you thought happened one way, but the way she tells it, you're thinking, "Damn, maybe she's right!"

If she "lost one hundred dollars," it would real easily turn into she "lost a thousand" by the end of her story, as she tells it. You can't really believe a word she says.

Living with someone like that is mentally taxing, as well as emotionally draining. It's from her I learned not to show no emotions, and it's also from her I learned what not to be. But to act on emotion with her would have me all fucked up: one minute, she's all lovey-dovey; the next, she's calling my parole officer making shit up. Then when the cops get there, she will be full on in tears and acting afraid for her life — an Oscar-worthy performance. Then, as soon as I'm in jail, she would come visit me, telling me I'm her favorite child/special son 'til the day I get out of jail or released from prison saying I can't live with them no more 'cause she took out a restraining order! I have literally watched this woman jump out of bed at 6am, stomp across the house, take off in her truck, sit at the courthouse 'til it opened at 9am, lie to the judge on how I'm beating her, get a restraining order, come back home with the cops, wake me up and be all like, "Why are the cops here?" Fucken nuts!

I have been around a lot of psycho people and crazy characters, but even up until this day, June 5th, 2022, 41 years old, I've yet to come across another person anywhere close to my mom's craziness!

Another time, (look man, some of these next few pages are gonna sound made-up, but remember I'm writing this for my family and for a lot of this they were there — you can thank my sister Jessica for helping me remember this stuff. Like I said, I didn't write this story to shame anyone, I just needed y'all to get somewhat of an idea of what I had to endure growing up with a mad woman. Even though I was physically beat for about twelve years, the pain I've suffered from this woman from seventeen on up until now is way worse. I would have preferred to just be physically abused than to be subjected to this woman's madness. I kinda feel like Eminem 'cause I'm about to clean out my closets. If there was ever any skeletons in my closet, it wouldn't be too crazy to find out it was minds 'cause I would have been in there hiding from my mama. I even wrote a remix to cleaning out my closet and shot it to my little brother Joseph.)

Like I was saying, my mom would overdose on her pills and one day — almost about the same time I went to the psych ward and my siblings were visiting — my mom comes out of her room running and screaming at me to get all the dogs out of the house and why is there a fire truck in the front yard?

All my siblings look at me like, "What the fuck?"

I simply look at them and say, "Welcome to my world."

To get an idea of how this lady's mind works, let's start at day one:

November 2nd, 1980

Garfield Medical Center

Monterey Park, California

My father—well, step-father, to be exact, but never in all my life have I ever called him anything but "Dad" (he has been the only father in my life, even though I always knew he wasn't my biological. He loved me so thoroughly, I never cared to meet my real father. Why I didn't get his last name "Guevara" at my birth is a mystery 'cause at six months pregnant with another man's child, Bill met my mother and fell in love. He was there for my birth! To show my mom's madness wasn't all-of-a-sudden. But it was evident she named her second child, a male, Kenneth James Thunderburk! Where she got "Thunderburk" is a mystery. She named my other brother Kelly James Thunderburk! I don't know why my dad didn't question that too. I've asked her where the name came from. She never gave me an answer. It's even crazier 'cause his father's name on my birth certificate is Victor Bocos....who that is is also a mystery.

At first, my real father was a Mexican drug lord who gave my mom her only wish: to get pregnant by him on her birthday. Then he just rode off into the sunset.

The second story — 'cause if you've ever seen me, I have Armenian features, so this story suits her even better — is even more spectacular than the first. I guess this father's name is Debby Zubat (pronounced *Debbie Zoo-Bot*). He's an Armenian terrorist on special assignment in the U.S.A. I guess she met this dude in a bar on her B-day too!

Then I come to find out in 2015 she found my read dad. His name was Jerry Castricon. He died a few years ago. She showed me a picture on Facebook. Some skinny-ass old puny white coke head. Yeah, nowhere close. She even had his sons convinced they was my brothers. I tell you all this to show you this lady been crazy a long time ago. You can look "Thunderburk" up on Google. I'm the only one in the world! Check. I'll wait...

Okay, back to the story.

My siblings leave. I can only imagine the story they tell my dad or their friends!

One day, my mom wants some meth, so she steals one hundred dollars from Irene. She'd always do that then blame me. Well, anyways, she says, "Here, go get some dope, Kenny," and hands me the hundred. So me and the homie Boboe take off. I guess Irene notices the missing hundred and they call the cops. I get back to the house with the meth, but decide to come in the back way. I can see through the window into the front room and I see my mom talking to two cops.

I listen and hear her say, "Yeah, he should be back. I overheard him saying he was gonna go get some meth then come back. So when he comes in, you should have him red-handed."

The cops say, "Okay."

I tell Boboe what she just said. He says, "Let's bounce."

I say, "No, I'm gonna hide the meth. Just go in 'cause if we don't, they gonna go looking for us. We ain't got shit on us fool, so we good!"

So we come back around the front like we don't know shit and go in the house. Right away, the cops is on us. They search us and don't find shit — nothing they can do. They ask me about the hundred. I say I don't know anything about it. The whole time, my mom is looking at me all smug and shit. The one cop asks me to step outside, so I do, and he says, "Son, I don't know what you did to your mom, but she's intent on putting you in jail. Be careful!"

I say, "Okay, thanks!"

I go inside the house. I guess my mom thinks they left. She says, "You got the dope?"

I say, "Hell yeah, I'm about to go get lit."

She says, "I want mines!"

I say, "Hell Naw, you ain't getting shit — you tried to set me up. I heard it all!"

She says, "Randy called the cops but I will just call the cops back and tell them you just robbed me."

"Oh yeah?"

I run outside and stop the cops as they are about to leave and tell them my mom wants them. They stop and come back inside.

My mom says, "Take him please."

The cop says, "I can't!"

They leave. So do me and Boboe. *Thanks mom!*

I never intended to burn her, but shit, she tried to set me up so fuck that bitch! Like I said, no emotion. I must admit though, all-in-all, she took that one on the chin. *Love you too, mom!*

Somewhere in all this, I turn eighteen. The day just passed like any other. I was at my homie Joker's pad chilling. Next thing I know, there's a whole lot of banging, then cops run up in the house, put cuffs on Joker. I go outside, police everywhere. I guess it's a parole sweep in the whole hood. I ain't on parole so I'm cool.

Joker goes to jail. His mom's like, "You need to leave!" So I go to the freezer cuz Joker has 3 sugar cubes laced with acid. I take them out and eat two.

I call Randy to come get me at the corner and take me home. I guess during the wait, I slip into my acid trip.

Randy pulls up, I get in.

He's talking, I'm tripping.

The car is an old "MG" convertible, top open, so the noise and air is tripping me out. Randy don't even notice.

When I get home, I go sit in my room and listen to some Bone Thugs and trip. Next thing I know, it's night. I look in the fridge and see a new bottle of After Shock liquor. I start to hit it. My mom sees me then starts yelling. I guess it was hers.

I really need some weed, so I walk down the street to this white fool's named Thomas. They all inside playing Nintendo 64. I take the little neighbor kid, a different Thomas, with me cuz he had the weed money. I ask the people in the house, "Who got the weed?"

Some lame named George says some dumb shit. So I step outside. I tell Neighbor Thomas, "We gonna rob these fools. Go in the house and get a trash bag." So he does.

I walk in, pull out my knife and grab one of the wires to the game console remote and start to wind it up. It's like, as I pull it in, dude's coming with it like I'm fishing and he's on the string. When he gets close enough, I punch him on the side of the head, top of his ear. The knife I had covered my hand from my thumb across my knuckles — like brass knuckles — so he starts bleeding. That wasn't my intention. I find out later that I clipped the top of his ear off. I guess now I know how pit bulls feel when you clip their ears.

No one else moves as I toss shit in the bag.

Once I'm finished, I give the bag to Neighbor Thomas and tell him to take it home, so he does, running.

I walk. Once I get home, I see Neighbor Thomas. He says, "Follow me." So I do.

We pull up to his house. Two little black kids answer the door. They turn out to be Thomas' friends, so we go in.

All the stolen shit from Thomas the white boy's house is in the front room! I call the homie to come get me. He's on his way. I then call Thomas the white boy's house.

He says, "The cops is here!" then a cop jumps on the phone, tells me to turn myself in.

I say, "For what?"

Then I hang up.

I call my mom's, she is panicking. She says, "There's twenty cop cars lined up, all the way down the street. What the fuck did you do?"

I say, "Nothing!"

Next thing I know, there's a knock at the door. I figure it's the homie.

Nope.

I'm face-to-face with the sheriff. The gig's up.

They cuff me and Neighbor Thomas, put us in two different cars. A while later, they pull me out of the car and say, "Look into the light."

I do.

"Positive!"

I've just been positively ID'd.

They ask me, "What happened?"

I say, "I don't know!"

The cop goes to the car where Thomas is. He's there for a good while. Thomas is telling it all! Said I made him do it and all that.

Neighbor Thomas goes home.

I hit the county jail for the first of many times. Honestly, I really didn't see the big deal. But I guess robbing a house full of white kids at knife point and cutting off a piece of ear is. *Damn, who'd a thought?*

Pretrial – Kern County Jail

I remember almost the whole first week.

I slept, coming off the dope. I kept getting woken up for count. I just wanted to sleep, man. When I finally came to my senses, I realized one thing off the rip — I wasn't in Kiddie Land no more.

But I still wasn't tripping. It was what it was. I didn't have no one to call or to visit me, so I wasn't really too worried about the streets. The homies asked why I was busted. I said, "I stole some fool's shit. Nothing major." I guess the courts felt way differently:

- Home invasion, first offense
- 6 counts of strong-arm robbery, residential burglary and mayhem

Mayhem?? What is that? Chopping dude's ear off is what that is!

My lawyer says something about 56 years.

I'm like, "Naw, I'm good. Try again."

I get back to the pod, I tell the homies.

They say, "Shit's serious!"

I still don't think so! I get on the phone and call white Thomas.

"What's the deal? Why you telling?"

He says, "No I ain't. George is the only one telling."

It's the truth!

I'm thinking, "Damn, what the fuck's he tripping on, he got all his shit back. Why is he still being a bitch?"

Then I laugh and think, *Naw, he didn't get all his shit back — he didn't get his ear back!*

He even put a dub on it.

He told the cops that after I cut off his ear, I licked the knife all Hannibal Lector-like! I kinda like it though. The homies say I'm a savage! Truth being told, I didn't do it though. At least not to my recollection!

Next time I see my lawyer, I tell him, "Only one fool gonna snitch, all that other shit out the window. Talk to the DA."

It takes a few months, but the DA finally caves — two years "with half", plus one strike — the strike being cuz it's violent.

"Three strikes and you're out" means life in prison — no questions! It's a new law. The courts really fucked up — it was supposed to be three consecutive violent crimes, but they put all kinds of twists on it.

To the fools with one violent case who had prior violent cases before the law came into effect, that one violent case could be enhanced using that prior violent case against them giving them two strikes, then any felony not even violent could then become a strike. I know plenty of fools who sit in California prisons for petty theft and simple possession charges doing life on three strikes. It's a fucked up law.

It was written by some dad whose daughter was raped and killed by a dude who was paroled on a prior crime similar to that. Its whole purpose was to impact violent criminals — not for what it turned into. After the dude who created the law heard the way it was being used, even he said the courts were misusing it! It's 2020, the courts have yet to fix it — although they did amend it, making it the judge's discretion.

"Two years with half" means with good behavior I only have to do about one year. So yeah, it's looking like I'm about to do two years!

I hit Wasco reception center. It's a state prison. My CDC*** is P-33042. "CDC" is "California Department of Corrections".

They put about two hundred inmates — I'm no longer a minor/ward, I'm now an inmate — on a long, cold bus, three to a seat, shackled and cuffed, absolutely no talking while the bus is in motion. It's about a two-hour drive. I'm scared, nervous and anxious all at the same time. I've heard crazy stories about prison.

We finally pull up. Big fences. Razor wire all over. Gun towers where you could see the cops and assault rifles. We pull through the fence, bus stops. They start calling out names.

"Thunderburk!"

I step up.

"Number P-33042."

I step off into line.

They are taking off our shackles. We're all in these blue paper jump suits too, no boxers! Back all stiff, my shackles get removed. I step inside the building. It's a rounded interior. All the way around is bullpens with a gang of fools in them — different county jails. In the center is all the desks and computers where the cops are. On the floor are yellow guide-lines that we're to stand behind, or follow. Inmates are wrapped all the way around the pod, all facing forward. About every ten feet, in-between inmates is a C/O.

They tell us all to strip naked. I look around, and there are female officers everywhere. They pay us no mind.

"Palms up, run your fingers through your hair! Run a finger through your mouth! Lift your nuts! Turn around and lift your left foot! Your right! Squat and cough three times! Get dressed!"

In front of us on the floor is an orange jumpsuit and some Jap-flaps, which are some black slip-on shoes, like the Chinos wear. Still no underwear.

They herd us all into a bullpen like cattle. One-by-one we get a "TB" shot, see medical, talk to the gang coordinator. Then do our fingerprints, then back to the bullpen to wait. Lunch is a 4-pack of bread and peanut butter and jelly. They took us out of our cells in county jail at 2am. It's now going on 7pm. Everyone is tired, hungry, and cold and ready to get to their cells and crash out!

"Thunderburk, last two!"

I reply, "Right here. 4-2!"

"Unit D-1, cell 248!"

I walk outside, grab my bedroll — that's two sheets, a wool blanket, a roll of toilet paper and plastic cup. Then I follow the walkway until I see the unit "D-1" in real big blue letters on the side of a unit. Also, on every single wall in the whole prison, big white signs with red letters: "WARNING: NO WARNING SHOTS". Even inside the units! You'll find out a little later what all that means!

I pull up to my unit, step into the "B-side" of the building: fifty cells on the top, fifty cells on the bottom. I swear, everyone is in their cell windows checking out the fresh meat. I go to my cell, step in. The fool is on his bed, jumps down, says, "Luney, Anaheim Penguins!"

He has a big moustache and glasses with a tattoo above his left eye.

I say, "Turtleboy, Varrio Bakers!"

He says I can have the bottom bunk.

I make my bed, go to sleep, jump up the next day, go to breakfast.

I meet the homies. They give me the rules:

- Always keep shoes on
- No sleeping in the daytime
- No fucking with the blacks for any reason
- Must work out every day
- No psych meds
- No talking to the police

Those are the main rules.

The usual stay in reception is about two months, then off to your yard. The purpose of reception is to classify inmates to assign what type of yard you go to.

Level One is a low. Usually short-term offenders and parole violators.

Level Two is still kinda low custody inmates, but it's behind a fence.

Level Three is medium security. Fences and gun towers. Plus they got Lifers on those yards, more serious cases.

Level Four is Max. It's for violent crimes and people who fuck up while in prison. I already know I'll be there soon...

I been in reception about a month. I really don't like my celly either. He thinks I'm not no threat to him, don't really give me the respect I got coming. Plus he acts like he's above the Sureño rules. He sleeps all day. He don't work out. He even talks down on the homies. I believe in if you my people, I'm with you 100%. Well it's actually 113%.

One day, Looney says, "I'm gonna jack off so shut up!"

I thought he was playing. A couple minutes later I stand up and this fool is jacking off! I think, *naw, what the fuck?*

We come out for dinner and I tell the other homie what this fool is doing.

He says, "Fuck that fool, we'll deal with him at yard tomorrow!"

I say, "OK."

The next day he don't go to yard so the homies tell me to smash him out. They ask do I think I can handle him, since I'm so small.

I say, "Shit! Hell yeah!"

I take my thick-ass state-issued cup and put it in two socks. Once we step out the cell for chow, I let him get a couple steps in front of me, then I blast his bitch ass in the side of the head — well, the temple. His glasses fly off, everyone scatters. I start beating him with that cup in those socks until the sock rips and the cups go flying. I jump on him with fists. I hear a loud ass BANG!! God damn. That shit is loud, scared the shit out of me.

Next thing I know, literally one hundred cops is all running up on me spraying OC pepper spray. That shit hits my face. I can't see or breathe. And I'm on fire like they hit me with a torch.

They tackle me, then cuff me up, take me out the unit, drag me for what seems like forever and put me in this phone booth-size cage and leave me in there.

The big bang I heard was the 40 millimeter block gun. They call it "Big Bertha". It shoots five soft ball-size blocks at a time. It's supposed to be non-lethal, but I have seen it kill. They also can utilize live rounds which they shoot from a mini 14 — 7.62 rounds, same ones they use in an AK. No warning shots. I'm happy they missed me with the 40 millimeter. Later on in my story, they don't.

I'm placed in a D-6 which is "Ad-Seg" — "The Hole" — for assault on an inmate! Right away the homies ask to see my 114 lockup order. I shoot it, I'm good! Once again I get a kite about the size of a post-it note — the small ones. It has the smallest writing I've ever seen on it. It has even more rules than the ones on the yard!

Our whole door is see-through. Every time we leave our cells it's hand-cuffed and secured by two big-ass cops. We're only issued two pairs of boxers, two t-shirts, two socks and a pair of sandals.

Every morning at 6am the Sureños do a roll-call. They call your name and celly's name out. Well look, it goes like:

"Turtleboy, Puppet."

We say, "Kema," which means "yes" in Aztec.

They say, "Qualli Ici," which is "good morning" in Aztec.

We say, "Qualli Ici."

Right now it's "Qualli Yoalli," or "Good night."

They do it to make sure we're all alert. If you don't wake up and miss it, you do 113 burpee's. The second time is you got to do burpee's literally all day. Since your whole door is see-through, they have no problem watching you. To miss it a third time is "court action" — usually three homies beat on you for 113 seconds. A fourth time, they stab you up and "X" you out. It's serious shit.

The same applies to mandatory workout: we get seven hours rec a week, Monday-through-Friday, no weekends. We work out as a group at rec, which is usually Monday-Wednesday-Friday, 3 hours-2 hours-2 hours, rain sleet or snow. The workouts are brutal and all in unison. If they call, say, 113 jumping jacks and someone loses count and does one extra, the whole group does them all over again. Plus, the homie that messed up owes 113 burpee's after the whole group is done working out. But you never let a homie roll solo, and usually the whole group does them with him.

They understand some fools ain't in tip-top shape and they work with him. They got two weeks to be tip-top shape or they considered dead weight—"X" him out, stab him up, send him on his way! The whole reason behind these workouts is to prepare us for war — literally.

On the yard, the riots can last for hours, several hundred inmates, pepper spray, tear gas, real bullets, plus all the inmates got knives or some type of weapons. The Sureños are a literal army. This is just the physical aspect. I'll also get to the mental in a minute. Being honest, just the stress from worrying about if I could handle the workout every day be fucking me up. You got to remember these fools are criminals, killers, thieves, drug dealers, schemers. The one perk about the Sureños is none of them have fucked up charges like sex cases and stuff like that — once you hit a yard they make you show your paperwork from court with all your prior cases. If you got any weird cases it will show! And if so, you will be stabbed up on sight, no questions. And trust me, you got fools lined up to do the honors.

OK, now aside from the military-type workouts, they make you learn nuhuatl, which is the Aztec language. The Sureños base themselves on the Aztec culture because of their warrior mentality. The reason we learn the language is so we can either communicate verbally or in kites, and if the cops hear or pick off a kite, they won't be able to understand it. They also encourage us to learn the history of the Aztecs as well. Also, it is encouraged to learn Swahilli and German to know what the opposition is talking about too. It's mostly Swahilli 'cause they are the number one enemy. They want well-rounded soldiers. No loose ends! They expect every Sureño to be in top shape. It's not just a gang, it's your lifestyle — it defines you as a person.

Being in a Hole or a SHU is like being in the Pentagon — it's headquarters. All the big homies are in there. Since I got an assault, they give me thirty days. I do my thirty days. The assault puts me at level 3 points. They send me to Corcoran State Prison. At the time it was under a lot of controversy due to the cops staging inmate fights on super small concrete yards, betting on the winners, then shooting the losers. They called it "Gladiator School". They even made a movie on it called "Felon".

It wasn't just the SHU that was crazy, it was the whole yard. Every race is segregated. The blacks have their own showers, phones, workout areas, dinner tables. Even though everybody is out together, no racial mingling is encouraged. They all know all the Sureños hate all the blacks. Same for the whites and blacks. The whites usually fall in with the Sureños too, but at times even they clash! You could literally cur the tension with a knife. And trust me, everyone has one. It's especially mandatory all Sureños carry one at all times, which is also super stressful.

To get caught with a knife constitutes no less than two years in the Hole/SHU, and almost 100% of the time, street charges and more years, if not life. The C/O's all know the deal too, so just imagine the feeling of knowing at any given moment you can catch a life sentence. It's so serious, you sleep with your knife, wrapped up and insider your ass cuz the cops do raids at like 2 or 3 in the morning and ain't shit you can do when they are at your door and your knife ain't put up! Trust me, there ain't no place you can hide your knife they won't look. Cops even took it a step further making us walk through metal detectors and body scanners to catch the knives in our asses. It sounds funny, huh? Tell that to the homie who got life for getting caught with his knife or better yet, tell that to the homie who got killed cuz he got caught without one. Trust me, ain't no laughing going on here.

So here I am, a young man, eighteen, 5 foot 6, maybe 100 pounds, in the so-called "worst place in America". I hit the yard for the first time. I notice how big all these fools is. I see how racially divided shit is. I remember the homie saying, "Prison ain't shit until you see someone get killed." I laugh, not knowing I'm about to see just that.

The Sureños have their own punching bag and I'm just watching this homie kill that bag thinking, "Damn, that fool's a beast!" The next thing I know is I see three fools run up on him, a quick flurry of punches, the dude hitting the bag is on the ground not moving. The three fools spin off. It's over in about ten seconds max, if that. No one helps helps the homie up. They call yard recall, he still down! Come to find our them fools stabbed him over fifty times — he's dead that quick! No suspects will be sought, them fools got away with murder, that easy. I won't lie, I was a little envious. I wanted to be talked about and glorified like they were doing for them three homies! But don't trip, I soon get my own fix and so much more.

They call us young fools "torpedoes" cuz they just set us on a target and we explode. I thought it was a term of endearment or respect but later I learned it was kind of an insult actually! Torpedoes are expendable, single use. They blow up at the end — the blowing up is you catching a life sentence.

The prospect of me catching life held no value; that thought got no play in my twisted head. I had just been doing me! An incident happened to where the Sureños and blacks almost fell out. In the end, it didn't though. I'm telling you I was super jealous 'cause them three fools was getting all types of praise. I told the homies, "Man, it took three of them to do that fool. I get down solo!"

The homies said, "Oh yeah?"

I said, "Shit, you'll see."

This one fool named Casper is half white and he says he's Mexican. Well when it almost fell out with the blacks, he got scared and told someone he was white. But once the coast was clear, he was a Sureño again. The homies don't play all that! I raised my hand to handle homie. I got the green light to handle him! I tell the homie from Colonia Chiques — his name was Mono — to keep point. So I called Casper to my cell and told him we was gonna get high. He slides in my cell, Mono closes the door. I immediately stab that fool in his face all the way through his cheek. He screams. I stab him at least seven more times: head, neck, ear, back, chest and arms. Then I flushed the knife and grabbed his head and started to bang it on the desk over and over again. I thought Mono had point 'cause I wasn't tryna get caught. I wanted to stay on the yard and get all my props but I guess somewhere along the way he bailed out on me.

The cops heard the screaming and located where it was coming from, and for the second time in my life, introduced me to O.C. pepper spray. That shit ain't fair — it gives you no chance. This time, instead of in an open pod, it's in an enclosed cell which makes it a hundred times worse. They follow the same routine as the last time, the only thing different is this time they read me my rights. The whole time I'm thinking, *The homies gonna be talking about me tomorrow,* plus I'm also thinking, *if I catch that bitch ass fool Mono he's gonna get it too.* In the end, he eventually does.

4Blleft: the hole in Corcoran; SHU. I stay there until I see ICC committee that decides my fate, such as amount of SHU time. I get a serious 115 which is the technical term for a write-up. It is also pending a DA referral which means the facility referred it back to the district attorney for further criminal prosecution: street charges, more years in prison. But considering it being Corcoran State Prison, hundreds of these case come across their desk every year; they won't pick it up unless it's you getting caught red-handed with the knife in your hand. They usually kick it back out, so my fingers are crossed!

The incident code is: ASSAULT ON INMATE USING A DEADLY WEAPON RESULTING IN SERIOUS BODILY INJURY

Minimum SHU time is 16 months. 90 days loss of good time.

A couple days later, this big ass cop who's all tatted-up like an inmate comes to my door telling me he needs my 114 lock up order; the homies need it. I'm like, "Move around cop, I'll send it myself."

Later I get a kite from the homies saying the cop works for us — his name is Paco Loco, he's cool. When he comes back I tell him, "My bad."

He says, "It's cool!"

He takes my 114 then later he comes back and tells me I checked out. He will bring me a TV later. In California State Prisons you can have a TV in your cell.

ICC committee decides 20 months SHU. I moved out of AD-SEG to 4Blright — the SHU unit. I trip out 'cuz instead of it being bunks, the beds are left and right, side-to-side. My new celly's name is Largo. He is from La Punte Basset Grande, "Big Basset. He's cool as fuck too. He tells me the run down. He right away likes me 'cause he sees I been laced up already. He says the homies request we do three integrated rec movements which means if they pull us out to rec with some blacks or Norteños, we have to fight them on the tiny rec yard with a high possibility of also getting shot by the gun tower. Add to that, we couldn't be the aggressors — we had to let them fools rush us first, so when the DRB (Disciplinary Review Board) looks at the incident, we're not in the wrong and we can still do integrated rec movements, which only means we get another chance to fight again. Lucky me, right?

A couple days later, we hit the rec yard and lucky me, we draw two huge ass black fools. I won't lie, I'm scared as fuck, but mostly of getting shot. The blacks make it easy on us — they rush us immediately. One hits my celly so I swing and nail the black fool with all I got. Yeah, that doesn't do shit. He then kicks me straight in the side of my head. I'm literally out on my feet. My celly saves me though. He smashed out the other black fool. No one gets shot. We get to our cell. I tell my celly, "My bad."

He says, "For what?"

I say, "'Cuz I didn't do shit!"

He says, "Fool them niggers were huge. Most fools your size would have curled up. I seen you rock that fool. Don't trip lil' homie. We gonna work to get your weight to catch up to your heart. Until then, I got your back dog."

That's what it was all about when I entered the system. The love and camaraderie of soldiers to soldier. The bond you create with a total stranger for one cause. All this new shit they got going on now is all watered down now. The same bond I had with Trippy and his family. Aside from all the crazy stress of being a Sureño also came peace of mind to know that no matter what you weren't alone! Maintain your integrity and you will always be good! I had no fear anywhere I went 'cause I was always a good soldier — loyal and dependable. I followed orders blindly — it was others that tried to take advantage of my loyalty and insulted my intelligence in all types of different ways. I learned to speak Nuhuatl, Spanish, I could literally break anyone off in working out.

"This time away just made perfection, did you think I'd die?"

- Makaveli, "White Man'z World"

I gained and learned a lot from being a Sureño. The main thing is I learned the mental capacity to assess situations and manage accordingly.

***

I did 20 months out of the 24 in the SHU on my first bid of two years with half.

Told you I'd do it all.

Up to this day, October 22, 2020, writing this story, I've always done my entire sentenced term. And most other times I've caught added time.

I parole out from the SHU, so I'm now "high control" parole, which is:

- zero tolerance
- report once a week in person to the office
- one home visit weekly from the parole agent
- no gang conduct

Can't be around any other parolee, drug tests, all types of stupid shit. I fucked all that up just on the first day. Shoot, on the 45-minute train ride from Corcoran to Bakersfield, I got drunk on the train using my $200 gate money. Got to my mom's house then she got me high.

I wend to see my agent the next day lit up. Only reason he didn't violate me is because he didn't read me my rules and conditions. Otherwise, I'd have been in prison again. He warns me. I say, "Cool."

A couple days later he does a home check. My little sister Alyssa lives with me and my mom. One day she comes in crying, saying the neighbor — some black kid named DJ — tried to rape her. I rush to his house, knock on his door. His mom says he ain't there.

The next day, my mom and me and my sister are driving down South Union, a ghetto-ass street full of hookers at this hour of night. She stops at this motel — run-down, been out of business for years. But they got extension cords running everywhere. It's obvious it's full of people. She tells my sister, "Here. Run this to room *so-and-so*!" Mind you I only been out a few days. I can't afford my mom to flash on me cuz first thing she gonna do is call my P.O. So I watch my 12 year old sister go. I'm sitting there stewing. The longer she's gone the more pissed I get! I say, "Fuck that, what room is she in?"

My mom says, "Don't worry about it. You're gonna fuck my business up!"

I say, "What room is it now bitch?"

She tells me.

I take off.

I get to the room, open the door. My sister is all the way on the far side of the room, on the other side of the filthy ass room littered with old porn magazines, and some old ass chump looking fool in his underwear with a hard on. It looked like he had my sister cornered and was blocking her exit. I punched the dude, dropping him, start to jump on his head. My sister runs past me. I stay smashing this dude out. I run to get to the car. I looks like my mom and sister are trying to leave without me, but I jump in the car. My sister is telling my mom what I did, so my mom goes off on me, talking about her business, her clients, all sorts of stupid shit! My sister chimes in too. I don't say shit 'til we get home.

Once in the house my sister starts running her mouth. So does my mom! I say, "Alyssa, if you ever do some shit like that again, it's your ass. I will beat you senseless!"

She gets up in my face. I smack the fuck out of her, knocking her ass out. My mom jumps in. I tell Mom, "If you ever put my sister in that type of danger again I'll slice your throat you evil bitch!"

I meant it too.

I slapped the shit out of her too! That sick ass bitch put my baby sister at risk. Who knows how many times she done shit like that prior to my release. She'd had all my so-called homies giving her dope, using my name while I was in prison then when I'm out they stop cuz I'll tell them to. She don't care about anyone, not even herself. All she does is take and breed evil! She even had Alyssa wrapped up in all this shit. I can honestly say I never had a chance.

About a week later I come to find out she didn't call my P.O. She even said I could come home, so like a sucker I do.

That night I'm at the homie's house a few houses down. Some big ass black fool with a full on beard is talking "South Side *this*, South Side *that*."

I'm all like, "Fool, this East Side Varrio Bakers. Fuck the South Side!"

I'm sitting on my bike. He opens his mouth so I rock his ass.

He falls, hitting his head on this homie's car door mirror. I stoop over him but he don't want no smoke.

I go home.

The next morning there's banging on my mom's door. I'm sleeping in the living room. I jump up, it's the fat ass neighbor DJ's mom. She's all, "Is Turtleboy here?"

That's me, but I don't know this lady so I'm all like, "No, why?"

She says, "He beat up my son DJ last night!"

I said, "Who? That grown ass man with a beard? Are you serious? Get the fuck out of here?"

She's all, "He's only 16!"

Damn.

I was like, *that nigger looks 40!*

A little while later my sister says, "Look outside, something's going on across the street."

I look.

About 30 people out on the corner at DJ's house and in the street. I see DJ and two other fools walking across the street towards my house. I grab my gun and step outside.

I point my gun at them and tell them, "Step in my yard, I'm gonna smoke all you fools!"

They stop.

Alyssa runs outside making a loud ass scene, all, "Give me the gun, brother, give it to me!"

My mom comes out too. She and Alyssa walk across the street and start talking to them fools. I go to the back yard, hit the fence. Soon as I get to the corner I see a bus. I jump on it, I'm gone!

I post up with my homie Joker for about a week. I call my mom's. She says, "Come home. The detective just wants to talk to you."

Yeah, I heard that before. I want to go get my clothes and shit so I wait 'til Friday about 7pm cuz they usually finish the parole sweeps at business hours, so I should be cool until Monday, so I'm at my mom's house.

I had this chick I just met there too. Joker was in the shower. I went out back to smoke and heard the side fence open. I look. It's the Gang Task Force! I got caught slipping. Fuck! Back to the county.

Three days later, I'm back in Wasco Reception Center, waiting on my parole hearings. You can subpoena witnesses. I'm being violated for hitting that kid DJ. So just to be a dick and make his mom have to come out of her way, I subpoena her. The Commissioner reads her my questions, cuz I'm not allowed to speak to her.

Any questions, we put them on paper ahead of time. They screen them then read them if they're reasonable questions. My question was, "Did anyone else witness me supposedly hitting him?"

She says, "No!"

The next question was, "Then why did you call the cops?"

She says, "I understand my son be in some shit. He's a gang member. I wasn't too worried cuz he said you only hit him once. What worried me was the next day, when your own mom walked across the street and told me if I didn't call the police you was going to shoot up my whole house. I have babies in there. I was scared for them. If it wouldn't have been for your mom, I would have never called the cops!"

I have no more questions!

The verdict: a year flat in prison.

Heartbroken, devastated, I began to realize how evil my mom really is — how conniving she can be, with no sympathy or empathy, not even for her own children.

I get to my cell.

All I want to do is hurt someone!

Alyssa too.

Fucking little two-faced bitch.

A few weeks later my homie shows up, says he went to check me out but found out I was already busted, and that he saw my mom and sister chilling across the street at some black fool's house!!!

The next morning the black orderly says some stupid shit to one of my people. I jump him. Instantly a riot kicks off. I'm at the top of the stairs fighting. I see a black fool running up the stairs, so as soon as he's all the way up the stairs I turn and kick him straight in the chest, pushing him backwards. He pretty much flips — back flips — landing on his head halfway down the stairs and continues to fall all the way down, hitting his head again. He's out of the picture.

I run around the tier, looking for another victim. The gun tower shoots. All the cops spray. Everyone gets down.

We all go to the hole — Sureños and Blacks.

The 115 write-up code is "Institutional Murder By Way of Route or Riot" which means someone died during the riot. They can't personally charge anyone cuz ain't no telling who done it. But dude on the bottom of the stairs was the victim. I guess only two of us knew the secret, and one of us is dead!

I ain't no stranger to the hole. I got ninety days to do there for all that. One day I shoot my sister Jessica an introduction letter hoping she shoots it to one of her friends. A few weeks later I get a letter from some chick named Nancy. *Jessica looks out again!* Her nickname is Shorty cuz she's tiny, but right off the rip I knew she's a good girl. We exchange letters for about a year. I don't fuck up no more in prison. I want to go home for once. I have something to look forward to, for reals...

It's June 2001. The Sureños are at war with the Fresno Bulldogs. The Bulldogs are a Fresno street gang that turned into a prison gang. They at one time used to fall under Sureño guidelines, but chose to do their own thing. The "Big Homies" of the Sureños didn't like all that so they put a "green light" on them. A "green light" is pretty much a hit; open season to take them out! In Wasco, up until this point, they had their unit which was "D-3". I was back in unit "D-1". They was talking about re-integrating them back with the Sureños. Uh-oh! All bad! Now I'm stressed. For once in my life I'm looking forward to getting out. I really like Shorty, and she seems the same way. They all supposed to come pick me up at the prison — my mom, Jessica and Shorty! But if I get into it with these Bulldogs it's gonna be an added 90 days minimum! I'm usually all for that free violence, but shit, I know this girl is way worth it. Fuck the bullshit!

The Administration bullshits about 'til August 1st to actually move those fools into our unit. I go home on the 3rd, so now if I get into it, ain't no way to notify my people not to come pick me up cuz I won't be getting out — ain't no phones. No mail ain't gonna make it either. Man, I'm all fucked up over this. A big part of me is "banged out". But an even bigger part of me wants to be loved even more!

Up until this point, you haven't heard me speak about nothing but 2 females: the big tittie Tweeker, and the chick I met the day I got rolled on by gang unit. The reason I ain't spoke on none is because there *wasn't* none! I ain't never had no girlfriend. I don't do no hood rats or hoochies. Plus I was always real shy when it came to females. I always felt I was ugly. I was super short and skinny. I was always fighting cuz I felt I looked like a weenie, so I'd fight to show I wasn't no weenie!

Getting to know Shorty in letters, plus she seen pictures of me, I guess she like me. I've never felt so excited about something! I sat in my cell literally visualizing our first encounter — what I'd say, how I'd bust my first move, every single detail. I literally did that every single day for a year. I literally thought that moment into existence — the law of attraction — cuz it happened almost to a "T" of what I imagined, with the exception of one detail I'll tell you about later.

So here I am two days to parole. I tell my celly, "Fuck fool, I'm gonna shit this one out. I can't afford to fuck this off!"

He ain't feeling none of all that cuz you know misery loves company.

One thing about inmates is they feed off hate and bitterness.

I tell my celly, "I would rather see you go home to be with your family, to be happy, if the roles were reversed."

He don't say shit!

It takes all day to move all the Bulldogs into the pod. We all on our toes, looking out the window to get a size check on all these fools. The rest of the day is uneventful, aside from the stress of knowing in less than 24 hours we will all be trying to kill each other literally all with knives and weapons just waiting for the doors to crack. Even though the Bulldogs didn't have the numbers, they were down as fuck — they put on for Fresno, California. Most of them tatted-up their faces so they bang. It's a Fresno street gang that turned into a prison gang but they don't have any shot callers so they all do whatever they want to. But they got heart — every single one of California gangs or disruptive groups goes hard as fuck. It's not even a possibility that you make it on these yards and you ain't earned it. I'm still on pins and needles — I'm sure it's gonna pop off first thing tomorrow. I literally don't sleep. I've always been super over-anxious, plus I'm ADHD. Plus I always expect the absolute worst. I'm feeling like, "Shit gonna pop off, I'm gonna catch more time, and Shorty is gonna say, *Fuck him*.

I tell God, "Man, fuck with me one time please! My whole life been shit, I need this."

I'm steady looking out my door window at the clock. The countdown is on. Any minute they gonna pop doors for breakfast.

The food cart is pushed into the building.

Here we go!

The guard starts to open one cell at a time, giving us our tray. We eat in our cell.

Thank God.

I won't keep you in suspense.

The warden already knew it was gonna crack first thing so he put us on modified program until further notice! Now I'm super happy. That night I still don't sleep, cuz I know I'm going home. I just hope I ain't got no stupid hold or detainers.

August 3rd, 2001

I don't get no sleep due to my anxiety. Plus I see my celly is hating. Oh well, fuck that fool! I hope he gets smashed in a riot.

I shave, then wash up and now just pace the cell until they crack the door to roll out. I yell to a few homies I fuck with, get a few numbers from the fellas so I can call their people for them and tell them they are doing cool. I'm not one of those fools who promise homies money or letters, but trust me I still reach out and touch fools from time to time. If I say I'm gonna do it, I do it!

About 8am they rack my door. I'm out this bitch!

I get to R&R – Receiving and Release. They say to go to the last bullpen.

"Do you need dress-outs?"

I say, "Yes!"

They bring this trashcan that has a bunch of donated clothes.

Shit, they even dirty.

I look for the best shit — ain't nothing good. I have to settle for some dirty blue jeans and wrinkled up grey shirt. But I scored on some decent shoes.

They call me to the desk, ask me some security questions. Mother's maiden name, where I was born, paroling to what address.

They count me out $200: eight twenties, two tens, three fives, four ones and four quarters.

Sign the receipt.

"We'll pull you in a minute. Go wait."

I'm waiting. I'm so anxious to see my sister and mom and be free. But mostly to see Shorty!

The prison van takes me out of the prison to the parking lot. I see my mom's car but just her and no one else.

My heart sinks.

I get off the van, walk up to my mom and give her a half ass hug and she's all, "What's the matter?"

I say, "Where's Jessica and Shorty at?"

My mom says, "They had to get out of school and take the Greyhound — they will be here Friday!"

I guess that is the only thing different from the way I had imagined it in my head. I had Shorty there to pick me up in my fantasy. Even though, it ain't all bad, I got a chance to get a haircut and some decent clothes before meeting with the girl of my dreams.

I have to go see parole the next day. I have a new agent — I guess the last one got shot by his ex-wife. The new agent gives me all my conditions and stipulations of my new parole.

Yeah, yeah, sure...

You better believe I'm on my best behavior — no weed, no meth, no alcohol, nothing is gonna fuck this up for me! Shorty will be here Friday!

On Wednesday, some girl I met named Paula — I met her at the mall, I gave her my number — we talk. Now I find out she is a real nut case. She looks really good though. All of a sudden she is calling me non-stop, all day blowing me up. She won't even let the phone ringer rest! For reals, it's getting real old fast.

I wind up turning off the phone ringer and fall asleep Thursday night.

Friday, I wake up early 'cause I'm anxious to get the call from Jessica and Shorty that they on their way.

All day goes by and no calls come in.

I'm thinking, *What the fuck? You would've figured they would've called by now right?*

It's a three-hour bus ride and it's now about 3pm so I'm starting to feel discouraged that they ain't coming anymore! My mom said that they were supposed to get to the station at 5pm. I try calling them but they don't answer! I'm about to just leave and right before I step out the door I remember the phone ringer is off so I run to the phone and turn it on. Right as I turn it on it rings!

"Hello."

"Kenny, what the fuck we been here at the station an hour now waiting and trying to call. What the hell y'all been doing?"

I say, "Sorry I had the ringer off. We be there in a minute."

I'm going nuts now with anticipation. My mom takes the trip to get them. I keep looking out the window like, *Damn, where they at? Come on already!*

I'm looking out the window so I see my mom and them are coming down the street, so I sit on the couch acting like I'm Mr. Cool as they walk in.

My sister runs up to me, "Kenny, hey brother."

"Hey sis what's good?"

She says, "Here is Shorty!"

I was well aware of Shorty as soon as she stepped in the room — even as soon as she got off the car. She was even prettier in person! *Oh MY GOD! I'm in love!*

"What's up Shorty? It's nice to finally meet you in person."

She says, "You too!"

My mom starts talking, taking Shorty and my sister into her room. I want to follow but I don't want to look like no idiot, so I just stand there looking dumb anyways. I'm so shy I can't even think of shit to say, even after plotting all this out in my head for over a year! *What the fuck?*

I step outside to regroup, I light up a smoke. I'm still at a loss for shit to say. My sister and Shorty come outside. I see the sunlight shining on Shorty. Her hair is kinda red so I say, "So your hair is red?"

Yeah, I know. Lame right?

She says, "What color does it look?" with an attitude.

I'm thinking, *This girl must think I'm a lame*, so I go in the house licking my wounds.

My mom says, "Who's hungry?"

Everyone is, so she says, "We'll all go to Burger King, who's coming?"

I say, "I'll chill here, no room in the car."

My sister says, "Shoot, Shorty, you can stay with Kenny and me and my mom will go. We'll be right back so behave."

Shorty says, "That's cool."

In my head, I'm super excited. I can have her all to myself for a little while. Hopefully I stop acting like a lop!

They leave. We are chilling on the couch, but she is way on the other side. I see her stretching her neck, side to side like it hurts.

I ask her, "Does your neck hurt?"

She says, "Yes. I hate riding the Greyhound."

I say, "Well thank you for coming. I'm super happy to see you. Do you want me to give you a massage?"

It took all my nuts to jump out there like that. In my head I said, *Fuck it, I'm going in!* But man, if she says NO it's over with. I won't be able to live it down.

Surprisingly she says, "Yes I would please. Thank you."

She scoots over. My hands touch her tiny shoulders.

It's over!

I fall in love.

I maybe manage about twenty seconds of the massage, then I kiss her and she kisses me back! I guess it's called macking so we mack the whole time my mom and sister are out getting the food.

She tells me, "You're a really good kisser."

She don't even know she is the first girl I have ever kissed!

My mom and sister get back and see us snuggled up on the couch.

My sister says, "Oh no!"

I guess my dad was tripping on them cuz they didn't ask him to go to my mom's — he wanted them back home.

I'm like, *Awe, man, what the fuck for reals?*

My sister says, "We got to be home tomorrow."

Fucking shit!

Shorty says, "I can stay to hang out with Kenny. You can go home though, Jess."

My mom says, "I'll take Shorty home when she's ready."

Oh my God! This is the best thing to happen to me that night.

Me and Shorty sleep in the same bed and it's starting to get real serious.

She says, "Stop trying fool cuz I ain't like that. You ain't getting fresh tonight, Kenny!"

I pull off and be all like, "It's cool. I really like you though!"

She says, "You're cool too," then giggles.

The next day we take Jessica to the Greyhound. We all say goodbye. We get back to my mom's. She leaves. Me and Shorty are just chilling. We go rent some movies and chill!

In the front room we have a sofa bed. We pull out the bed. My mom and everybody are asleep. Me and Shorty are going at it real hard.

She surprises the fuck out of me and says, "Do you got a condom?"

Shit, fuck, goddamn!

I say, "I can get one."

Before she even has a chance to say, "Never mind," I'm flying out the front door, my dick still hard as a rock.

I pull up to the homie's house about three houses down. I'm sure one of these fools has a condom. They always talking bout how much pussy they get but it turns out ain't none of them got a condom!

Fuck.

It's too late to go to the store and even if it wasn't, I ain't got no bread to buy any condoms.

As I go to leave, I see the least likely person to have a condom. The nerdiest fool in the bunch, but shoot, I ask him and surprisingly he says, "Hell yeah I got one. Here fool, take it!"

Thank God.

I snatch it up and speed back to my house and jump right into the bed all happy and shit. I'm about to get laid!

We get into it once again. I finally got her naked. She has a sexy ass little petite body too. I'm loving it.

I go to put the condom on and the mutha fucker's too small! Mind you, it's my first time doing any of this so I'm thinking, *Maybe that's how they supposed to fit,* but naw, something ain't right. I play it off. I ain't trying to throw no dub on my shit but 4 reals it was super small it barely rolled down halfway but fuck the bullshit, I'm past the point of no return!

I won't be too nasty — like I said, this is a book for my family and they all know and love Shorty — so let's just put it this way: it was a great night!

She even laughed about the condom and said, "Next time we get you a Magnum XL."

Like I said, no lies, all truth.

She didn't even know she took my virginity and when I told her, I don't think she ever truly believed me. She said I was too good. I'm good at everything I do though, for reals!

Man, that was the fastest weekend in history 'cause now we are on the 5 South coming down the Grapevine into LA County. We pass Wayside Jail and Magic Mountain getting close to Shorty's house. This sucks but all good, things must come to an end sometime, right?

We get to Shorty's spot. I kiss her goodbye and tell her I'll call her as soon as I get home. I watch her cute little booty all the way to the door.

We get back to Bakersfield. I call her right when I get in the door! Right after I hang up, my mom starts talking about "NO LONG DISTANCE PHONE CALLS!" *Really?* Like I said, this woman is crazy and will switch up in a heartbeat. Mind you, I'm still on parole so the next day my agent comes to my house. It's all good, I'm clean. That same day my homie Joker comes over. My mom likes him so she ain't tripping.

Later that night, my mom's weird ass tweeked-out friend comes over. He's tweeked to the max. I pull up on him and say, "Ay Sundance, if I washed my dick would you suck it?"

He looks at me all scared-like and almost as if I was gonna actually make him do it and says, "NO! NO I WOULDN'T!"

I say, "You dirty dick sucker!"

Joker starts to laugh. So does Randy. It was just a joke. I'm sitting on the couch weeded out. My mom comes out the room.

"What the fuck did you do to Sundance? He's in the backyard crying!"

I start busting up. The next thing I know my head explodes — I'm literally knocked the fuck out.

When I come to, I feel all kinds of warm, syrupy liquid all over my face and my head is bleeding at the temple. I stand up. I see Joker. He grabs me, 'cause he knows I'm about to snap. My mom is standing there with this weird look on her face. I'm still trying to put it together, I see a soda can laying on the coffee table; it's looking like it has a hold in it. I hear my mom start talking shit like, "Disrespect my friends again you piece of shit!"

I realize that stupid bitch blasted me in the head with a full can of soda. I pull out my knife — I'm gonna end this lady's cheap ass life. If it wasn't for Joker, she would be dead and unable to inflict anymore heartache upon the world.

Joker pulls me out of the house. I'm fucking pissed.

I hear the phone ringing, then, like nothing happened, my mom says, "Kenny, Shorty is on the phone!"

Instantly I forget anything happened too. Love will do that, I guess.

A couple weeks later, I'm at the bus stop. I meet some chick named Lorena Juliette — she's another tiny cute chick, real pretty. I take her to my mom's house. I fuck her in my lil' sister Alyssa's bed. Alyssa realizes I fucked homegirl in her bed only <u>after</u> she gets into bed! She's pissed! I guess she's yelling about a wet spot in her bed so she's going nuts, yelling and shit. So now my mom starts to yell too, so now everyone is tripping on each other. I was getting ice from the freezer. It's in a big ass bag. I get pissed off and throw the whole bag of ice across the house and against the wall. It puts a hole in the wall. My mom then calls the police. I take off 'cause of the type of parole that I'm on, which is: High Control 1192.7c — any police contact is an automatic violation.

A couple weeks later, my sister Jessica talks me into going to see my parole agent. She came down to Bakersfield with my homie Ron.

I tell my sister, "If I go see my agent, they are going to lock me up fool."

She says, "No they won't!"

But I guess everybody knows better than I do, right? So yeah, we all show up to the office, four of us: me, my mom, Ron and Jessica. I bet you can't guess how many of us left together? Well if you guessed THREE, you're right 'cause I also bet you can't guess where I went. If you guessed Disneyland, you're wrong — I just got me a 100% free ride to the county jail.

Sitting in jail I'm thinking "FUCK THE WORLD".

Then, "Thunderburk, visit!"

What the fuck? Who could this be? Probably my stupid ass mom playing her bullshit games again talking 'bout, "I'm sorry son, I love you and I'll see you when you get home, bye..." I'm thinking, *Fuck all that.* I almost don't even go to the visit, *fuck that bitch!*

I pull in to the visiting room and I see an angel — it's Shorty! If I didn't already love her, well then I fell in love with her that moment all over again. She was like a breath of fresh air in hell. I tried to play it off like how much time I was getting wasn't no thang, but it would more than likely be a year flat.

I told Shorty, "It's just a year!"

She stole my heart when she replied, "But you're not the only one doing time."

She meant that too! Man, I ain't never had no one outside my family care for me like that! That lil' five-foot-nothing girl broke me down all the way! I died inside 'cause now that year flat was gonna seem like forever.

I go from Wasco State Prison reception center to High Desert State Prison — B yard. It's literally the farthest from home prison they can send me to — it's an hour from the Oregon border up north.

The whole prison is on lockdown due to a riot between the Sureños and the Blacks. They have been locked down for eight months, which means I'm just in time for the next riot.

Lucky me!

All I wanna do is get home to be with Shorty. I'm telling you, having someone to love out in the world can at times be a burden!

A few weeks later, the lockdown is lifted. It's Winter time so snow is everywhere.

We all go to yard. I see all the homies clearing all the snow off the basketball court, so I go help. It takes about thirty minutes but we get it done. We only got two hours out. We hurry up and pick teams. I don't get picked so I ride the sidelines watching the homies run and slide all over the place, attempting to play basketball in the snow.

A while later, this black fool comes up and says, "We got next, how long y'all gonna stay on the court?"

The homie says, "Shit, we cleaned the court so all rec homie!"

The black fool gets mad and says *Nigga, nigga, nigga, something, something something* — it don't even matter what he really said 'cause after he referred to the homie as *Nigga,* it was over with

In California, all prison yards are all RESPECT—the Sureños run almost every single yard. We give everyone respect and if we don't get the same respect back, it's all bad every single time! One thing you don't do is disrespect a Sureño!

The homie tells the black fool, "It's cool. Yeah, y'all got next!"

He was just rocking him to sleep.

As we walk away, he tells the homies in the immediate area he's about to kick it off! We then alert all the other homies!

We walk to the pull up bars — the homies is all using the toes of their boots to dig at the ground. The homies bury they knives on the yard to beat the metal detectors so they got them at yard for times like these.

Everybody got they shanks, we ready!

I follow the homie, he finds the black fool. I see all the homies is ready — the blacks don't even have a clue!

The homie don't even hesitate, he runs up to the black fool so I follow. He then stabs that fool in the face. The black fool turns and runs right into me so I tackle him to the floor. The homie is on him, stabbing him all over. I roll over and jump up, all I see is groups of people going at it. It's all white too 'cause of the snow! I run into the group and start swinging my knife at anything black!

I hear a loud ass BANG! all over the place. I see smoke all over the yard. Cops come by the hundreds, expelling O.C. pepper spray, tear gas and utilizing their billy clubs to max potential! The fighting goes on forever too, but due to my training and discipline, I ain't even tired as I'm well aware of all going on around me.

I then hear over the bullhorn, "LIVE ROUNDS WILL NOW BE USED. STOP FIGHTING!"

That means all eight building towers plus the main yard tower utilized their maximum eight rounds each from the .40 millimeter Big Bertha block guns and now they can and will be using live 7.62 rounds on us. Just like us inmates love riots 'cause it's free violence, so do the cops — they are shooting to kill!

I hear the Sureños all start to yell and we all pull back, grouping together for safety. The blacks are doing the same thing.

Once at a safe distance, I see the blacks start to get down first 'cause they all know ain't no Sureño gonna hit the ground otherwise. Once they are all mostly down, the Sureños start to get down too. I see this one dude, a bystander, is right in the middle of the two groups. He is looking like he knows we about to jump up and start again, and he is caught in the middle, so he jumps up and starts to run.

BLAM, BLAM, his head explodes. It's over for him, just like that.

That easy to die!

The cops leave him. They then start to zip tie all the inmates and separate us by race — blacks and Sureños. All the other races not involved get escorted to the buildings they lived in. They keep us on the ground in that freezing ass snow forever.

Finally I get back to my cell. I'm so happy to be in my cell. I almost froze to death for reals! I know we are gonna all be on lockdown for well over a year, so I also know I'll make it home now too!

I write Shorty every day. I also get letters from her at least four times a week — she's such a good girl. I love her so much!

My crazy ass mom moved to El Centro which is ten minutes literally from the Mexico border. So, 'cause it's the only place I can go, I have to parole out to her house. Shorty comes to see me a couple weeks after I get out.

My mom had this young girl who was her friend name Ari. I won't lie, she was super bad too! She lived next door. Well, Shorty was super jealous 'cause Ari had a bad ass body but shit, my Shorty did too — I adored my Shorty! Well, whenever my mom would get pissed at me she would always yell and scream she was gonna call Shorty and tell her I was cheating on her and it would really fuck me up 'cause I wasn't. The only time I ever cheated was when we first got together with Lorena Julliette, and this goes for our whole relationship!

I met this fool named Cyber. He put me in the dope game so I'm doing this parole shit, doing what it takes to beat the drug tests and put on that face for my agent. I'm doing ok. One day my mom flies off the handle. I come home and my whole room is tossed up — my mom is in there tearing shit apart looking for my dope or my money. I was like, "What the fuck?"

She said, "I want some dope now!"

I told her, "Man, get the fuck out of my room!"

So she takes off. She goes to her room.

I hear shit being thrown around in her room. Then she yells, "I'm calling Shorty and telling her you been cheating on her!"

She picks up the phone to dial but I guess she forgot she took off the long distance calling just to be a bitch and put added strain on me and Shorty's relationship.

Well anyways, so she attacks me.

I grab her in a bear hug to stop her from attacking me. Once I let her go, she picks up a knife and swings at me, almost slicing my whole chest and stomach open.

She cut me pretty bad.

Then she picks up the phone and calls the police. I'm standing there as she screams into the phone how I'm supposedly beating her and at the same time she's knocking shit off her dressers — she even pulls the TV off too! She is telling the dispatcher I'm keeping her trapped in her room and that I'm in a rage tearing shit up. I'm just standing there like, *This evil ass bitch!*

I know the cops is on the way. I know it's 100% I'm going to jail. I know I didn't do shit but I don't know what to do. What can I do, I'm hit no matter what!

She then hangs up the phone and starts to yank on the collar of her shirt, stretching it all out, making it look like she got dragged or some shit. She also starts to bite her lip so it bleeds, making it look worse on me!

She then runs out of the house down the street. We live in a mobile home park. Everybody knows this bitch is crazy. She's yelling and screaming that I'm trying to kill her. The whole time I'm sitting on the porch. Nobody does shit! She realizes ain't no one tapping into any of all that shit so she goes back into the house.

A while later the cops show up. My mom puts on an Oscar-worthy performance.

Off to jail I go!

While I was in jail, I had to action at calling Shorty. My mom told her all types of stories and shit. Shorty got her heart broke. She didn't know my mom to be the vindictive person she really was so she believed what my mom said. She thought, *Why would his own mom lie to me — lie on her son like that?* I guess Shorty just took it all at face value when she should never have believed word one!

While I was in jail, my lil' sister Alyssa came to live with my mom. They got into it and I guess my mom hit her in the face with the phone and got herself locked up for child abuse. The whole time I was in jail on a parole violation telling these fools my mom was crazy; she made it all up!

I go to my parole hearing. They got all the evidence — this lady is nuts, plus she is in jail. I figure they give me a chance or a lil' love — maybe I get six months, then I may have a shot at salvaging my relationship with Shorty. But fuck no, the stupid ass unsympathetic commissioner gave me a year flat!

I spoke to Shorty a few times before I left county. I knew she was hurt for several reasons:

One, all the shit my mom told her. Adding insult to injury, she told Shorty it was Ari I cheated with. Stupid bitch knows how to put in on, right?

Two, Shorty knew I was gonna be away again for another year flat.

She said she loved me and she would wait — I had no reason to doubt her. She always been solid in the past.

I get to Donovan State Prison. I'm writing to Shorty like crazy.

About two weeks go by, no mail. I'm in reception so ain't no phones to call home with.

Now it's almost two months later — still no word from Shorty and I'm sick as fuck going through it. I know full well now the meaning to the song "Ain't No Sunshine". You don't know the feeling to be 100% helpless, 100% at the mercy of someone else. Wasn't shit I could do at all! I could write all day everyday, a thousand letters, but if she didn't want to write back, I was helpless!

I have experienced heartache, torture and physical pain, but keeping it real, nothing could compare to this. I kept seeing her with someone else in my head. Trust me, you don't want to know what goes on in my head. I literally kill myself in it every single day! I'm a beast!

After I get classified, they tell me I'm going to New Folsom State Prison — yeah, the infamous Folsom Prison you all heard about. I'm thinking, *This should be fun!*

It's a level four 180° design so that means it's a maximum security yard. It's also in Sacramento. It's also one of the craziest yards in the state so, so far I've been to the top three worst prisons in California: Corcoran, High Desert and now New Folsom.

When I get there, we on lock down again and it's the same as before: the blacks and Sureños.

As soon as I get there, I get a kite from the homie Cartoon. We were busted together as kids so he knows I'm a rider.

He says, "They about to let us off lock down but they gonna put us all on the concrete rec yard — fifty and fifty — to see if it cracks off again," and he's gonna sign me up!

The rec yard is a super small concrete enclosed cage in the back of the unit directly under a gun tower.

Lucky me!

A couple days later, they start the rec movement. They start pulling two Sureños, two blacks, all the way until they hit fifty each. It's a modified rec movement they always do after a big riot to see if we will get along. Most times we fake the funk and be good so they can open the main yard and we can really get it, but not this time.

As we get on the yard, we are all pulling our knives out of our asses. I'm super scared, keeping it real, but fear can be utilized as an ally if you use it in the right way.

The Sureños, we ain't fucked up. We let all fifty of them fools make it to the yard before we kick it off. We're all for that — the more, the merrier.

It finally cracks off: we smash them fools.

It only lasts about seven minutes 'cause we are literally fish in a barrel. The cops got guns, pepper spray, billy clubs, stun grenades, plus they were ready for it to happen.

The blacks, I guess they don't like sticking things in their asses. Fuck it, their bad.

All in all, after it was all over, it was kinda fun, once I realize I made it through without getting hurt. Plus, from start to finish, it took my mind off of Shorty!

My celly is a two-faced fool from Walnut Street. His name is Puppet — go figure. I guess he feels the amount of time he has makes him more gangster or high power. I laugh. I tell these fools, "Look, most you fools only on this yard 'cause you got life sentences. I'm doing violations on these mutha fuckers 'cause the work I put in!"

Puppet one day trips out 'cause I guess he don't like the way I'm flicking the pages to turn them in his magazine. Some stupid ass petty shit, to be honest. He feels some type of way so I throw his magazine on his bed. Next thing I know is I'm looking out the window and I feel movement. I turn just in time to block him as he attempts to stab me. I elbow him in the face and split his eye open. I beat the shit out of him too! The black neighbors heard it too. I used to talk to them cool though, so they call over like, "Everything cool?"

I say, "Shit, I'm good. Ask my celly."

I don't want to push no issues so I don't say shit to the homies.

We stay on lock down the rest of my time I am there. It's a good thing too 'cause the shot caller just put a green light on the cops!

My release from New Folsom is not only my parole date, it's also my discharge date — I am no longer on parole. It took all four years but since I didn't catch no new beefs, my parole ran out. I did two year-flat violations that each turned into almost two years each, plus the time I stayed on the streets on parole — I was finally free!

Like an idiot I went back to my mom's house.

I didn't have anywhere else to go. I can't say I was fully over Shorty, so as soon as I get to her mom's, I call her aunt's house. She never answers so I say, *Why pick old scabs?* The last letter I wrote and sent to her mom's house had come back "return to sender" with "no longer lives here" written on it in handwriting!

Right off the jump I started to sell drugs and to get high and wouldn't you know it, my mom kicked me out again.

So now I'm back on the streets.

One day — well, it was actually June 6th, 2006, they call it "6-6-6 Day", I guess — I went on a mission to get some meth with some fools. Well, it ended up I was in Mexico, stuck trying to cross back over into the United States with a backpack full of meth — thirty-two eight balls to be exact. While not a whole lot, it's just enough to catch a serious federal case. I was super sketched out.

Well anyways, on the Mexico side, the gate/fence is about thirty feet high and has a screen on it so you can see through it into the United States. I know just on the other side of the fence is Calexico, USA — it's the United States side of Mexico. I keep walking along the fence line and the next thing I know, in the distance, I see a Bronco SUV — the immigration officer vehicle — and it turns on its flood lights and lights me up. It's still a good distance away but I'm like, *Oh fuck!*

I start to run back towards the border but ain't no way, it's too far, so I hit the fence. I shoot straight up it and gangster flip over it. I'm thinking, *I'm just gonna land and be home free*, but shit, I'm still falling. *What the fuck?*

Finally I hit the hard, sandy ground. I land on my stomach. I feel all types of sand stuck to my face and whole body in El Centro, Mexicali. It's literally 120° all day in the summer, plus I'm super tweeked out and sweating everywhere. Plus I'm all scraped up.

I jump up and run across the street into a little park then into a bathroom.

I go into a stall and rip open the backpack, tear into a bag of dope and start to eat some. Instantly, I feel way better — like Popeye after he eats his spinach! For reals!

I'm only wearing a tank top and some shorts. I come out the stall to wash up and look into the mirror.

I'm shocked.

I'm looking at my reflection — all I see is a tatted-up, bald, all dirty and bleeding fool with no shirt on. I almost just walked out the restroom like that!

I say, "Fuck!" 'cause reality sets in 'cause in my mind, it was still dark when I went into the restroom and now it's daylight and there are people everywhere — ain't no way I'm getting out this city with this backpack full of dope. I ain't even got no ride or no money or no phone!

I walk back into the restroom. I stick the backpack in the trashcan. I say, "Fuck it." I formulate a plan. I walk outside.

I walk right by a cop.

I know he's gonna stop me instantly. It's 6am, ain't no way he don't.

He does.

I'm not on parole, so I'm cool.

After he runs my info, he asks me, "What happened?"

So I tell him, "Shit, I was chilling with some broads and they spiked my drink. I knocked out and they robbed my ass," which is pretty common in this area.

I ask him for a ride home, he says, "Naw," so I tell him, "Man, you're the fifth cop to stop me. Can you at least radio your fellow officers and tell them I'm clean so they can leave me alone and I can try to find a ride home please?"

He gets on the radio and gives my description. They say, "OK."

Once he leaves, I see this Mexican setting up shop. I ask him if he can give me a shirt, so he does. He gives me one with a Mexican flag on it and some writing in Spanish. I don't even stop to read the shirt, I just put it on.

I go back into the restroom. Fuck it, I grab the backpack, go back outside.

I see an all-white transport bus that takes all the *paisas* to work in the fields. I jump on it!

Men and women looking at me — they been working with each other for years — I guess they are wondering who I am!

About forty-five minutes later we pull up to some fields and everyone gets off. So do I.

I look for the boss.

I find him by his Ford F150 truck. I tell him I want to work for the day but I don't want no money. I will settle for a ride to El Centro.

He looks at me for a while, then he says, "OK, but only if you work good!"

I get my work ethic from my pops, so I work like a Mexican right away. He sees that I get down — I work all day.

At the end of the day, he says, "Get in. Where do you want to go?"

I tell him, "To El Centro, Adams Street!"

While driving to El Centro, he says, "I watched you work and you work good. Do you want a job?"

I say, "I do, but I don't want to waste your time. It wouldn't be worth it to you right now. Thanks though, man."

We pull up. I go to get off the truck.

He says, "Here is my number, just in case. And here is your money for working today."

He hands me two hundreds.

I'm all, "Good business homie, thank you."

I use that $200 to get a motel room. I get some chicks and a couple of homies over and we chilling, plus I got all that dope too. I'm telling them this story I just told you.

I say, "Fuck homie, it wasn't looking good for a minute. I thought I was over with!"

I'm still wearing the shirt that paisa gave me and my homegirl looks at me and says, "Si se puede."

I say, "What?"

She then says, "He gave you a shirt that says, 'Yes, it's possible!"

I say, "Yes it is!"

I'm staying in motels just selling dope.

One day I send my little homegirl which turns out to be Ari to this one Mexican who stays in a different motel so she can buy us some cigarettes 'cause for ten dollars I get three packs. Well she comes back all shook up like, so I'm all like, "What happened What's a matter with you, why you acting like that?"

She says the dude tried to rape her!

He had her trapped in his room and wouldn't let her go! Add insult to injury, that fool pulled out a knife on her too!

I tell Ari, "Don't trip, I got this."

The next day I go knock on dude's door. He opens it, but he just cracks it to see who it is. When he sees it's me he tries to close the door real quick, but I push myself all the way in and I close the door.

He runs into the bathroom and slams the door.

I start to look in all the drawers 'cause I know he gots money.

I find it. I start to put it in my pockets.

He comes out of the restroom and tried to stop me so I pick up a big ass spoon like the ones they use to get soup and I hit him in the face (I find out later I broke his nose).

He yells and I flee the room.

I'm running down the stairs to jump on my bike and some old ass lady sees me and says, "What's going on?"

I say, "Nothing" and take off on my bike.

When I finally make it to my room, I pull out the money and notice it's all cut in half. *What the fuck?* But for the next couple of days, Ari has fun putting all the money back together.

A few weeks later, while I am outside using a pay phone by dude's motel, the police run up on me.

Hands up! You know the deal.

I guess that fool had the nerve to snitch on me!

I'm in the county jail and my mom comes to see me, telling me she's gonna move to Oklahoma and she's marrying her cousin.

I'm thinking, *OK, weird ass bitch.*

What can I do? I take a deal for two years with half. I leave the county jail and wind up in Donovan State Prison in San Diego by the border. I stay there for a couple uneventful months and wind up being shipped off to CRC — California Rehabilitation Center, also known as "Hotel California. The Eagles even made a song about it!

This place is crazy — it's a thirteen story facility with a dorm on each floor — you need to use the stairwells to access each floor. The stairwell is treacherous too — everything from fights to homosexual activity go down in there.

I know immediately I do not wanna be here so the first chance I get, I smash some fool out with a lock in a sock. They then send me from the hole in Chino called Palm Hall to Iron Wood State Prison in Plythe, California. It is literally the hottest prison I even been to with no air conditioning. It's horrible, but at least all the homies act right!

It's back to business! Sureño program!

I wind up tattooing the whole right side of my face with a big ass "VB" for Varrio Bakers! I also fully tatted my whole back — the homies paid for it. They wanted to keep me out of trouble so they moved me in with the tattoo artist and told me to sit down until he was done.

My homie Lazy from Verdugo runs the yard. He has his squad which is me, Speedy from Verdugo, and Thomas, also from Verdugo, Downer from Delhi, Psycho from Long Beach, and out of nowhere came fat ass Happy from Orange County — I guess he just got out the hole.

We all held each other down — none of us wanted for anything. We ran that 2,000 man yard well.

One day all the homies was playing softball versus the white boys. It was game three of the best of three and a lot of money was on the line. Me, Lazy, Speedy, Psycho, Downer and Thomas was in the bleachers drinking and smoking, just watching the game when the homie "P" gets caught in a pickle — back and forth. The white boy tags him in the back, kinda pushing him, so P eats shit. *HE'S OUT!*

Keeping it real, P was in the wrong 'cause he should have never tried to get that extra base, but he did and now he jumps up all mad-like and starts to bark all up in the white dude's face. So we all jump up just waiting to see what's next. The homie Lazy and I see the white boy catcher pick up the bat — now, maybe he was just picking it up to toss it aside, but who knows? All I know is that is all it took! Lazy jumps out the bleachers. I follow him and he cracks the white boy catcher that has the bat. Instantly it's a full-fledged riot — the white boys don't stand a chance either.

It's like 300 to 100 so here I am fighting, I turn to see where more action is and I start to run from the center field spot and I see a white boy laying on his stomach with his head laying on his arm like he's taking a nap. I'm sprinting full speed as I reach him. I field goal kick his head with all I got. I'm also wearing state issue boots too.

He flips, lands on his back and makes no movement.

We all gravitate back together — all the homies.

All the homies are talking about "I stabbed...", " I cut...", "I hit so and so" and on and on it goes. So the homie Lazy says, "So I should see at least 50 fools stabbed, all that shit y'all fools is talking about." I say, "I don't know about any of all that but you can see my work right there!"

We are all on the ground on our stomachs. All the homies look up and we see them putting that white boy on a stretcher for the life flight out of dodge.

The homie Lazy laughs and says, "That's what's up lil' homie."

It's the same protocol as every riot, just a different prison: zip-tied, escorted back to the unit and an undetermined length of lock down — no one really goes to the hole in riots 'cause there won't be any room.

A few weeks prior I had shot out a hail Mary letter to see what was up with Shorty. I sent the letter to her mom's house never thinking I would ever get a response. Then one day at mail call:

"Thunderburk, mail last two!"

"Four two, here I am."

The cop shoots the letter in my cell door. It's from Shorty!

I won't lie, my heart literally stopped. I didn't know what to think. I immediately tear the envelope open to see what she had to say!

She tells me she loves me and she's still in love with me. She misses me and she wants me back! I never ever truly got over her and to have her telling me all this was mind-bending. It was a miracle. I couldn't think anything could get any worse for me. I didn't have any prospects or plans for my life, but now with her back it put everything back into perspective.

But then I was like, *Oh shit, what about this big ass tattoo on my face?*

I didn't even tell her about it the rest of my time, and she was gonna pick me up at the prison gates on my release date. I was nervous as fuck thinking she would be all like, "What the fuck? Naw, hell no I ain't fucking with you."

My release date comes and next thing I know I'm in her car and we are driving and she says, "So I see you got some new tattoos, huh?"

I smile and say, "A few."

She don't even trip, nor does she ever ask me to take it off or hide it. She is that kind of girl — that real unconditional love that's so rare to find these days. I love her so much. She is still the best thing to ever have happened to me. I'm grateful to have ever had her at all!

Now I'm in El Centro with no home to parole to, so I request a transfer. But in order for the transfer to happen, my agent has to request it and it takes a few months. Meanwhile I need to find somewhere to live until it goes through, so I am forced to go into a Salvation Army church rehab.

Hell naw, for reals that shit is like a real-life cult!

So I skip out and start staying in motels.

So now I'm working and fucking up at the same time. I find work every day at the labor ready work source. It's a daily temp job agency where you need to be there at like 5am every day to get a job. If not, you're hit and won't work so it's very important I work every day so I can pay for my room every day.

I'm staying in ghetto ass motels all week. Then when Shorty comes to see me on Friday through Sunday, I get a nicer room in a different area — it's more expensive but somehow I manage it.

It is super hard to juggle two lifestyles bu I never want Shorty to see that side of me, and she never did. But I think if I would have let her see that side — all the shit I came from — she would have kinda changed how she really saw me and things may have turned out differently that they did in the end. I feel like she never really truly knew me 100%. She didn't realize all the demons I had to overcome and fight daily to be the man she saw me as. She never knew exactly all I had to go through — what I had to sacrifice for her — but then again, no one really did!

One weekend she can't come see me. It turns out for the best that she couldn't make it 'cause at about 4am that same morning as I'm sleeping, I hear a knock on the door. I jump up to answer the door. It's the cops!

I'm on parole so they don't need no warrant. I think it's a parole sweep but later I find out someone said I robbed their house and they identified me by the tattoo on my face. They said it was me and a female so if Shorty would have come, she would be in jail too!

All the evidence they had on me showed it wasn't me — they had muddy shoe prints, fresh ones, and none of my shoes had mud on them 'cause they were all brand new. They also had fresh bike tracks from I guess the suspect rode away from their house. Well, the bike in my room was flat. Also, they couldn't even identify the tattoo on my face. The local newspaper didn't help either — they ran a story about "A Tattoo on the Face: A BAD Idea!" They pretty much had me convicted and all that in that story. 100% honest-to-God truth, I had nothing to do with any of all that! I didn't even know the people. I still don't even know why they said I did it!

I was just chilling in El Centro County Jail playing cards one day when three homies stabbed another homie to death up in the corner cell. One homie, the homie Vala, comes out the cell all covered in blood and screams, "I want his heart!"

Then Vala goes back into the cell and starts to dig in dude's chest. I don't think he got his heart. Well, he comes out of the cell and is walking around the top tier to make his way downstairs. He has a towel draped around his neck.

Vala is about six foot four — pretty tall. He walks down the first part of the steps and is on the landing. Right on the side of the landing are the phones, up against the wall, and some fool is on the phone.

Vala leans over the railing with the towel in both hands hanging down. He wraps the towel around dude on the phone's neck, then he raises up using the rail like a wench and pulls dude up off his feet like a noose. Dude on the phone is kicking, going nuts and struggling to get free — it ain't gonna happen. After a while he is real still, just hanging. Vala still holds on to him forever then lets him go. He then walks down the rest of the stairs and hides dude's body under the stairs.

I'm thinking, *With all the blood all over the three homies, it's 4 sure they gonna get caught*, so I tell all the homies we all need to strip and everyone throw all they clothes in the shower, so everyone does. The entire pod is deathly quiet. You could smell the blood from upstairs.

The cops come to do their rounds and see us all in our boxers as soon as they enter the pod — they know someone died.

They radio backup and tell everyone to lock up, "Back to your cells!"

I feel sorry for the homies who have to go back to their cell up in the corner with the dead body in it! Everyone refuses to lock up though!

A cop still does his rounds and finds the dead fool in the cell. They send in the troops this time — they ain't playing around anymore!

Everyone is handcuffed and removed from the pod. A count is then conducted — they are missing one person. About an hour later they find dude under the stairs. The pod cameras make it easy to find the suspects — they take them fools to a max pod.

The dude who got strangled, well somehow they brought him back to life. He testified on the whole case. They found the homies guilty too. They day after he did all that he kills himself!

Crazy right?

Amongst all this I cop out in court — I take another two years with half. I really didn't have no choice, I can't chance a trial with my criminal past. They would convict me just on that. Plus, I was most definitely gonna get a year flat violation anyways.

I tell Shorty. She's all fucked up about it cuz she knows I was innocent, but yet again here she is "doing time" with me again!

I go back to Donovan, then to Corcoran B-yard — Level 4. Remember I told you about the Bulldogs earlier? Well, they just opened B-yard, they put three hundred Sureños and three hundred Bulldogs on this yard. For a while the war was supposed to be stopped.

One day my building is out for rec. Everything is cool, then a couple homies chase a Bulldog into his cell and stab him up. They lock us down, but everyone makes it seem like it was personal, not political, so they let us off lock down in a couple weeks!

So now we back at yard. The homies go to meet up on the yard to talk. The Bulldogs rock the homies to sleep: when the homies was walking away, the Bulldogs struck. They stabbed the homies in the back. It happened so fast, no one could react cuz the cops was on it!

They lock us down.

One day Shorty comes to visit me, driving five hours to come see me. I love her so much! I'm the only one from my block that gets a visit. My visit goes good. I get to kiss my baby and watch that fat little booty as she gets up to put my food in the microwave! The visit finishes. I kiss her real big and squeeze my fat little ass. Tell her I love her.

I always feel fucked up after a visit. One, cuz I miss my baby already, two, cuz while I'm laid up in my cell, she's still driving home! I'm all in my head about all this. I walk in the block, look up and see fools in the shower. Next thing I know the 4 top shower doors burst open and fools is running at me!

What the fuck?

It's four Bulldogs! Two are coming down the stairwell, right in front of me, one fool goes to kick at me, I side step him then pull his leg, pulling him off the stairs. He lands in like an awkward splits, he screams. I know it's 'bout to be three-on-one, all bad. So I tell myself, *I can at least smash ONE out.*

I jump on dude on the floor and beat him out. The other three jump on me. I'm just waiting to be stabbed. I hear the whole pod erupt in yelling — it's the Sureños and the Bulldogs kicking the doors and yelling! I get cracked in the head, they fucking me up. These is fools that be on that shit — warriors, not just regular dudes. It's not just the Sureños who train for war, everyone does!

It's starting to get bad! I hear *bang, bang bang!*

I feel them fools let me off, so I get up trying to find my bearings.

BANG!

My whole back explodes, knocking me on my face, taking all my wind! The fucking gunner shot my ass with Big Bertha! Add to that I'm on my way back to the SHU!

I get 120 days in the SHU, I can't do no workout cuz my back is super fucked! It's the longest 120 days ever!

I get back out the SHU. I'm getting close to going home.

One morning I guess the tower racked the whole bottom tier's doors, so as soon as I come out, my neighbor, a Bulldog, rushes me. Everyone's fighting, the tower is shooting, the cops is all running into the pod. The cops finally get ahold of everything and put us all back into our cells.

About two months go by.

They start by trying to let us program together. They start by letting us sign up for the phone. If by chance they let a Sureño out with a Bulldog, well you know the business. All the cops know I'm short to the house, so I sign up for 12.

The cop is all like, "Naw you don't want to do that!"

I say, "Why not?"

He says, "You already know, I'ma make sure you go home!"

I was all like, "Hell yeah!"

The next day at 12 they let a homie out then two Bulldogs. That homie got butchered. I felt bad but glad it wasn't me. I had been working on transferring my parole to my dad's house in West Covina. I only seen him a couple of times since he dropped me off at my mom's. Shorty was putting work in extra time to get all this done. I won't lie, I was super nervous cuz now I really had to man up. Plus I knew my dad has his wife tripping out on me coming to live there cuz my little sister had robbed them due to her drug use. Even stole her wedding ring. So she was real scared, plus she knew I had been in prison my whole life. She didn't know what to expect. She wasn't the type to risk shit.

I know my dad's decision to allow me to stay there put pressure and strain on his marriage. But this time I was 100% focused on changing my life. I wanted to show my dad how much I appreciated him. But before I could transfer I still had to go back to El Centro until the transfer was complete.

While in El Centro I have to stay in rehab. Man, that shit sucked. It was all I could do to not say, *Fuck it,* and leave.

Just when I thought I couldn't take it no more, the transfer finally went through. I was a little worried cuz a few days before I had smoked some weed. But finally it was happening!

I called Shorty. She bought the bus ticket, and I was on my way home! Finally after all these years, I was coming back to my family. More than ten years of bullshit, a totally different person. Now as a man.

First thing, my dad has us meet at Shakey's Pizza, which is crazy cuz as a kid he's always take me to Shakey's. Me and Shorty pull up, my dad's inside. He hugs me and it's as if nothing has changed. Shit, he even looks the same. I'm kinda nervous cuz the big ass tattoo on my face! He don't even comment on it.

Later we all go to his house, which is where I'll be staying. I meet his wife Esther, her daughter Jessica and son Diego. Also my little brother Joseph fresh out the Marines lives there too.

Since I transferred my parole, I have to report in to my new parole office the next day, so Shorty takes me the first time.

My parole agent says, "I can terminate your transfer at any time for any reason!"

It's a female too, so I'm thinking, *God damn!*

She says I need to drug test!

Oh shit!

Remember I told you while in El Centro waiting for my transfer I smoked some weed? Well here it is, biting me in the ass.

I tell her, "I'm dirty but my parole agent in El Centro already took care of it."

She ain't hearing none of all that!

I test. I'm dirty.

She says I'm fucking up, but I get one shot. That shot is now I got to do the STAR (Substance Treatment And Rehabilitation) class. It's from 8am until 4pm, Monday-Friday all the way at the parole office. I have to start Monday and it's Wednesday.

Oh fuck!

So I try to go leave. As I'm heading to the lobby she follows me, sees Shorty. She greets her, then tells Shorty I'm lucky she didn't kill my transfer. I'm all like, *Fuck, here it comes!*

Shorty says, "Why?"

She says, "He tested dirty!"

If looks could kill, Shorty would be in jail for murder! I already know my little five-foot-nothing girlfriend 'bout to let me have it! I'm feeling super stupid too. After all she was doing to get shit straight for me, I was getting high. But it wasn't even like that. I hit some weed a couple times, it wasn't like I was out there getting high. But I can only imagine what Shorty was thinking.

We get into the car. I'm just waiting.

She looks at me and says, "I'm a stupid bitch, huh?"

I don't say shit. What could I say, "I'm hella wrong"? Plus I feel stupid as fuck. I really with all my heart and mind love this girl. She's only been amazing to me. A blessing. I never had to stress on her while I was busted, she always held me down. And her I was fucking shit off. But like I said, it wasn't like that. I do stupid shit at times.

She says, "If you ever lie to me again Kenny, or go back to prison, I'm gone. I won't put up with it no more!"

I say, "Ok!"

She then says, "Since you got yourself into this mess, don't think I'm getting up early every morning and taking your ass to that class or picking you up, that's on you. If you want to show me, it's all on you!"

I ain't got no money or no car, and the parole officer is about 45 minutes from my spot.

Fuck!

She drops me off at my dad's. I explain to my dad my situation.

He says, "Let's figure out the bus schedule."

He gives me twenty dollars.

The next day I'm up at 5am. I learn that down the street, if I walk up to the freeway entrance, I can catch the "Silverstreak" bus for $1.50. It takes me to El Monte bus station. I can then walk to the parole office or catch another bus. I soon find a short cut walking through the canals.

I do the program.

About a month into it during a lunch break, I Google "Homeboy Industries". I ask the receptionist for the tattoo removal department. She patches me over.

"Tattoo removal, how can I help you?"

I told them, "Yeah, I'd like to schedule an appointment!"

She says, "Uh, sir, it's a year-long waiting list just to be seen!"

I say, "Fuck! 4 reals?"

She says, "Yes sir!"

I say, "Well do you think you can put me on that list pretty please ma'am?"

I guess she liked how I spoke to her cuz then she said, "What's your tattoo and where is it at?"

I said, "It's my hood and on my whole face!"

She said, "Give me your name, I'll see what I can do!"

"Thank you, I appreciate you!" I tell her. I hang up.

About an hour later, I get a phone call, it's the receptionist.

She says, "Come in next Tuesday, don't make me look bad!"

I say, "Hell naw, never that, you'll see!"

I come to find out later cuz she told me she hit my Facebook up and thought I was cute, but she liked my girl better!

I call Shorty, tell her the news. She didn't even know I was trying to take it off — she is super excited.

The day finally comes. We show up, it's a big yellow nice building — it even has a café called "Homegirl Café"! All pretty ex-homegirls work there. The place is in downtown LA. Almost every minor employee is gang-related, from the clerks to the janitors.

I step into the tattoo removal room. *Damn, the little receptionist is sexy as fuck too!*

She recognizes me, not to mention, like I said, my last name is one-of-a-kind.

She greets me warmly, then she sees Shorty and shoots darts at her. Later, Shorty says, "Damn, I thought she was gonna jump my bones right there babe!"

I told her, "Cuz you sexy as fuck" and she really was!

We go into the tattoo removal room, it's a really pretty Asian woman. I see Shorty all looking at her like she knows her. Mind you, my Shorty super respectful and always real professional.

She says, "I'm sorry but you look real familiar!"

The Asian woman says, "I do the show 'Dr. 90210'!"

Shorty blushes then says, "I watch you every week!"

The removal process is using a huge laser — it picks up the green ink pigment and literally burns it out of your skin. Each session is set three months apart and every session the laser is set to a higher degree.

It hurts.

All I can say is it feels like someone is taking a torch to my face, literally! Thank God it's pretty quick!

They say I need to keep it covered for 24 hours after each session and put sunblock on it for the whole time I'm getting it removed. If the sun hits it and turns it brown, the laser can't pick up the pigment and it's never coming out. The number of sessions depends on how deep the ink is set, how dark, what the ink is made of, all types of stuff. It's a slow, gradual process. My shit is super black and done right so it's gonna take a while.

The sexy little receptionist gives me my next appointment. She then tells me, "Miss one appointment, you're done, it's that serious!"

I tell her, "I won't, I promise you. Thank you."

I know she feels somewhat proud 'cause she took a chance on me — I think she could sense my dedication. I never missed a single appointment, she was there the whole time. It took five years with a session every three months.

I completed the STAR class — my parole agent was switched. I was doing super good so he wasn't tripping on me. I had moved in with my baby in Ontario. My homie from the STAR class gave me a job lead so I took it.

One day Shorty was at work. I was feeling like a bum at home. She came home at lunch and told me I got a job interview at Pacon, Inc. I was super stoked. The interview was the next day.

Shorty took me during her lunch hour. The company wasn't but a few miles from my dad's so I told her I'd walk to my dad's and wait for her later.

This was my first job interview ever, plus this big ass tattoo on my face is usually a deal-breaker. The HR guy Mike doesn't even trip on the tattoo. He says, "I'ma show you the machines you'll be running!"

I was super excited. I had a job!

The machines were huge, and super hot. One thousand degrees hot, no punk! I start the next day.

I literally almost run to my dad's house, so excited, I can't wait to tell everyone.

My dad is the first to get home so I tell him. He's happy for me. Then Shorty gets there, I tell her, she's happy too. I'm still supposed to be living at my dad's, by the way.

Next thing I know my parole agent shows up. Everything is all cool. He tells me since I'm doing so good he's gonna put me in for early discharge. That's the best news ever!

I tell Shorty I'll stay at my dad's to figure out how to get to and from work. She says, "Ok."

I get to work the next day and they say I'm in charge of three extruders which extrude hot plastic. The company makes mesh netting! It's called Pacon, Inc. in the city of Baldwin Park. The main part of the entire company is the production of the plastic mesh netting being extruded from these giant extruders! They are extremely dangerous and unforgiving. Super, super hot, over one thousand degrees hot, extremely greasy, hot grease, loud and unyielding! The work can be back-breaking and tedious, it's really sensitive too.

I won't lie, standing in front of these machines I was a little overwhelmed. My trainer was a Mexican guy Miguel. He starts me out explaining the concept of the machine, how it works, how to set the dials for certain types of material, the length and weight of the net, the different types of material, how to fill out the production sheets, how to mix the color and plastics, it's a whole bunch of shit!

I'm there about a cool month. I'm actually handling those machines. One day I'm at lunch standing in front of the company building smoking a cigarette when this old man is walking by. He looks at me, he stops, starts to walk toward me, zoning in on my face tattoo.

He says, "You work here?"

I say, "Yes sir!"

He shakes his head then says, "Who the fuck hired you?"

I go to say something but he cuts me off and says, "Where you working?"

I say, "I run the extruders sir!"

He says, "How long you been here?" and "Do you know what you're doing?"

I say, "A month sir, and yes, I know what I'm doing!"

I told you, these extruders are no joke. He invented them — 'he' being the old white man that's talking to me. That white man is Bob Austin, the owner of Pacon, Inc.

He says, "A month, huh? I call bullshit, let's go inside!"

I follow him. He stops at a machine and says, "Shut it down, run yellow super VU. I want it done in an hour!"

He turns and leaves.

Fuck, fuck fuck.

These machines are super technical. Ain't no simple 'shut it down'.

To do this I first need to lower the die, stop the unwinder, slow down the chain slowly, stop the material. It has a die cast attached to the gear wheel. The die cast has $12^{3/16}$ allen head bolds that anchor it to the shaft — they all get full of plastic.

Using a wire brush, I clean out the bolts.

First I need to take off the inner die's six bolts using my allen key. The whole time I'm wearing these huge high temperature gloves. It's a bitch, especially to not strip a bolt. I remove the inner die, hold it using some needle nose pliers, then clean it using the wire brush. The same goes for the outer die cast.

Now I need to put a new die cast on.

You put the outer die on first—you put it on like you do a car tire, one bolt at a time on one side, the next directly across and so forth. The same for the inner die. Once attached, I leave it to heat up.

I have to empty the hopper which holds the material/plastic that melts into the netting — one five-gallon bucket at a time. It's about thirty gallons to empty the hopper.

Now I have to make the new material super vu, which is two different plastics! Four five-gallon buckets, one at a time, I throw into the mixer, toss in the dye/color then let it mix, then pour it into a one hundred-gallon barrel until that barrel is full, push it to the machine so it can be sucked into the hopper then melted to use for the type of net we are gonna run.

I put the form on which dictates how wide the net is gonna be.

I start the machine, adjust the controls, weight, and the stretch that dictates the material.

Once running, I need to check the samples to make sure everything is good to go.

The hardest part of this whole process is setting the die: one false move and you could burn the die, costing $10,000 a die — that quick.

I get it all done, and I'm taking care of another machine when I see Bob come to my machine. He has Miguel with him.

He asks Miguel, "What you think about this one?"

Miguel says, "He's good boss, real good!"

The next day Bob calls me to his office. I'm stupid nervous. He hands me a white envelope and says, "Get back to work!"

I stick the envelope in my pack. I'll check it out later at home.

When I get to my dad's, he's home.

He says, "What's up Foolio?"

I say, "Just about to open this envelope the owner gave me."

So my dad snatches it out of my hand then opens it and says, "You're in trouble...and me and Nancy want dinner on you, we love steak!"

I don't know what he's talking about, so I take the envelope.

It's a check, a $1,000 check. Hence my introduction to real money.

I settled in at my job. I won't lie, for a while things were great at work, at home and in my life. My parole was discharged so I was a free man. I had been living with Shorty in Ontario. I'd take the train to Baldwin Park, then walk the rest of the way to work! It's been almost a year and a half of doing this, no drugs.

Well, I lie.

After work, sometimes I'd smoke some weed with my three work homies, but then I'd be all on the train stupid high and somehow always wind up sitting next to a cop, only thing going through my head the whole time is, *They gonna know I'm high, search me, find the little weed I have on me and make a big deal. The outcome, I'd be banned from the train and go to jail.* I couldn't have any of that! I didn't want to let Shorty down again!

My Shorty was always great, I loved her, I still do with all my heart, she taught me all about being a man: How to open a bank account, use a checkbook, pay bills, keep a job.

Mind you, all this is still new to me. I literally went from being banged out to fully caring and staying away from any and all bullshit. The tattoo on my face keeps getting lighter too. It seems the more the tattoo fades, so does my relationship.

I hate fighting and arguing with people. Let alone my lady.

In 2008 I proposed to Shorty, she said yes! I thought that would be it, we'd be happy. But with all her great ways, she had some fucked up ways too. She'd stay mad at small shit forever. Almost every night, I'd fall asleep in the front room. Every night she'd jar me awake. I'd jump up flustered like, "What the fuck?" She'd get mad, stay mad, so that anything I did after she would get even more mad. I couldn't win!

I'd come home from work and she'd leave the living room, go to the room and close the door, so I'd say, *Fuck it.* I'd go downstairs to my homie's and chill!

I ain't never once — aside from old girl way in the beginning — cheated on Shorty. I changed my whole world for her, for us! The drugs, the gang, the tattoos. The lifestyle, the friends, I literally started all over.

She got a new job at Kaiser Hospital. I worked my ass off to support us and she only worked 10 to 15 hours a week. I didn't know why she was always so mad at me. I knew it was bad cuz at work she had these three fat man-hater coworkers. I'd see comments on her Facebook about me. *Really?* I guess they was getting in her head. My relationship, my whole world was falling apart! I didn't know what to do.

I excelled at work though. One day, I was at work scrubbing the floor on my hands and knees and some Mexican fool laughed at me saying, "I'd never get down on my knees for the man!" I guess that's why I lasted and he didn't! Bob Austin, the owner, was a great man — even though he could be the biggest asshole in the world.

One day, on a Saturday, I was super hung over cuz my little brother Joseph was just back on leave from the Marine Corps and we all got fucked up. I was even late for work. I had all my machines up and running, then I sat down and I guess I dozed off...to be woken-up by none other than Bob.

He says, "Ain't no sleeping on the job, son!"

I say, "I'm not asleep sir, I'm watching the machines with my eyes closed!"

He says, "Get your ass in my office!"

I'm all like, *Damn, I fucked up!*

We walk to his office, he sits down, tells me to sit down. Then he says, "Son, I'm taking you off the extruders!"

Right away I think I done something wrong!

I say, "Why? I like the extruders!"

He says, "Life ain't all about what you like. I'd sure like to keep you as a lifer here Kenny, but at the same time I want to teach you skills you can take with you everywhere. Those extruders, I'm the only company that has those in the world. Sure, you can run those but it gives you no world experience! I'm trying to teach you stuff you'll need later in your life!"

So I start my new position that Monday. Just like the extruders, at first it's overwhelming but I soon learn the trade. My specialty is changing the extruders' main bearings when they need to be changed. Being in maintenance, there is a lot of downtime and changing the bearings takes about two and a half hours, so I keep busy! I also got a good raise too!

So as things at work are looking up, at home things are starting to fall apart. And it's starting to affect my work!

The stuff Shorty would normally do like make my plate of food, drive places together, watch TV together, she no longer did. If she was sitting in the living room watching TV, when I got home, she'd get up and go to the bedroom. So instead of fighting, I'd go chill downstairs at my homie's. This became normal. So for about a year or so, we pretty much were just roommates.

In 2010, July, Shorty breaks up with me. She tells me to pack my stuff and leave, but I refuse. The next day when I pull up to the security gate, I can't find the gate opener. So I wait until another car goes through then follow it in. Once I get to my apartment, I notice I don't have the door keys no more. Shorty must have taken my keys when I was sleeping.

I try to call her but it goes to voicemail. It's about 7pm, she should be home soon, so I wait.

10pm, 11pm, midnight...

Pissed, I drive to my dad's and sleep there!

For over two weeks I can't reach Short not get into my apartment. Good thing I used to live at my dad's and have clothes there or I'd be fucked.

I won't like, I go nuts losing Shorty, calling every two seconds, numerous texts, the only thing I don't do is call her work. But she's sick of all the calls and texts, I guess. She's staying at her mom's for the time-being, and the step dad is all scared so he makes her get a temporary retraining order. I don't know about it, so about a week into it my aunt Vivian — whom Shorty works for at Kaiser Hospital — comes to my dad's house. She serves me the order!

I'm pissed — even more so that my aunt would get in the middle of it!

As much as I want to, I can't call or text. It's a felony in California to violate an order and with my record, two strikes, it's a potential life sentence. Mind you, the order was issued July 2010 and I wasn't served until early August 5th or somewhere around there.

As time does, it heals, so it's now Halloween 2010 — three months passed. I'm still hurt, but not so much. I'm at a Halloween party when my sexy ass homegirl shoots me a pic of her in a naughty nurse costume and says, "Wanna chill?"

I been about four months with no sex, a bad breakup. I'm all like, "Sure, why not?"

So I jump in my ride and speed off. It's 2am, I'm on the freeway going about 100mph when I get lit up.

They pull me over for excessive speeding, they run a field sobriety test and they determine that I fail!

I blow a 0.68, under the legal limit of 0.81, but they still take me to jail for "wet reckless" and almost a "DUI"!

My court date is February 5th, 2011. For a DUI. Well, I show up to court. When the judge calls my name he reads me my charges, they wind up dropping the DUI but the judge tells the bailiff to detain me on a 250 thousand dollar fugitive arrest warrant. *What the fuck?*

Two days later I'm getting arraigned on violating a restraining order.

Come to find out, during the initial report to get the restraining order, Shorty said I've never harmed her, but that I constantly kept calling and texting. The officer took her phone and made a record of all the texts and calls.

My lawyer argues that I never contacted the complainant after I was actually notified of the order. All the calls were prior to the order being served so the DA storms out of the courtroom, to come back later and say, "If I can't get him for violating an order, well then I'll get him for stalking!"

All it takes for a stalking case to stick is phone calls, and text messages, and a person to complain, and with my record, they got a case!

My first deal is seven years. I refuse but wind up settling for sixteen months only, to do half.

I sign.

I was guilty but in all reality I didn't do shit wrong. This female was not only my lady for 10 plus years, she locked me out of my own house and refused to speak to me. I was an emotional wreck. I didn't deserve to go back to prison for no texts and phone calls. But I was! She even took the stand and said I've not bothered her since notice of the order. But this is a fine example of how corrupt the California penal system is!

2011 April

I'm now in Tehachapi State Prison Reception Center awaiting transfer to a yard. The Sureños check paperwork — my charge is "stalking". It don't sound good, so I tell the fool checking my shit to actually read my paperwork so he can see it ain't no creep shit. I guess he doesn't cuz I catch him telling the shot caller, "We got us another victim!" Meaning me, and they gonna stab me up over my case!

Once homie leaves his door, I run up to the shot caller's door and tell him they got me fucked up — my case ain't all like that. If he was gonna appoint someone to do a job they needed to do it right.

He says, "I'll holla at you when I come out."

After dinner, he comes out and we chop it up. He reads my paperwork, it's all cleared up now.

They have inmates on bunks in the dayroom due to overcrowding. I'm one of them. I'm naturally loud, so at night while fools is sleeping — not on purpose, it's just my nature — I'm all talking hella loud. I guess people complained so now I got to do discipline which turns out to be smashing on some dude and taking kites back to the hole.

Kites are notes we wrap in plastic then stick in our asses to take to the back. The kites usually consist of the reason I'm in the hole, plus whatever else they want to relay to the homies in the hole. Sometimes drugs or razor blades.

At dinner they lock everyone's door. I watch for my victim to step out of his cell. But instead of it being the dude the shot caller said had to go, I chose to smash the shot caller. Like I said, I've never been a victim to anything but circumstance. I was also mad 'cause Sureño policy is six months or shorter to the house, you get to chill. So I felt he was wrong!

As soon as he comes out of his cell, I run at him. When I get close enough to hit him I Superman punch that fool. I hit him in his right eye-socket, then his head hits the wall. A loud ass 'crack', then he falls forward like a sack of dead meat.

His head hits the concrete, another loud 'crack', blood starts to pool around his head — it's super dark, black blook, and then he starts to convulse, spewing white foam out of his mouth.

The floor cop seen the whole thing and I see him walking towards me shaking his can of pepper spray, getting the tower's attention, so I say, *Fuck it.* I jump on dude on the floor and start punching him. I know and feel with every punch I'm fucking dude up way worse. I guess they think I'm stabbing dude so they shoot the real gun — a mini 14 — at me.

I scoot away and lay prone on the floor, the cop still sprays me and hits me with the billy club. I'm then handcuffed and escorted to the hole/staging area, stripped, searched, then placed in a little phonebooth-sized cell.

Because it's an assault, my rights are read. It's a new street charge, so I have to sign the paper stating I know my rights. But at the top where it says the charge, it's left blank. So I tell the cop, "I ain't signing it until I know the charge."

He laughs then says, "Well ok, it looks like it may be murder!"

All in all, dude was unresponsive the whole ambulance ride. He went into a coma, his body shut down so they put a shit bag on him. The end result was 'extensive intracranial skull fracture, and a right orbital break in his eye-socket". The charge was 'assault on an inmate causing severe bodily injury'. Another DA referral plus an aggravated SHU term at sixteen months, so no more eight months — it's sixteen plus whatever the DA gives me.

My entire sixteen months in the SHU, I literally stress every single day. Every time a cop or outside agency comes into the Pod I would swear they are there to serve me the new charges filed by the district attorney.

While in the SHU the big homies decide o impose a state wide hunger strike that is mandatory for all Sureños. The reason being, the SHU conditions:

- While in the SHU, the only clothing assigned is two pairs of socks, two pairs of boxers, two t-shirts and one pair of slip on shoes and shower shoes, also no phone calls.
- To get a visit it first needs to be scheduled months in advance and when it finally gets approved, it's through bulletproof glass for one hour.
- They give you an all-white one-piece jumpsuit.
- The commissary is $25 a month and if you buy soups they are all taken out of the wrapper and put into a brown paper bag.
- All the hygiene is squeezed into a plastic bag such as shampoo, toothpaste, deodorants. All plastic containers are not allowed.
- No pencils — you get a pen filler that most people wind up rolling in paper to make it useable.
- No pictures are allowed through the mail and in facilities, your mail is not allowed in your cell. Once a week, all your letters for the week are saved then they, the cops, bring a projector to your cell and each letter is projected onto the back wall in your cell for five minutes per letter for you to read.
- The rec is in a 10-by-10 dog kennel with not workout equipment.
- The showers have no hot water.
- While assigned to the SHU unit you're labeled a 'disciplinary' inmate so you're doing 100% of your time which means if you're sentenced by the courts to do, say, ten years with half time, that means with no rule infractions you only do five years, but since you're a SHU inmate you're doing 100%.

Now, for fools that break the rules to come to the SHU, that's understandable 'cause they can still behave and leave the SHU and when placed-back on the main line a re-classification will be made and their date will be adjusted accordingly. But say you have been validated, and every time you come back to prison you are placed in the SHU even after your disciplinary time has been exceeded. To be 'validated' means you have been validated by the administration to be a 'validated' member of a security threat group or STG. To get validated they have to prove you're doing stuff to aid your gang. It's on a point system — three points, you're out. Get caught with a hot kite, get told on for being a shot caller, putting in work, in California the administration knows Sureños don't ever fight amongst themselves so if you're in the SHU for stabbing, it's usually three Sureños on one, and it's political so that's one point.

Any combination of circumstances and sometimes it only takes one reason to be validated. All the certified members of the Mexican Mafia are validated and it's those men pushing the hunger strike. Like I was saying, for the validated people who come back to prison, they have to do 100% of their time, even though a judge says they only have to do half.

It's not fair 'cause they already did their time for the initial disciplinary reason. Now it's just an administrative decision to keep them in the SHU. So now they are utilizing the hunger strike as one of the few means they have to get the attention of the administration for the living conditions and all the above reasons, but it's mainly and primarily the latter.

To partake in a hunger strike is also one point towards that validated status 'cause it's a group demonstration. All the administration knows the Black Hand call all the shots, we just implement them!

The Black Hand acts as God and literally we must worship them and will kill or do everything they say to a "T". No questions asked. It's crazy 'cause all Black Hand in the state are locked in single man cells in the most secure prisons in California and are still obeyed blindly.

The first hunger strike lasted twenty-seven days. Once the police were aware of what we were doing every inmate involved was removed from their cell and taken to medical, weighed, blood pressure taken, and blood was taken as well, I guess to see if we were eating secretly. Our cells were then searched to look for food we may have hidden and this was every day, not to mention the Sureño workout was still in play five days a week.

I won't lie, it was the worst experience of my life, not to mention the mental stress of waiting any day to be served those new charges, but like everything else in my life, I survived it. The fucked up thing — nothing was accomplished. The administration did not grant a single one of our demands, it was almost like they broke the Black Hand! I was like, *Fuck, finally.*

I lost twenty-two pounds. I was already skinny. I looked like a smoker just all cut up. I couldn't be happier it was over, but it turns out it wasn't, not even close! Stupid me for being optimistic, huh?

Man, I couldn't catch a break, cuz even my celly was a piece of shit, some lame ass fool tryna act all political Super Sureño. All the doors to our cells in the SHU are clear and see-through with holes drilled in 'em from the top to bottom so not only could everyone see into our cells, they could pretty much hear you too.

I literally sat in my cell and stewed over all the bullshit that was completely out of my control to change. I didn't do shit that was beneficial to my growth. I couldn't concentrate, not to mention, at best, I could have gotten something out of all the working out but the fucking hunger strike set me back years. With the food rations they serve us wasn't no way I could gain the weight I lost back.

All this in my mind, I was done with all the stupid shit that in no way benefitted me. All it did was cause harm to me, literally, in every single way. Being alone, broke and hungry with stress consuming me, I felt trapped in my own mind. I still had that type of pride that instead of making me feel proud of who I am, it was killing me. I'm a very conscious man so I knew all this was detrimental but almost 100% I was helpless to change the circumstances. Just like a captured animal in a trap, backed all the way into the corner, even if I were to fight I couldn't win!

After being in the SHU eight months, I been watching the shot caller Spanky from East Side Baldwin Park make bogus calls. He had good homies doing stupid hits when it was mostly personal — fools that had beefs with him were being stabbed by homies and being told lies as to why they were to be stabbed such as, "He's a rat," "He fucked up on another yard," etc. Spanky was full of shit. He been single cell for the last ten years in the SHU while us soldiers coming into the SHU was on the front lines subjecting our lives for the cause — the cause being whatever the shot caller decided it was at the time.

I couldn't respect that shit.

Us soldiers is out there fighting with knives against the other races while these fools is in a cell safe fighting with pens and kites.

Fuck all that.

This was my introduction to the first hand knowledge of the inner workings of being a Sureño and I didn't like it. Not at all.

"Turtleboy, shoot your line!"

I shoot it.

"Pull!"

I pull. It's a kite.

Fuck. Ain't shit good ever come in a kite. It's usually a hit or something new that's gonna fuck shit up.

Sure enough:

"Starting tomorrow, all camaradas will participate in the hunger strike!"

Oh my God, no way!

First thing literally in my mind was, *How can I get out of this?*

Second thing was, *If I do this I'm probably gonna get validated, adding fuel to the fire that is all these current situations I'm currently stressed out over!*

Water, fingernails, water, toilet paper, water, I even considered eating my toenails, I don't even know what this hunger strike is about — I assume it's just a continuation of the first one, but this time it's not just the Sureños, it's the white boys and a few blacks.

So here I am, on my second hunger strike in three months. This one lasts seventeen days. I guess the administrative staff granted a few of our demands such as:

- They allowed us to buy shoes, all white, gray sweats and sweaters
- The commissary went up to $35
- They welded pull-up bars in the rec cages and
- Allowed us one fifteen minute phone call per month

They also said they would see what they could do about the 100% time on non-disciplinary inmates such as validated and PC inmates.

This hunger strike, I lost twelve pounds. My overall weight was 128 pounds standing at six feet. Yeah, I know, I looked horrible, but hey, they all got what they wanted. I didn't give no fucks about none of that petty shit.

Finally, with 57 days left 'til my release, my sixteen month SHU term is up. So now I have to be moved from the SHU unit to the AD-SEG unit, a policy implemented by administration that any time you move in with a new celly you need to do a meet and greet and meet the new celly. Both need to agree to live with each other which is easy 'cause a Sureño is-to never refuse a celly if it's an enemy — you are to move in then take care of business which is fucked up 'cause at the end of it, you can't just allow dude to simply move out or let him just tell the police he can't live there. They literally want you to kill dude or get caught in the act which constitutes PC pepper spray being administered by the ton into your cell. All bad!

After both inmates agree to celling up, they make you both sign an agreement they call a marriage chrono. It states:

"I agree to this living arrangement. Any and all adverse actions, the blame will be placed solely on the inmate."

It's signed and dated then placed in your central file.

My new celly is an older man named "Perro" or "Dog" from Blumas, which is short for Bloomington. We both agree to the terms and sign. In my mind I'm super relieved my ordeal is almost at an end. The cops escort me in cuffs back to my SHU unit and cell and I will be moving the next day.

Once back in my cell, I hear Spanky yell, "Turtleboy!"

I respond, "What's up?"

"Buenos Tardes camaradas, say homito, who you moving in with over there?"

I say, "Perro de Blumas!"

He says, "Ok, give me a minute, I got a kite for you, read it and give a verbal that you understand!"

I say, "Ok fool just let me know."

Like I said, ain't shit good ever coming in a kite so I'm wondering what it could be. I'm just hoping all it is is he wants me to pass word to the homies in the hole unit. I'm super anxious by nature so I'm going through it waiting on his fool's kite plus I don't even like this fool, all the bullshit calls. I'm glad this is the last time I will have to fuck with him.

"Turtleboy, manda tu linea camarada."

"Here I come fool."

I shoot my line, he pulls me in. A couple minutes later I hear, "Pull it dos veces" which means pull it two times, meaning two things are tied on the line.

"Ok I got it two times homie."

After I pull the line in my door I see immediately one is a kite and the other is a knife.

Man, what the fuck?

I open the kite:

"Mixpanzinco techpa, look lil homito, Perro ain't no good,

here you go, handle it. T'loc Techpa."

-Spanky Es Bolen

A black and white logo

Description automatically generated

"Mixpanzinco techpa" is "greetings and respect".

"No good" means like it sounds. He done fucked up somewhere.

"T'Loc Techpa" is "always respect".

"Es Bolen" is East Side Baldwin Park.

- is "13"

It's all in nuahtl or Aztec.

No fucken way. I'm thinking, *What the fuck am I gonna do?*

If the DA don't pick up my first case, for sure, after this next case for stabbing my celly hits her desk, she's gonna pick them both up.

What the fuck am I gonna do?

Spanky yells, "Turtleboy, you understand homie?"

I reply, "Yes, I got it homie."

He says, "Gracias homie, mucho gusto." Thank you, nice to meet you.

That whole night I sit and pray God would somehow intervene on my behalf and cancel the move or put it in Perro's heart to kill the move or anything so I wouldn't have to do it. I'm not scared — that's not it at all — I just don't respect Spanky. But it's Sureño policy to follow orders blindly. If he was making bogus calls then someone of a higher rank would deal with him. It wasn't on me to make that decision — my duty is to follow orders. They say "SUR" stands for "Soldier Under Rules" or "Soldier Under Recognition".

Somehow I fall asleep and at lunch, the next morning the cops say, "Pack up Thunderburk, after breakfast you're moving."

Here I go.

I yell to a few homies my saludos and I say my goodbyes.

"Cuff up Thunderburk."

I stash the knife in my waistband and cuff up. They open the door.

As we are walking in the annex that connects the buildings, in my mind I am getting my game plan on how I am gonna get Perro once I am in the cell, wondering if he knows the play 'cause if he does I am in trouble. All types of thoughts are tryna be the first in my mind like a crowd of people all rushing to the exits during a fire We pull up to the unit, "Hey, Thunderbird. We're going to put you over here in this cell by yourself since you're going home soon. You're so short. The administration didn't want to mess with you, so..." I'm thinking in my mind, what the heck, God, did you just rescue me? I'm thinking in my head, like, no way this is true, bro. I got the burner on me right here. I'm ready to go. And now it's... Oh, man. Thank you. All right. Yes, sir. Let's go.

That's what I said. I walked into the unit, into my own cell, all the way in the corner. A cop was telling me, "We're just going to put you back here and forget about you. Go home in your 57 days. Take care of yourself. Stay out."

The first couple of days sitting in my cell, I started thinking about all the programs and all the mental stress and anguish that I had just gone through facing this new case and the potential new case from the district attorney. I wasn't supposed to be back in prison. I was innocent. I caught a whole bunch more time while I was in there. I was just done with it, bro. You know what I mean?

There were just a lot of rules I had started following, and it didn't matter how much work you put in. There were also all kinds of other reasons. So sitting in that cell by myself, I told myself I was done with the gang life. I was given an opportunity to focus on myself for the last 57 days before going home. And that's what I did.

One thing I decided to do while I was sitting in those last 57 days was grow my hair out. But I decided to grow it out the entire time I was in the SHU, the whole 16 months.

I sat in the SHU my entire sixteen months stressing on if the DA was gonna pick my case up. I put it in my heart I wasn't never gonna come back to prison so I had to denounce all my gang ties

I also decided to grow my hair out.

The cops keep me in a single man cell until I go home.

I get released. This time instead of parole, I'm out on 'AB-109 Supervision". California had done away with parole. The only fools who get parole now are violent offenders. It is a new law to help battle prison overcrowding. AB-109 consists of just one monthly office check-up, no drug tests, and it's only for one year max! If you violate, the most they can do is give you three months in the county jail. Even if you don't report, all you have to do is stay free a year and it will fall off.

I take the Greyhound from Tehachapi State Prison to West Covina. My little brother Joseph picks me up at the station in this new Dodge Charger. He trips out on my new long hair. We go to my dad's house — once again my pops is gonna let me stay there 'til I get on my feet again. He has a nice dinner made, so we all eat. My sister Amanda lives around the corner with her husband and two kids, Joey and my princess Nevaeh, so they all come over.

I'm surrounded by all my family and I love it. You can't fathom the two conflicting scenarios from one, being surrounded by killers and hate and violence and having to be leary of all around you at all times to being surrounded by pure love. It's mind-blowing and deeply emotional. I love my family deeply.

The next few weeks I just chill and catch up with my friends. Really no rush to get a job now, it's just me, my dad and little bro Joe living in the house 'cause pops got a divorce from Esther. It's crazy 'cause my dad still takes care of her too! He even pays her rent — like I said, my dad is a real-life saint! I love him so much.

A few weeks later, I cleaned out my room and I go to move a green-covered book and I notice it's my little brother's journal he kept while in the Marines. I remember before I went to prison last time I was reading it so I opened it and a sack of meth fell out. *What the fuck?*

Oh shit, now I remember. I put it there the day I had this little Asian chick at my house and she's all like, "You wanna get high?" so I told her "No, give me that shit" and I put it in that journal and that was that. Here it is four years later, so I say, *What the fuck?* I do a line.

All that *dope has a shelf life,* shit, I was lit the fuck up!

So now I'm tweaking and you already know the deal with meth, you can't just do it once! So now I'm in my dad's house tweaking and trying to be all sneaky.

My sister's husband gets me a job with him working at his company. My little brother Joseph gives me his old car cuz my dad bought him a new Charger. My dad had paid all the fees to transfer Joseph's old car into my name, bought the insurance, and helped pay to get my license. Well, the day before I'm supposed to start work, I tell my dad I need money.

He says, "Man, every time I give you money you get cross-eyed."

He still gives me the money though, so I go buy my work boots, which is why I asked for the money. I then decide to go see some female I just met at a real shady motel.

We chill and when I go to leave, I guess I forgot to turn on my lights when I pull out. I turn left and immediately pass a cop. He flips a bitch and lights me up. I'm pulled over. They know this motel is a high traffic meth area so they know I got meth — I really don't though. What they do find is a meth pipe, so they take me to jail and they impound my car.

It's only a book and bond but it's about 3am so I won't be let out until about 7 or 8 — there goes my first day of work, plus my car.

I get released and have to walk home. I get there, my dad sees me and he's all like, "What happened to work?" So I tell him the truth.

He gets pissed. He really don't want to get the car out but like I said, it was my little brother's so he tells me to get in the truck, "Let's go get it out, but once we do, I want the keys and it parked at the house." *What the fuck.*

The first place I went after getting my car out the impound was to my new job. I talked to the boss and told him half the story of why I missed work, minus the meth pipe. He said, "Ok." I start the next day.

I sleep in my car, I start work the next day.

I been working about a month. We are adding on a six-story addition to Chapman University. We do all the steel framing, the foundation of the building. Well, it's lunch so everyone is gone eating. We are the local iron union at the job site — they got all the electricians, carpenters and plumbers, union, all doing their thing. My position is using the acetylene torch, cutting down all the I-beams that were marked "no good" by the city code inspectors due to the weld not being correct. I loved it cuz I'm a beast at the acetylene torch.

Well anyway, I noticed a cool-looking torch that had a hose on it so I was all like, *Shit, I want that,* so I took it. It belonged to one of the plumbers. I guess someone saw me so here it is, after lunch I'm up on the scaffold cutting down the I-beams and notice a crowd of men just staring up at me. So I turn off the torch and the man says, "You took my torch!"

I say, "You're tripping I got this big boy, what would I do with yours?"

Anyway, they found it. My brother-in-law told me to leave the job site to avoid issues. The plumbers versus us iron workers. In the end I was fired. Keeping it real I did take the torch. I thought it looked cool and I wanted it. I just wasn't thinking of the repercussions. Stupid me, cost me my job and the embarrassment of having to face my sister and brother-in-law but I never told them the truth.

I'm homeless now but at least I have a car and my last paycheck so I start to sling dope once again. Well, one day I had just re-upped and was waiting at the 7-11 for my weed man to come. I must have fallen asleep cuz next thing I know I am woken up by knocking at my window.

I wake up startled and see a cop at my window. I also have a fat sack of dope sitting in my lap. *Damn, I'm slipping.*

I get cuffed, taken to LA county jail, booked in on possession with intent to distribute.

While in LA county, I was in 3500 fish row. It's 100 cells on top, 100 cells on the bottom, three tiers, all cells, the smallest cells in the world, literally non-stop yelling and screaming 24/7. It will drive you crazy. It literally makes a person take the first deal offered just to get out of there, so I take 36 months at 85%.

Off to prison I go. Once again. New Folsom's level 4 one eighty B yard. The first thing I thought about was the decision I made the last time I sat in a cell to no longer be part of a gang. As soon as I got to the yard, I got situated, met the homies, chilled out there for a couple of months, and then I pulled up on the shot caller. I told him, 'Hey, check this out. With all due respect, big dog, I think I'm going to go check out my religion, my Native American people. You know what I mean? I'm going to go ahead and do that.' And that's what I did. Nobody said anything, nobody had any issues with it because I just did it. I stood on it, and they saw it and respected it. Nothing more, nothing less."

I meet the Indians and fall in with them since I'm Native. I start to learn my Native ways.

The first time I go to the lodge or sweat grounds, while in the inipi (sweat lodge) my water pourer tells me if I have any issues while inside to just raise my hand. I'm all like, "OK."

They close the flaps and it's 100% completely dark black. They got eight huge glowing rocks that been sitting in the fire for hours. The water pourer named Digger starts to speak in Lakota. It's already super hot and I'm thinking, *Oh shit, what did I get myself into?*

I then hear hissing. Digger is throwing water on the rocks, making it steam. *Oh shit.*

Then I feel hot wind like a dragon is breathing on me. Come to find out brother Wayne is fanning his hawk feathers around. It goes from left to right, each brother either sings or prays. Eighteen brothers in the lodge. *It's gonna be a long round.*

I won't even lie, I really didn't think I could last all four rounds but I did. I found out that I could literally withstand anything if I put my mind to it and focus.

Coming out of the inipi, I felt reborn fresh and full of life. I couldn't wait to do it again. The whole point of sweating is to suffer, to pray, to cleanse yourself. Man, I had lost everything coming back to prison this time. I let down my whole family so I was in that inipi praying my ass off. I won't lie, cuz I been in there for about a year praying and ain't nothing happening. I see all my brothers getting blessed and I'm still in the same boat.

About five months 'til my release, which is actually coming six months early due to the 85% dropping down to 65%, I receive a letter from my mom in Oklahoma. The first line says, "Son, it seems you may need a change in your life, I'm inviting you to live with me in Oklahoma."

I won't lie, I had real doubts about going to live with my mom, cuz of all the crazy shit she's done to me in the past. It's like every time she's get mad at me she'd either call my P.O. or kick me out or usually both. Plus now I would be in a different state, away from all I've ever known. So I prayed on it. In the end I looked at it like this — I'd been praying for my family to come back to me and Grandfather sent me my mom so I wouldn't refuse her offer.

While in prison I worked in the meat plant. My job was sanitation.

One day an inmate who was my supervisor told me I needed to stop bullshitting and get back to work. I told him, "Stop doing the cops' job and get the fuck away from me."

Mind you, this inmate had been down twenty-five years plus and doing all he could to stay out of trouble so he could make parole. Everyone knew he had a parole hearing coming up pretty shortly too. Well, he told me something I felt was not very respectful so I called him out. I really didn't think he would fight, considering all the circumstances — him being a supervisor plus the parole hearing coming up any day. Any misconduct, write-ups and his shot at going home is over.

Well, sure enough, he followed me to the bathroom so I turned around and punched him twice, knocking him out. He fell and hit his forehead open, all bad.

Well, somehow the cops caught wind-and they reviewed the camera and seen it all. The end result: we both get written up and the overall outcome, I get an additional 90 days added to my sentence and he, well let's just say his parole hearing didn't go as planned. I won't lie, to this day I still feel a little fucked up about that.

My release date comes up. I'm in R&R, receiving and release, waiting to be taken to the Greyhound station. My grandma helped my mom pay for my ticket to Grove, Oklahoma.

They finally tell me, "Let's go."

I jump in the prison van, we pull up to the Greyhound station, I go to the counter and get my ticket. The CO's leave and my bus comes. I'm now on my way to LA Greyhound station from Sacramento. It's about a four hour trip so I sit in back and just chill. My whole bus ride should have only taken two days but in the end turned out to be a week until I actually made it home to my mom's and I'll tell you why...

The bus ride to LA was pretty uneventful, but when I get to the LA Greyhound station, all that changes. The downtown LA Greyhound station is huge. Out front in the parking lot area you can literally find anything you're looking for and I mean literally. So I go out front cuz I'm looking for some weed. I got my $200 gate money. I right away find it. What the hell, I'm already running from probation, might as well. I also get some rolling papers. As I'm smoking, some hick hillbilly white kid walks up to me and asks me where the closest Western Union is. Now mind you, we're in downtown Los Angeles, super ghetto. I look at Opie and tell him, "Bro, you don't want to go walking around this area alone, they'll kill you."

So he tells me that the bus he was on left without him and all his shit was on it too. He's diabetic too, even his insulin is on there. He's from somewhere in Alabama, I'm thinking, *Ain't no way. This kid ain't gonna make it.*

So me being me, I tell Opie, (that's what I named him) "Come on, let's go inside."

I walk all the way up to the front of the service desk and at first I'm polite like, "Ma'am...", "Sir...", all that, but no, they ain't gonna give us no attention, so I yell, "AYE YOU STUPID ASS BITCH!"

Right away I get a reaction.

"Who the fuck you calling bitch?" says some ghetto ass black female employee.

I say, "I need your supervisor."

She's all looking at me all stupid like she don't know what the fuck I'm talking about.

I tell her, "It's easy, pick up that walkie talkie on your hip, stupid, and call a supervisor!"

So she calls for security. They come immediately.

The employee is all ghetto, talking, weaving her head from side to side, fingers all snapping as she tells the cops what I said.

The cop says, "Sir, what's the issue?"

I tell the cop, "Look man, this kid," he looks at Opie, "the bus left with all his shit and he needs to alert the driver cuz he also left his insulin and he needs that." I ask, "By any chance can you contact the bus driver and let him know, and how can we go about retrieving his stuff?"

The employee is saying some shit like, "Sir, that's impossible, we don't even know which bus it is and we can't call either."

I then tell her, "Well look genius, the bus left from this bay *** and its destination is Alabama. And if you look at that thing on your desk it is a computer. It may magically have all that info or if you're too stupid to figure it out you might understand why I asked your stupid ass to call a supervisor. You see how that works, sweetie?"

Here we go again, fingers snapping, head weaving, she goes on refusing to call a supervisor, telling me not to tell her how to do her job!

The cop finally shuts her up and he tells her to call a supervisor, and she hesitates like she's about to go off on him too when finally another male employee comes over to see what's going on. When he does, he uses that magic black box to call a supervisor. The whole time she's looking like she's never seen how that black box worked. Why she even has one still amazes me. She must have thought it was just a cool accessory to her uniform. Stupid bitch.

The supervisor finally comes.

"What's the issue, sir?"

I tell him.

He says, "Ok, let me see..." jumps on the computer and the whole time ghetto employee is looking at me like she wants to kill me. I don't even know why she's still hanging around but she is, so I start to goad her. I'm all like, "Look, ooh magic, com-put-er, make words..."

The whole time, Opie is just standing there like he don't know what the fuck to do.

Opie has a cowlick haircut, he's super pale, skinny, wearing one of those Bart Simpson t-shirts that says, *Cow-a-bunga dude!*, the neck all stretched-out with some hole-y jeans and like size 15 white Converse. Yeah, if he would have set foot outside that Greyhound station they would have killed his ass. I couldn't let that happen.

Anyways, the supervisor says they contacted the bus and they will leave his stuff at the San Bernardino station. She prints him out another ticket and tells him not to miss the bus again.

I ask the lady, "What stop do I get off to get to the San Bernardino station?"

She says, "The Montclair transit station." So off we go from the LA station to the Montclair station.

Now mind you, I used to live in Ontario and take the train — well, the Metrolink—every day for almost five years. One of the places I'd catch the Metrolink was the Montclair station and I don't remember no Greyhound station. I know the Greyhound used to drop people off there but as for a station, I never seen one. But shit, I just did a couple of years so they may have just built one...

It's about 9pm when we get to the Montclair station. The first thing I do is look around for the Greyhound station. Man, just like I thought, ain't no station anywhere in sight! The bus leaves so now me and Opie just standing there in this bay and parking lot looking for the station. I already know we ain't gone find one. The stupid ass supervisor gave us bunk into!

Like I said, it's about 9 to 9:15pm. I know one more i is gonna come going towards San Bernardino, so I go to buy two tickets from the machine.

It says $50. I'm like, *Fuck all that!* All I got is about $100 left from my $200 gate money.

So the train comes and we both jump on, but I almost forgot...

Me and Opie walked all the way across the huge parking lot to inspect the other businesses to see if one of them were the station — they weren't — so while walking back, the train started to come so we had to race all the way back and jump on the train. We were out of breath and sweating then some cop-looking ass fool is all like, "What's the deal?"

So I tell him the story.

He then is all like, "Ok hey buddy, just calm down! Calm down!"

I'm looking at this fool like, *What the fuck?* I'm hella sketched, all it's gonna take is a train cop to ask for my ticket then I'm hit! So I go hide in the restroom until I hear the San Bernardino stop. When we get there I tell Opie, "Come on."

It's now about 9:45pm. We at the San Bernardino Metrolink station. I don't know where the Greyhound is so I look around, all I see is one dude way off in the parking lot leaning on his car talking on his phone so I tell Opie, "Come on."

We pull up on dude and I'm all like, "Hey can you tell us where the San Bernardino Greyhound station is?"

He shrugs us off all like, "I don't know."

I'm like, "Can you Google that shit?"

He's about to give some lame excuse then I say, "Fuck that shit homie just do it!"

So he does.

He says, "It's ten miles away in Ontario on San Bernardino Street."

I say, "Naw homie, I said Google 'Greyhound in San Bernardino.'"

Then he starts to type in "Greyhound, San Bernardino".

I get pissed and snatch the phone out of his hand, he jumps back.

I type in "Greyhound station in San Bernardino", it says it's a mile away!

I tell dude, "You want your phone back, give us a ride. So all reluctantly, he does.

It's about 10:15pm when we pull up.

The first thing I notice is it's right in the ghetto. The Greyhound employee is chasing some bums out of the station with a broken fishing pole. For real. I look at Opie and he looks scared as fuck. I tell him, "Come on fool, I got you!"

We go into the station. I was all worried about it being closed when we get there but nah, it was still open and they had all Opie's shit. They had to fix both our tickets and now we had a twelve hour layover. It would have been okay but this station didn't have a reception area. All bad. So this means we'll have to wait out front all night.

I see some black females walking down the street, three of them, so I holler, "Hey, where the weed at?"

They all look at me then at each other. One says, "What you looking for, cutie?"

I say, "Shit, 4 reals, you!"

They all laugh then start to walk up to me. The girl who talked to me looks hella cute too 4 reals. She says, "You just got out, huh fool?"

I tell her, "Yeah."

She says, "How long you do?"

I say, "A few years!"

They say, "How long you stuck waiting for the next bus to come?"

I say, "Shit, all night. Why, what's up?"

The cute one, who turns out to be Diamond, says, "Do you wanna come chill with us? We live just down the road."

I'm all thinking, *Man, I kinda want to but then again these bitches nowadays be on some extra shit, ain't no telling what will happen.*

So I'm all like, "Man, y'all ain't got no jealous dudes do you?"

Diamond giggles and says, "Naw, hell no! Come on, let's go smoke, y'all good!"

So I turn to Opie and tell him, "Let's roll!"

We walk with these girls down the street about two blocks and I notice all kinds of black fools is out and looking at us. Now, it's California so all that racial tension don't just end in prison, it's out in the streets too. I'm thinking, *These fools is gonna trip any minute! 'Cause what they seeing is some tatted up long hair in corn rows Mexican they don't know in their hood plus a super hick-looking tall skinny white fool!*

I could only imagine what these fools is thinking, nor do I care, all I'm thinking is, *Fuck, fuck fuck, I should have stayed at the bus station!* But I was thinking with my other head!

We pull up to Diamond's spot, step inside and she immediately closes the door and locks it. We all in her front room chillin'. Opie is just watchin' everything.

I hit the blunt, and all of a sudden I'm in chill zone. When I smoke weed I get super lyrical and love to rap so I ask Diamond to turn on the music so she does and I start to spit. It feels so good too 'cause for that last couple of years I've been musically starved. It was hella cool to have this sexy woman enjoy what was coming out of my mouth. I was really feeling myself, even Opie was digging my shit.

It's hard when you walk the yard
And niggaz want to kill you
It's hard when you spit this hard
And niggaz can't feel you

For reals, these ladies was good company. The sexual part fell off and I was just feeling myself and feeling them.

But the dudes outside weren't feeling it at all.

I could hear them just outside making death threats. I love sexy females and a good time, but even more than that I love my life and just wanted to make sure Opie and I both made it home safely. So I asked Diamond to let us out the back door so we could jump some fences and double back to get to the station where we would wait it out.

She said, "Ok."

So now I got Opie hitting back fences with me in the hood.

It was funny.

At the end of the day, after I though about it, Opie just followed me with absolute faith. I'd keep him safe. And I did. Helping him fucked my whole ticket up too, but helping him made my whole trip what it was...you will see what I mean in the next few pages.

We get back to the station. None of those fools came by either, I guess they thought we was still in the house. Ha! Got 'em.

The rest of the night was uneventful.

The bus comes in the morning and we leave. We pull up to the station in Tucson, Arizona. New people get on the bus, I'm in the very back seat next to the restrooms, I see a kinda chunky white girl in some daisy dukes with all kinds of bags on her walking towards the back. I say to myself, *I know she ain't coming back here.* It's all types of open seats throughout this whole bus but sure enough, "Can I sit here?"

I look at her like, *For real?* but I tell her, "Yes, take the window seat," 'cause she has all that shit and I ain't tryna be trapped in there.

She sits down, then I sit down and she takes out this pillow that wraps around her neck and this thing with a flat surface on one side and a cushion on the other, and pulls out an iPad. Finally she's all settled in.

I close my eyes.

Next thing, I'm feeling her shaking my shoulder to get my attention. I open my eyes and she says, "Do you wanna use one?" referring to an iPad.

I say, "Hell yeah!"

So she takes another one out of her pack and I say, "Cool, I'm Kenny, nice to meet you, and thank you!"

"No worries," she says.

Somewhere we start a conversation. Her name is Kayla. She tells me she's running from her abusive boyfriend that she robbed for $200,000 and around four pounds of hash oil she has in a bag under the bus. She's from Northern Cali, going to Florida to start over with the money.

I'm thinking, *This chick is cool but the $200,000 and four pounds are an exaggeration but hey, it's her story.* I also notice she keeps this one backpack in her possession on her lap at all times.

I ask to use her phone.

She says, "Why don't you have a phone?"

I tell her, "I just got out."

She says, "Ok, damn. Well here, you can have this one. It's paid up for the month."

"Damn, for reals? Shit, thank you!"

I try to call my mom but no answer.

Later I ask Kayla, "Why you choose to sit way back here when you passed all kinds of open seats?"

She says, "You see that group of white boys up there?"

I say, "Yeah."

She says, "Well that one right there," she points to this skinny blonde haired kid and says, "well he started coming on to me at the station but he was a little too aggressive and I didn't like it. Like, I'm running from my boyfriend 'cause he would beat me and he started to remind me of my boyfriend. I told him to chill a little but he didn't listen and no matter where I sat, he'd sit either right next to me or very close so when I say your tatted up long haired ass, I figured he'd keep clear." Then she laughed.

"I guess it worked huh?" I asked her.

"Definitely," she said.

Later she says, "You smoke?" and passes me this metal pen-looking thing. She says, "Hit it but be cool, it's good shit."

So I hit it and my lungs explode. I'm coughing like crazy, but I immediately feel super stoned. *Hell yeah.*

The crazy thing is it don't even smell. So we sit there for hours smoking, high as fuck, and no one had a clue! I thought, *This chick is cool as fuck.*

We wind up pulling into another Greyhound station. The bus driver says, "You got an hour."

We depart the bus and Kayla still has that black backpack clutched tightly. It looks kinda heavy so I say, "I can carry that for you."

She says, "Yeah, I know you can!" and looks at me all weird.

I'm thinking, *Ok. What was that all about?*

We walk to a McDonald's and I'm super hungry but really don't want to spend any more of what's left of my gate money so I say, "I'm cool, you eat."

She says, "Fuck that, it's on me."

So we order and get our food, and we walk back so we are near the bus. I see Opie still sitting on the bus. I laugh and tell Kayla his/our story and she laughs and says, "It looks like his ass learned his lesson, but you're really sweet for helping. I could tell, aside from all your tattoos, you were a nice guy. And thank you for being such a gentleman with me too!"

I say, "Shit, the trip ain't over yet."

We both laugh.

It's time to leave so we both jump back on the bus.

Later she's all, "You ain't got no money, huh fool?"

I still have a few dollars, so I say, "Not much."

She says, "Where exactly are you headed?"

I tell her the whole story about not seeing my mom in years, jumping probation, all that.

She says, "You see, I knew you were a sweetheart. After all she put you through you still love her and are going back to help her."

I tell her my fears of how once I get there she won't hesitate to go nuts and put me out.

She says, "Here fool, just in case..."

She opens that black backpack but just a little and hands me a stack of money! I was shocked. At the time, I didn't count it, but later I did and it was $1,000.

I said, "Thank you!"

She said, "No biggie," then put on her headphones.

At the next stop somewhere in Texas, I noticed a liquor store so I rushed to buy us some smokes. I also bought a 32 ounce beer and snuck it on the bus 'cause I didn't have time to drink it.

So now we are rolling down the interstate in Texas somewhere. I open my beer, but I'm just babysitting it. Kayla is asleep.

Next thing I know is we stop, all the bus lights turn on. It's at least 2am, so almost everyone is asleep. I'm like, *What the fuck?*

Next thing I know, a border patrol agent steps on the bus and says, "Everybody needs to have their IDs out" and he's loosely checking bags and scanning IDs. I notice Kayla panicking but shit, so am I. First off, I got this big ass beer on me, second, the only ID I have is my California state prison ID and I'm already absconding from probation.

Fuck, fuck fuck! What do I do with this fuckin' beer?

I tell Kayla to have her ID ready so they don't have to wait on us since we in the very back.

I notice on the back of the seat in front of me is like a cargo net to hold stuff, so I put the open beer in there and I'm wearing some big ass gray pro club shorts so I scoot all the way up in my seat and put the right leg of my shorts over the beer. I look over at Kayla and she's going through all her bags. I'm like, "Fuck, what's up?"

She says, "On the phone I gave you in the contacts it says 'mom'. If something happens to me, call my mom and let her know please!"

I say, "Ok."

I could hear the agents also looking under the bus in the baggage compartment.

The agent checking IDs pulls up on us, "IDs, please."

He takes mines, scans it and hands it back. He does the same with Kayla's, then turns around and walks off the bus.

A few minutes later a different agent steps on the bus and says, "Miss Kayla..." I didn't catch her last name. But Kayla says, "Fuck that's me!"

She says, "Over here" and the agent says, "Please gather your stuff and exit the bus with me!"

She looks at me and says, "Call my mom please!"

I say, "For sure!"

I watch her exit the bus. All the lights turn back off.

I'm looking out the windows so I can see what's up. The last I see of Kayla is her walking towards a building with all her bags and two agents walking with her, and one pulling one of those suitcases with wheels on it. I feel so bad for her. She was sweet.

I call her mom.

She says, "Hello?"

I say, "Hi, is this Kayla's mom?"

"Yes it is."

I tell her the story and she responds, "Good, that stupid little bitch deserves it!" and hangs up on me.

Damn, that shit is identical to the shit my mom would say...

A few hours later, the bus pulls into the downtown Dallas Greyhound station. Me and Opie hit the ticket counter and they say he leaves in an hour and I have a 32-houre layover. *Ha! Right, just my luck.* But I don't trip. I'm actually having fun on my journey.

The hour passes and Opie gives me a hug. I give him my mom's number and tell him to call when he finally makes it home.

He says, "I will for sure brother, thank you for all you did to help me too."

I tell him, "It's not a problem Opie, just make it home safe and we even, ok?"

"Yes sir," he replies.

I watch him get on the bus and I go sit down.

I'm bored as fuck so I go outside to the little gated area where you smoke at. It has a door that opens to the front sidewalk and I notice that every couple of minutes, some black fools peek their heads in and say shit like, "Who needs some weed," "Who needs some pussy," "Who needs some meth," they got whatever you need so I walk out front and say I got twenty for some weed and some head.

Dude says, "Ok, I'll be back!" He leaves.

Next thing I know, some cute white girl peeks her head in and says, "You looking for that green and dome?"

The only reason I said, "Yes" was 'cause she was cute. If she would've been ugly I wouldn't have said shit.

She says, "Money first."

I hand her the twenty and right there in the smoking area she sucks me up. I won't like, she pretty much got the twenty just to breathe on my shit, 'cause you already know a homie just got out. Then she gives me a couple joints and leaves. That quick. It's dirt weed but shit, it beats a blank so I sit outside and play on my phone until I notice it's about to die so I go back in to find somewhere to charge my phone.

I notice in the seating area along the wall are these outlets, so I go to see if I can find an open one, but everybody is all crowded around them and the open ones ain't worth shit — your charger port won't stay in the plug 'cause the plug port is all worn out — so I walk away and say, *Fuck it.* I decide to go play some video games to kill my time.

I sit down in one of those racing games that has two driver seats with a canopy over it like you're in a car so I post up plus I can lean back and chill in it — way better than a lobby chair/seat. I look around and notice a multiplug just peeking out from under the game so I pull it out and bingo, I plug my phone into it and slide it all the way under the game. *Hell yeah.*

So I'm just chilling in this car game and I see this sexy ass girl who looks to be black mixed with white. She has a lot of shiny, curly black hair pulled into a ponytail. She's wearing some all black yoga pants and like a sport top of the same material, all form-fitting — she looks sporty. She has nice small titties and a very nice ass too. She's perfect.

Well, I notice she's frustrated 'cause her phone is dead and she realized the same thing I did about all the sockets being pieces of shit. She puts her phone in her purse. She is only about five feet away from me. I tell myself, *Shit, why not? You only live once.*

I yell, "SKRRRRRT!" real loud like I'm slamming on the brakes. It works 'cause now she's all looking at me like, *What the fuck?*

I act like I'm rolling down the passenger window and I lean over to the other seat.

I say, "Let me holla at you, shorty."

All cautious like she thinks it's a real car, she approaches. She bends over like as if to look in the window and I say, "Jump in."

She's looking like, *What the fuck?*

I say, "I ain't gonna abduct you."

She's still all looking all skeptical so I lean over and push the multi-cord that my phone is charging on out from under the game. Once she sees it, she catches on and sits in the other seat and plugs her phone in, then pushes it back under the game.

"SKRRRRRT!" like I just peeled out.

She goes to push the button which changes the music to the game and I smack her hand.

"Don't touch my stereo. And put your seatbelt on!"

I'm just being silly but she surprises me 'cause she's sill right back and acts like she's putting her seatbelt on and says, "Where we going?"

I say, "Anywhere you wanna go, beautiful."

She laughs. We chill. I even put some quarters in her side so we can race. She beats me every time. I find out she's in college at Riverside University in California. But she's on break going to Florida to chill with her family. Her name is Katrina. I ask her if she smokes.

She says, "Weed?"

I say, "Yeah."

She says, "Hell yeah, I got some kush but no papers."

I say, "Don't trip we will figure it out, let's go outside."

We walk to the smoking area. I spark up my dirt weed joint but at the same time I'm at the gate looking for one of those convenient black fools. I spot one and say, "I got five for a blunt."

Dude says, "I just lit this one."

I say, "Shoot it."

I give him the five, turn around and Katrina is looking at me holding the dirt weed joint.

"I know bae, it's trash, but it's all I had. But let me split the blunt and we will twist that kush. Start to break it up, bae!"

Blunt split, weed broken up, then placed in the blunt.

After I twist it up I say, "You do the honors and lick it so it seals."

She likes that too 'cause she smiles and the smile is all the way in her eyes.

"You spark it too, bae. Ladies first."

I strike the match 'cause it tastes better when you use a match to light it. I don't know why, it just does. Try it!

I explain to her just exactly what I told you and she agrees.

So here we are about two hits into this blunt and I notice one thing right off the jump: I am STUPID high. I don't even want to hit it no more. She's passing it to me too, *Oh fuck.* I barely manage to shake my head. "No, I'm cool."

She's too fuckin fine, I'm too fuckin high, this is only gonna end with me lookin hella stupid.

She starts fucking with me like, "You don't smoke weed, do you fool? Why you so high?"

I manage to tell her, "I just got out."

She says, "Oh shit, that's cute. How long did you do?"

I say, "A little over three years."

She asks me, "This your first blunt then, huh?"

It wasn't but I didn't want to ruin it for her and I said, "You the first."

She says, "Yeah, I like that. I got something else I also wanna be the first at too. Can you guess what that is?"

Honestly I was super high so I really didn't have a clue what she could be referring to, so she says, "Come on, let's go inside."

She puts out the blunt and grabs my hand. We get to the game section but we pass it and she's pulling me behind her until we pull up to the women's restroom and she pushes me into the last stall — it has a changing station with a platform that looks like an ironing board. She pulls off her yoga pants and damn her body is so sexy. Then she jumps up on the changing table and opens her legs.

I sober up asap.

I kiss her coochie and she says, "Naw fool, all this is for you. Put that dick in me."

At first I was going slow tryna not nut but she says, "Just get that pussy fool, it's cool, I'll give it to you again, just get this one out." So I hit that shit about ten pumps and explode. She pulls me to her, so I'm standing up bent over her, weenie all soft. She pulls up her shirt. I see them sexy ass titties and in no time my shit is swelled up again. I never even pulled it out of her and this time I give her a run for her money.

We finish and she says, "That was fun."

I'm still so turned on by her body, I push her facedown bent over the changing station and hit that shit doggie again, and she loves it. Shit yeah, I know right?

So we get dressed, she unlocks the door so I slip out.

A lady attempts to enter the restroom but Katrina locks the door again. The lady is mad dogging me and I say, "My lady is changing our kid and needed diapers."

I wonder what she thought when Katrina came out that restroom a few minutes later with no kid!

Katrina finds me back in the game and sits down. She asks me about where I'm going and why so I tell her the same story I told Kayla and she feels the same but she says, "If my mom were to ever do me like that I would never fuck with her again."

She says her bus is leaving soon so she gives me her phone number and messenger info and says, "Look boy, I wanna spend some time with you. Let me go see my family for a couple weeks then I will come get you in Oklahoma and we will chill, I promise."

To me it sounded good, but I didn't really think it would happen. But I said, "I would like that. And I'll be ready. I can't wait to get you in a bed."

She says, "Fuck a bed, I wanna go crazy with you, you'll see."

A while later we kiss, she gets on her bus. Now I'm all alone and I fall asleep.

I wake up and get some food and my bus is here.

It's like ten hours to Tulsa. The entirety of my bus ride is going over the events of my trip so far and laughing, saying to myself, *You a nut, Kenny!*

Now I'm on to another roller coaster journey in my life and this ride is called, "Wendy."

It's an emotional roller coaster.

Enter at your own risk!

My introduction into true evil and this time I am entering her lair as a willing participant on her own turf.

Keeping it real, I pretty much just sat down at the typewriter and up until this point freestyled this book. I had a lot of anxiety about actually getting to this introduction in my life. I figured that by 2015 I was already grown and as you've already read, I've experienced all different types of pain and heart confusion. I figured I was calloused enough to protect myself from whatever new blisters may arise from my decision to come back to my mom's.

I wholeheartedly felt it would be different, something spiritual. I soon find out it is none of these things. I will now know evil has many different forms and faces.

Throughout my life, I can say that the only face of evil I've ever seen is my mother's. I'm a creature of instinct — I don't plan in advance, I live and survive off of instinct.

I truly feel I've done a lot of wrong, but it was never intentional. I also believe I've done a lot of good, but it seems people miss that. All that is noted and recognized is all the wrong I've done — just look at my criminal record. I've sat and read my own rap sheet through the eyes and mind state of a civilian and it appears that I'm a savage. Yes, I will be the first to admit I am all those things which all my cases — with the exception of a couple — I've been guilty of; maybe not to the full extent but still guilty. I've never made any excuses or placed any blame with the exception of saying I blame my aunt and uncle in the very beginning and I stand on that. It's not blame, it's just the facts. My entire family knows it. But in the end they had a reason for doing what they did and to be honest, as much as I don't agree with it, I have to admit that the ends may have justified their means. What they did served a purpose because every one of my siblings, plus theirs, turned out fine, so it did some good, but as for my mom, none of her madness had any reason behind it — it was just premeditated acts of evil 'cause she had to know it would turn out the way it did. Even worse, it never affected her adversely in any way aside from turning the only person who tried to love her unconditionally away.

I won't lie, the only reason I didn't put too much thought or worry into what it was gonna be like when I finally got to my mom's was for one, all the energy invested in actually just getting there and two, I was now on the run once I got on that bus and decided to head towards Oklahoma. But if I were to stop and weigh the pros and cons, I would have already known the ending result — it's like it always was in the past: ALL BAD.

Like I said, I already knew what it was gonna be hut I still decided to go on through with it. Hell, I was already on the bus and almost there. I would have been homeless in California 'cause I wore out my welcome at my dad's house. Then I would have been right back in prison. So I thought *If I put some distance between me and the State of California...* It would make it harder on them if they decided to be petty and pursue violation charges.So here I go.

I have always known my mom to be very spiteful and vindictive, as well as just plain old evil — not to mention heartless and cold — whenever the situation was not in her favor or even slightly against her. It was like she was always on the offensive defensive, just waiting to strike, looking for the slightest reason to strike.

Damn, I was literally a trained soldier for the Sureños and even I didn't have that cunning and devastating ruthlessness. I've seen interviews with serial killers that weren't as cold-or guarded as my mom, for reals. I know she will never change but neither will I, and I love my momma, fuck the rest. It has to be the only reason I keep coming back.

It's like I've had so much negative in my life that I will take any positive, even if it's a false positive and I still know it — I'll jump every time. I set myself up for failure. I can't really blame my mom. I knew what it was, I just was expecting it to be different. I literally had nothing to even hint it would be though, except the few years in between the last time we saw each other, figuring, *Burn some bridges to gain some distance...*

I don't agree with most of my mom's actions and the way she treated us by the end, but like I said, in my mind I expected it, but in my heart, I wanted something different. I've always been a dreamer, even though all I've really lived was a nightmare! And the boogeyman has always been my mother. Physically, mentally, and emotionally she abused us to a degree that would shame the devil. I was her child, I couldn't even fathom why she would treat me this way, even considering I'm the only child who keeps coming back to her, time and time again. I really guess I'm to blame 'cause like I said, "I keep coming back!" I really can't say why except maybe out of desperation 'cause must times I had nowhere else to live so I guess my desperation got the better of me. But another part of me says it's 'cause I feel sorry for my mom 'cause after she ruined our family, we all turned our backs on her.

I once told my mom I wanted to show her my unconditional love and love her fully for the person she was and at the time I meant that, I still do. But it's hard to keep loving when someone fucks you up over and over again, and each time in a different way.

I once called her a mental vampire because she sucks your mental state until it's dry and you're left hollow.

In this next episode of my life, you will see just what I'm talking about. I love you mom, but it's time I get all this off my chest.

I finally get to downtown Tulsa's Greyhound station

"Mom, I'm here."

"What? Where? When do you mean?" she says. "Son, I can't pick you up for a couple days, you got to stay there, I can't leave my house."

Right off the rip. This Greyhound station don't even have a lobby, it's just a drop off and I don't even have but a few dollars. And I don't know where the fuck I'm at besides I'm in Tulsa, Oklahoma. Plus this crazy bitch just literally hung up on me!

I find out the homeless shelter is directly across the street from the Tulsa Greyhound station, and so is the jail! It's about 6pm and they say to be able to stay in the homeless shelter, I need to be in there before 7pm so on that note, I head to the shelter.

I find it with no issue. I go get my prison style mattress — how ironic, right? I'm laying down just thinking how my special reacquaintance with my mother suddenly just turned to shit. What could possibly motivate her to leave me stranded like this? Was she full of shit?

I'm brought out of my daydream by the chirping of the Facebook Messenger ringtone — it's a video call. Guess who it is? Katrina!

I answer. Damn, she is so pretty. I'm thinking she looks so sexy and comfortable, laying on a bed in some small ass shorts and a tank top.

She says, "Hi bae, where you at?"

So I pan the camera around so she can see my surroundings. She sees all the showerheads and says, "What? Are you at a YMCA or a gym?"

I say, "Naw, it's a homeless shelter."

She blurts out, "Why? What the fuck, you still ain't made it home?"

So I tell her I arrived in Tulsa at about 4pm and called my mom and she told me it's flooded in and she can't come get me until the flood clears up.

She says, "Bullshit! Give me the exact location and also give me yours too."

So I give all that to her and she says, "Give me about twenty minutes, bae, I'll call you right back." She blows me a kiss.

I want to kiss those lips so much.

I say, "Ok."

I'm chilling, waiting for her to call back. She finally does and says, "OK, now bae your mom ain't lying to you. It's flooded, her whole area is in red with flood advisory. I checked the weather map. Sorry sweetie but look, if you walk north up Main Street 1.5 miles, you will see a Studio 6 Motel and I got you a room for a week. I would have got you a nicer room but it's the closest motel and I don't want you out there walking the street and also I can send you a couple hundred to the Western Union.

I say, "No, I'm good on the money." I tell her how Kayla gave me that $1,000.

She says, "Huh, I thought I was your first."

I says, "Don't worry, you were bae, I promise you. And if you keep it up, it's looking like you also gonna be my last. I'm already in love."

She laughs and says she'll let me go so I can get to the motel and to call her when I get there. I promise her I will.

I make it to the motel, get into my room and finally shower. I order a pizza to eat, talk to Katrina, then fall asleep. I literally sleep almost three days.

I sleep talk with Katrina every day and on the fourth day, my mom calls.

"Where you at, I'm on my way. It should take about three hours. See you soon, son."

I call Katrina and tell her how my mom is on her way and she surprises me when she says, "Shut up real quick. Let me pray with you."

Oh my God, I'm in love!

"I got to go bae, I think that's my mom calling. Bye!"

She blows me a kiss. Damn, those lips...

I answer my phone, "Come on, get your ass out here, I ain't tryna sit around this ghetto ass motel."

I'm on the third floor, so I hurry down and notice for the first time how ghetto it really is. I see a bright red Chevy Colorado lowrider truck, so I assume it's my mom 'cause it's the only vehicle waiting. I approached it and assumed right. I jump in.

"Hi son." She give me a huge hug. I won't lie, my heart melted 'cause fuck all the bullshit, I love my mama, no matter what she's done. I even cry a little. I'm a little choked-up and she notices so she starts to cry too. It feels good. I have been around some fuck shit in prison. I'm with family now, so ain't no shame in my tears.

"Let's go eat."

Driving away she's all telling me about how she lives on the lake, all her dogs' names, all she has accomplished since she's been in Oklahoma. I'm proud of my mom 'cause last time I saw her she was pretty much living in Mexico in a single-wide trailer all tweeked-out. I can tell she's somewhat sober. She looks good.

She's telling me how much she's missed me. She asks why it took me so long to arrive. I give her my condensed version but I tell her all about my sexual exploits 'cause that's my mama, she don't give no fucks.

She says, "Well good thing you got you some pussy 'cause you won't find none anywhere close to where we live."

I just laugh.

We're crossing this big ass bridge all surrounded by the lake she says we live on: the Grand Lake. It's the biggest man-made lake in the USA. We then turn and are driving around some curves and bends. It's pretty rural.

About twenty minutes later, we're passing a big ass state park on the lake.

She says, "That's Bernice State Park, we live right over that bridge."

Damn, two big ass bridges in twenty minutes.

We cross the bridge and turn right, go up a little hill, then turn left and down a steep ass hill, all in a wooded area like a forest, huge trees everywhere on both sides of us.

Then we pull up a hill and turn into a circular dirt driveway, to a comfortable cabin-looking house.

She stops and says, "Here we are son."

I say, "Fuck, you said you lived on the lake, not in the woods!"

She tells me, "The lake is down that hill, son."

I won't lie, it's really peaceful and beautiful. A real change from the city.

She opens her front door, five small dogs all race out the door. She introduces me to all of her dogs: Toby is a wiener dog, Play is a white Shitzu. Bella is a black Maltese, and Junior is a mix of Shitzu and Maltese, he's all white. All my mom's dogs came from my grandma who lives down the street. She breeds Shitzus and Maltese and literally has no less that forty puppies around her double-wide. Yeah, I know, she's crazy but she sure does love her dogs. She lives with my grandpa but I'll get to them later.

Moms is, amongst other things, a great cook and she's proud of it. She loves to cook Mexican food. She knows I love tacos and homemade salsa with Mexican rice so she's cooking me a homemade dinner. I won't lie, I was in heaven. I was seeing my mom in a new light, figuring she really changed and wanted me there and she just needed a few years to herself to find herself. That first night I said to myself, *I could do this forever.*

Katrina calls and I introduce her to my mom via video message, then step outside to talk to her. She asks how it's going and I tell her, "I really think this may work out."

She says, "I'm really happy for you" and, "You better be ready for me 'cause I'm coming for you soon."

I laugh and say, "Oh yeah? We'll see."

She tells me, "Yes you will," then blows me a kiss and says, "Bye."

Fuck, this girl is so sexy. I'm sprung on her already.

Mom brings me my dinner on the patio with a beer. Sitting outside looking into the woods eating my favorite food, it couldn't be better.

Then mom says, "Alyssa will be here tomorrow."

"What?"

Mom tells me, "Your sister, she lives in town. She will be here tomorrow. Oh shit, I forgot to tell you she moved out here in July. She's been here about a month."

I've missed my baby sister so much. I can't wait to see her. I'm so happy.

My sister don't actually show up for about a week, and when she does, she's all hugs and kisses. She's crazy just like I am, so she's all over the place. She stays for a couple weeks, all in all. Minus a few minor arguments with my mom, shit is cool.

Then one day, in about early September:

"You need to get off your ass, Kenny and get a job."

I'm all like, "Ok but we live on an island, plus I ain't got no car, so how do I manage that, mom?"

She tells me to "Figure it out!"

I wind up pulling it off, finding a job at the trash company called 'Bernice Sanitation'. I convince them of my true identity but they say I got a couple months to provide the documents they need such as ID and social security card. My mom says she already ordered my birth certificate online, so it's just a waiting game.

It seems now that everyday is a worse day.

My mom is starting to show her true face, always bitching about money now that she knows I'm working. I'm only making $400 or so a week, and she wants $300 or get out of her house. I also realize she still on this meth and hydro pill she snorts when the meth is gone, and when she does, her demons come out 'cause she's coming down, plus she's already nuts.

My job tells me they got to let me go until I provide the identity documents and my mom flips out.

One day I'm in my room, it's like six in the morning. I'm laying with my homegirl Lacy and I can hear my mom stomping down the stairs. She literally kicks my door down and throws a jug of cold water on us. It's late December so it's freezing outside. My mom is going nuts.

"Get her out of my house, she's a rat bitch! OUT! OUT! OUT! I'm calling the police!"

She's hysterical.

Me and Lacy are in our pajamas and we both jump up. Somehow my mom herds us out to the front yard. It's freezing, ice and snow everywhere, we don't even got no sweaters on. She slams the door and screams, "The cops are on their way!"

Like I said, I was running from California and wasn't trying to go to jail, but I was 100% fucked, no phone, no money, no car in a rural lakeside town with no neighbors. What the fuck was I gonna do?

I have shoes on but Lacy is wearing sandals! Ain't nowhere to go, my mom is still in hysterics, so I tell Lacy to jump on my back piggyback and I start to walk down that steep ass hill.

We walk all day, then pull up to Bernice State Park. It's a campground, so it has showers in the bathroom. It's winter though, so ain't no campers. Me and Lacy go into the restroom and sit in the hot shower for hours. We fall asleep in the restroom but turn all the showers on full blast to make some heat.

The next day it's a little warmer but still snow on the ground, so we walk all day and finally we reach Tomcat Corner — it's a filling station. So we chill there. She's from this town so it's only a mater of time before she sees someone she knows.

A few hours later, she sees some tatted up fool and says, "That's Matt, let me go talk to him."

They talk for a minute, she comes back and says, "He's gonna give us a ride."

I say, "To where?" and she tells me, "He knows your mom and sister, he said he's gonna talk to you in the car."

We get in the car.

"What's good homie, I'm Matt. Your mom is nuts, I already know."

I say, "Cool. I'm Kenny, what's good, what's the plan?"

He says, "I'm gonna take Lacy where she wants to go, you roll with me, cool?"

I ain't got no other option so I say, "Cool."

We pull up to this compound that has a double-wide trailer on it. We all get off. Once inside I see like four little tweeker girls all half dressed doing different shit. Also an old white man sitting on the sofa. I already know it's a dope whore safe-haven. Lacy is just the latest addition, but I like her so I'm happy she will be safe, plus I know where she will be.

The old dude is Chris Parcel. He and Matt been doing business for years. Chris is the money man, Matt sells the dope, does the dope, makes a little money, gambles even more — it's a losing venture on Chris's end but it's good for Matt. The old man doesn't mind but it's backwards hustling as you will soon see.

Chris also knows my mom and sister. Matt gives him the rundown on me. Chris has a little sympathy for me, so he is somewhat cordial to me.

"Want a bump?"

What the hell.

"Shoot it."

Once I do that first bump, I always tell myself, *This ain't gonna end well.* And here I am, doing exactly what I moved eight states away to avoid. I came out to Oklahoma to do different but it just proves you can find bad anywhere you live.

I wind up staying at Matt's with his wife and two daughters. I'm selling his dope for him too. I'm not even making no money. When Matt leaves town to re-up, I stay behind to watch his house so no one breaks in. He also takes me along with him to all his clients. He's sloppy when he does his business and he's shady. I notice the type of clients are mostly the stay-at-home, work-oriented type, not the type to go out and look for meth, so if they give him a grand for an ounce and he only gives them a half ounce, they just accept it usually. After having to wait days to finally get it. Like, they just settle.

I keep record of all his clients' info on my phone for future reference. I notice Matt is also a pervert and I don't like that.

His main plug is some fool doing life in Oklahoma behind the walls! I'm doing all the dirty work, kicking in doors, smashing people and collecting money. The dope I get that's mine, I just save.

I meet this little white girl named Misty. She's a dope whore. Once day she is desperate for a ride, so I help her out. I soon find out she hit Chris for a couple ounces. I hide her out and help her make a few dollars. Chris didn't even find out. But honestly she didn't even really know the value of a dollar. She was so pretty and sexual she didn't need no money, she just wanted to stay high. So I helped her do just that, plus I sold the dope she stole.

I meet this midget named Tristan Bulger. He pretty much winds up being my personal driver. One day I have to go meet a client in the casino, so we pull up to the casino and I tell Tristan to stay in the car. Ain't no way I'm taking no dope inside, so I leave all my shit in the car so I can go in and find this fool. When I come back out, I notice Tristan's car is gone.

What the fuck?

Even my phone is in the car...I don't even know where I'm at. Once again I find myself in another helpless situation.

I go back into the casino, I see this little white girl named Tana I sold dope to a couple of times. I tell her the deal, she says she don't know where he lives but her homegirl might, so we leave to her homegirl's house.

Her homegirl don't know exactly where, but says it's a little service road somewhere off the interstate — *I know, right?* — but I could use her minivan to go look for him.

So I take off in this minivan that don't even have the side sliding door on it. All bad.

I'm driving down this interstate with no clue as to where I'm going. I look behind me and it's a highway patrol. *Oh fuck.* So I see this gated up little area and bust a left just to get this highway patrol to pass me. In the side of the gated area is a little dirt trail, so I follow it and right when I turn the bend, I see Tristan's car. *I just found a needle in a haystack.*

I see a nice house set off in the back too, so I jump off the minivan and knock on the door. Some 60-ish lady answers the door.

"Can I help you?"

I say, "Is Tristan here?"

She tells me, "Yes, but he's asleep."

I say, "It's urgent. Can you wake him?"

She's reluctant so I say, "Please!"

She leaves me at the door. When she walks away I step all the way in and close the door 'cause ain't no way I'm gonna leave without talking to this fool.

To my left I notice a bookshelf full of books and I glance at it.

She comes back.

"He won't wake up."

Before she has a chance to tell me to leave I say, "What's up with all these books?"

She says, "I read them all."

I say, "So have I."

She looks at me, all tatted up with long hair, plus I'm there looking for her son. I can't be on anything positive. But she's intrigued.

She says, "No way."

I say, "Pick a book and I'll tell you about it."

She winds up testing my gangster and picks four different books at random and just like I said, I read them all. So I think she decides that anyone that's read all those books can't possibly be on no shit. Little does she know that if her son don't have all the right answers to my questions he can real easily be dead.

She says, "You go see if you can wake him up."

It's like they say, "A vampire can't enter your home unless you invite it in." I was now invited in, and it was all that I needed to hear.

I walk to Tristan's room. I don't even knock, I just go in and close the door behind me.

Tristan is fast asleep. His room is a pig sty.

I pick up these brass knuckles that are sitting on his dresser and I knock on his head. He immediately wakes up.

The first thing he does is extend his arm. He's handing me something.

I go to take it, and it's his car keys.

I say, "Listen real good fool. Whoever you're scared of, I promise I'm way worse. Now where is all my shit?"

He can't even look me in the face. I already know this fool would never even think of robbing me so I say, "What happened?"

So he tells me he was sitting in his car waiting on me and Matt jumped in his passenger side seat and saw all my shit and took it then told him to go home. He says he was scared so he went home 'cause he didn't want to face me. I tell him as long as his story pans out, I will make sure he is ok.

Tristan lets me use his phone so I can call Matt. He don't answer. *Right...*

So I call Matt's wife, Christina and tell her to tell him he gots my shit and I'm coming for it. Mind you, I'm still staying at his place.

When me and Tristan get to Matt's place, I notice all my stuff is on the porch — even the shit he took from Tristan's car — so I load up Tristan's car and we drive down the street to Chris's spot to see Lacy. She ain't there but Misty is. I ask her if she knows anyone who wants to buy dope. Boy, did she ever!

Literally at least twenty fools show up back-to-back. Misty don't even want anything, she just wants to stay high, so I tell her that whenever she brings a customer, I'll hook her up. She's down.

I guess before she would get her cut by pinching the sack. Say her customer has a hundred and wants a gram, she will take his money and go get the dope but she will take some so he's getting shorted but one of the reasons these fools buy dope through her is usually 'cause they also want to fuck her too. And it's a chance since she knows they got a sack she will leave with them too and take the short.

I figured that out real quick.

I'm tryna make a name for myself 'cause I plan on taking this little area over, so I tell her, "Look sexy, whatever I put in these fools' sacks, give them all of it. You don't need to pinch it, I will take good care of you. Also, you don't need to sleep with no one for no dope as long as you're helping me out, ok?"

She's with it.

I would literally sit in the front room of Chris's trailer as he is all stuck in the back room tweaking and catch all his customers and the customers Misty would bring over all day and they never caught on. The same for all Matt's clients. He said he didn't know the shit in Tristan's car was mine. His bad. I could still stay with him, so I went back to his spot too.

Matt had surveillance cameras aimed at the main street on the other side of the house and he would get all tweaked out and literally sit and watch that street on camera on the TV in his room all day and night and wait on customers to come but they would pull up on the front street. I would sit in my car out front as a client would get off they car, I would say, "Matt ain't here but I got the sack," and I would short stop them and get the swerve plus I always gave them exactly what they paid for. Matt would always short them. Chris would get the money and buy, say, four or five pounds. He would give some to Matt and keep some for himself — they both were using that fool in the pen's plug. The dude in the pen doing life, his name was Slint. He been down twenty plus for killing a cop.

Well one day Misty calls me in a panic, I need to come get her ASAP. So I tell Tristan, "Let's go."

We pull up, Misty jumps in the car and says, "I got this much dope."

I say, "God damn girl, where did you get that?"

She says, "Just take it but drop me back off, I don't want Chris to know I took it."

I drop her back off.

"If you need me, call and I'll drop everything, ok?"

She is all happy to see she made me proud. She's a lot like a little girl.

I ask Tristan if he knows any place we can go chill.

He says, "Yes! My homie Andy."

So I say, "Ok, let's go!"

We are now driving on some cobblestone road in the back of some ranches, then he turns down a dirt road that wraps around to some forest-looking trailer park. We go all the way to the back. We stop and some Italian-looking fool comes out of a trailer, sees us and tells Tristan to come in. I'm checking out the whole scene 'cause I got a lot of dope, I don't even know the exact amount yet, but it's a lot...

Anyways my mind is now in a different mode. "Survival mode", "Grind Mode," cause I know with the amount of dope I got I can come all the way up. I'm now on full alert to anything that I can utilize to aid my come-up such as a spot to sell dope out of, and be as safe as possible. This trailer is soon to make me a ton of money.

We go in.

The trailer is hella small and it's messy but it's warm and safe. I ask if he has a scale and he does. I weigh the dope and it's a straight pound. *Damn!* At the time, an ounce of meth in this area is $1,600 and I got sixteen ounces! If I nickel and dime it, I can get way more. 448 grams at $200 a gram, I'm rich...

I ask Tristan, "Do you know anyone who wants to buy any dope?"

He does and just like with Misty they come by the pack. I just found my million dollar spot. I post up there a few days just selling all this dope.

Matt calls me and tells me he needs me to come watch his house while he goes out of town so I do. As soon as he's gone I call Tristan and I pull up on all Matt's "homebody" clients and give 'em my best sales pitch and way better business. Almost all of them fuck with me, so when Matt comes back they don't fuck with him no more. The best part is he didn't have a clue. I had all his big plays and most of his small swerves. I'd even sit at Chris's trailer and snatch all those sales. These fools loved it too, they all knew they would get exactly what they were paying for with no bullshit.

One day I was with Matt when Slint called him from the pen and asked him if he was ready to make a run to the city to re-up, 'cause by now he should be out of dope. Matt said he wasn't ready, he still had most of the dope. Slint went nuts.

"How is that possible?"

Matt said, "Ain't no one got money or they ain't buying no dope."

I was laughing my ass off inside. Fuck these fools, even Chris wasn't doing his usual numbers but my numbers were great. I wound up buying the empty trailer next to Andy's and called Misty to come clean it. I told her I would pay her so she came...and never left.

At first it was all business plus I loved all the clients she brought. She also kept my spot super clean. Between her and Andy's clients I racked up my 12 thousand I needed to make a California trip to get fifty ounces for ten grand — I figured 2 grand for the trip.

I rent Misty a car and another one for myself, tell her to get a homegirl in one car and I drive and meet them in the prearranged spot in California.

We all take off.

Once in Cali we all take my car to different spots, every trip, the beach, Disneyland, comedy clubs. A couple days later we drive back to Oklahoma the same way we got there — only difference is her car weighs three pounds heavier. She never figured it out either, she just loved to drive.

The Cali dope was "P2P" dope, about 100 times more potent than any Oklahoma dope. These fools were gonna love me!

I was telling Misty how good my dope was so she called all her people and they all came through — every one of them — 'cause by now they knew my business was legit.

Well now it's been a couple days and ain't none of them came back or called and one thing you can bet about a tweeker is they're coming back, and often, and if they don't it's only for a couple reasons. So here it is about two days later and Misty is talking shit.

"That shit is bunk. Ain't no one coming or calling. You're whack!"

She's mad 'cause I wouldn't give her no dope. It's my principle, I spent 12 grand and until I make all 12 grand back, ain't nobody smoking! So here she is running her mouth and the next day it's like the floodgates opened 'cause they all come flooding in talking about "God damn homie that shit had me so high..." all different reasons but all the same principle: that dope had them lit the fuck up.

I look at Misty and she look at me all pretty and says, "I want some please."

I make my 12 grand back by the middle of my third ounce! I still got 47 to go so you do the math. Here, we'll do it together: 28 grams at no less than $200 a gram is $5,600 an ounce, nothing less, all happy customers, million dollar spot.

I was making hella money, but I had a casino addiction. That is the worst addiction ever 'cause even if I spent all my money on drugs the very least I get out of it is the high, but if you spend all your money in the casino you don't get shit but being broke and usually stranded at the casino outside 'cause security seems to know just when you get broke and if you're not playing anymore they ask you to leave. All bad.

I helped my homegirl out and bought some dope off of her. It turned out to be some bath salts. Well you already know I was full on in my addiction so I didn't know and even if I would have known it wouldn't have mattered. I'd still have done it.

Well, my birthday comes around on November 2nd. My mom was hearing all the talk of how I was balling now so she tells me to come to her house so she and my sister can cook me a birthday dinner. It's a rare birthday I've spent on the streets so I said, "Ok." I've been up literally weeks.

I'm at my mom's house and I smoke some weed and the last thing I remember is I'm sitting up in the bed and my mom brings me a plate of tacos. I take a bite. The next thing I'm jarred awake by an incredible shock. I sit up and it seems I'm now on the floor by the door. I'm in the front room.

"Sir, sir, relax."

I see a woman in a white button-down shirt, then more people all dressed the same. I'm sitting up. I got no shirt on.

"Sir, you just died. How do you feel?"

I'm in a trance, it's all hazy, my fucking chest hurts, I got two big ass stickers on my chest. I see some type of box-like machine on my left side with wires coming out of it. I stand up.

"Can I leave?"

I'm freaking out 'cause I see the flashing lights of the emergency vehicle outside. I'm on the run plus I got dope on me. I'm in survival mode. I ain't going back to prison.

"It's not advised."

I guess I just walked away...

I black out for who knows how long.

I come to as I'm walking across a bridge. It's like the world just turned on like someone just turned on the TV in the middle of a TV show.

I'm freezing. My entire chest hurts. Somehow I have a shirt on. I pull the neck open so I can look at my chest and it's all bruised plus I still have those big stickers on my chest.

What the fuck? Where am I?

I pull out my phone and call my mom.

"Oh my God, son where are you?"

I tell her, "I don't know, I'm on a bridge, what's going on?"

She says, "Stay there, I'm coming. I'll be there in five minutes."

So I walk to the end of the bridge and she and my sister pull up. Alyssa, my baby sister jumps out of the truck.

"Oh my God we thought you were dead brother. You died last night then came back to life, then ran out of the house and we couldn't find you!"

She was crying full on. We both got in the truck, Mom drives us back to her house.

Later, after we're all settled, my sister curls up next to me and tells me everything that happened.

"I went to see if you wanted more tacos. When I looked at your face brother it was all black and you had white foam coming out of your mouth and chewed up food on your chest. You choked on your food. You must have fell asleep eating, so I jumped on your chest and beat it until you spit up the food. You weren't breathing. I was screaming and crying so Mom came in and saw what was going on so she called the ambulance. I gave you mouth-to-mouth brother but you weren't breathing. It took thirty minutes for the ambulance to get here. They couldn't find a pulse brother. You were dead. They had to shock you three times with those things, then you just jumped up and ran off. You're fucking nuts, Kenny, where did you go?"

I just sat and listened, putting it all together. All this happened in 2015. I didn't know it at the time but all this that transpired turns out to be a very pivotal experience that takes five years to manifest itself in full. I had glimpses of pieces of these events such as I saw myself rise out of my body and I saw myself with my face all black with the foam. I saw my sister hysterical, beating on my chest. I saw my mom frozen in the doorway with the phone in her hand.

"Call the fuckin ambulance, he's dying."

That's all I remember until five years later. I'll tell you all about it, just keep this introduction close...

Me and Misty wind up hooking up. Everybody hates her. The females 'cause she probably fucked all they men and she always got whatever she wanted, and most of the plugs 'cause at one point or another she probably robbed 'em or stole something from them or they already fucked her and she dissed 'em afterwards. But for whatever reason they all hated her. They all pretty much grew up around each other or knew one another and like I said, it was a small county — a bunch of Natives and white people on meth or in the meth crowd.

"She gonna rob you too, once she sees ain't no more dope, she's a hoe!"

I was hearing it all. I didn't care anyways, I liked her sexy little Miss America-looking ass. She was 23 but already been through some shit. Buried a son, been beat on by every man in her life, was molested by all the men in her family and when she told her teacher what was going on, he molested her. Even after all that she still was optimistic. I guess in our demons we bonded. She was super honest 'cause she don't give no fucks...

She been tweaking and going hard since the age of 16. The bond I had with this girl was crazy, but our entire relationship was toxic...

She knew exactly how to get me to respond to her.

She loved to be physically beat then right after, have sex. Shit, I ain't never hit no woman and now her I am beating this pretty little white girl almost every day. It's like the only time we got along was during sex 'cause shit, even moments after we would be fighting.

I won't lie, I loved what we had. Who wouldn't?

She found out that if she left I would hunt her down and now she's jumping out of bathroom windows and running on me, so I'd have to hunt her down.

I'd be sick when she was gone, I would put everything on hold until I'd find her. It got so bad, none of her people would even let her in their house if she wasn't with me. They knew if I caught them hiding her I'd get violent. I was sick over this girl and she knew it and exploited it.

One time we went to see her son in the cemetery and she sat on his grave and did a shot of dope and said, "I promise on my son I will never stop using meth and that this pussy will always be yours!"

I guess the meth kept her demons away 'cause if she didn't slow down they couldn't catch her. I had no choice but to respect this crazy ass girl. She was that real...

My mom was envious 'cause I wouldn't give her no money so she was trying to make waves by telling the police I was a drug dealer. Even though we were only miles away from each other it may as well have been continents. She would put all types of stuff on Facebook about me and assassinate my character to my other brothers and sisters. Misery loves company, but all her company was in her head.

I was selling dope, making money and gambling like crazy. I was actually getting somewhere. I had no police contact. I had my own spot. I finally came up and I wasn't looking back. I couldn't see myself losing, everything was going so good. Even all the fighting with Misty couldn't bring me down 'cause I liked it. The fact that she stayed around was all I needed but she didn't need or want for anything. What could go wrong? I soon would see my whole world collapse in a Walmart.

My sister Alyssa who was taking care of some fool with full blown AIDS on his death bed introduced me to her old man, Scott. He turned out to be my Oklahoma dope plug, among other things.

We did a lot of business. Every time I'd go to his place I'd leave with all types of cool shit, like guns. He had so much shit he never noticed it was missing.

He had three storage containers full of shit. He'd steal the whole semi truck with the storage container still on it — Best Buy, cigarettes, liquor — then he'd auction them off every weekend. He'd get like a cool million. Every weekend I'd stand in as security. But he had all this new shit all over the place. It looked like being in a store — even the guns were brand new and hanging on shelves like a store.

One day Scott called me and told me to be at his place that night. I show up, he tosses me an orange vest and a hard hat and says to put it on. We jump in his truck. He then hands me a plastic box full of roadside flares. He tells me to start placing them in the road whenever he stops. He stops, I jump out, light the flare, then jump back in his truck. We do this for about ten miles and pull up to a worksite. He pulls his truck up and parks, jumps out and tells me to follow him. I see one of his friends followed us, some other fool jumps in Scott's truck and takes off.

Scott says, "We gonna take these three bulldozers to my spot. Let's go."

I'm talking about full bulldozers, huge, with the boom and claw, all that!

I was like, "Let's roll!"

Keeping it real, I thought the whole gig was legit. So here I am driving this bulldozer down the highway at 3am. I get to his place, pull up all the way down his driveway to the backyard and he pulls up next to me.

He tells me to get all the impact drills and sockets ready, we gonna take these things apart and put the pieces in the empty storage containers. I get to work.

Scott has forklifts in his yard too. We get all three bulldozers taken apart and packed in the storage containers.

He says, "Good job" then hands me ten thousand dollars cash. Just like that. I guess he said he hauled them off and sold them! They were already gone that same night!

Well we'd been doing good business for about eight months or so. My little sister was in and out of jail. Well one day Scott comes to my spot and he's all depressed. I'm all like, "What's up fool?" Mind you, Scott is about 50, old school meth cook and cowboy. It's me, my girl Misty, Scott and his friend Rita. Scott says he just came from Tulsa hospital visiting his brother who is dying from AIDS and man, he is hoping he doesn't go out like his brother!

Right then when he said that the whole world just stopped.

I saw myself picking up my gun and blowing his brain out! It all happened so fast, like it was in warp speed.

As I am thinking about what I should do next I see Scott's mouth move, like he is talking to me. I snap back into reality and hear him say, "Are you okay?"

I'm all like, "What?"

He says, "You just zoned out on me."

I'm all like, "Yeah, fucking meth got me tripping!"

Inside I am dying. All I can think about is my baby sister getting HIV from this fool. I really want to smoke his ass. The one and only reason I don't is 'cause my girl is there and I don't want to have to kill her too. I'd have smoked Rita no problem, but I loved my little dope whore Misty. So I play it cool until he leaves.

Misty knows me so well, as soon as Scott leaves she says, "I thought you were gonna kill him! I picked up what he said too baby!"

She is happy when she says that 'cause she wants me to see how perceptive she is. Like she did good. I tell her to shut her ass up.

That whole night I sit there with that shit on my mind, hoping my sis would call me from jail so I can tell her to go get checked, but she never does!

When you're ADHD, tweaked on meth, no sleep for weeks things tend to slip your mind, but this I can't shake, it says on my mind. What really fucks me up is his nonchalance towards the whole thing, like he didn't give two fucks who else he fucked over. Maybe to him his people don't mean shit, but I done knocked my own mom out over some lesser shit. This fool had no clue I held his life in my hands literally! I will literally stew on something until the remedy presents itself. It's a quirk I got from all the books I've read.

"48 Laws of Power" – conceal your intentions

"The Art of War" – make every strike deadly

"The Holy Bible" – an eye for an eye

So I sit and continue normal program like everything is all good.

February 24th, 2015, I am in my trap. I usually never carry no meth on me unless I have to. I am on my way to get my hair cut. As soon as I'm leaving I get a call — someone wants a gram so I have my homegirl turn around so I can wait and serve them. I handle that, then I go to leave again and someone else calls wanting another gram. *Shoot.* At the time, I was getting point for point so that's another quick $100. So I just pick up an empty pill bottle and scoop it into the big bag of meth. I put the top back on it and tell my homegirl let's bounce.

Somehow we end up at Walmart so I jump out the car and shoot inside.

I go to the phone section and grab two Galaxies plus $50 straight talk cards. The total is like $1,280 so I throw 13 hundred at the clerk and tell her to keep the change, but she makes a big deal out of it, so I take the change then shove it into one of those charity things.

I head to the phone protector section and next — I won't lie, I was super tweaked out and I did look suspicious, but I wasn't doing anything wrong — the section that has the phone protectors is all full of open cases from people checking to see if they fit their phones so I was just checking to see if any of the open ones fit my phones. I keep having to squat down and my pants are a little tight, not to mention I have two full wallets open the long way in my back pockets, so I take my wallets out and place them on the floor next to me. I keep going up and down the aisle, leaving my two wallets on the floor but keeping an eye on them. I hit the end of the aisle and then the 'secret shopper' or better yet loss prevention dude comes into my aisle.

He sees the wallets on the floor and goes to pick them up and I yell, "Thief ass dude, keep moving!"

So he looks back at me and all stupid like leaves the aisle. I can see him all peeking at me from around the corner. I had been in this Wal-Mart literally every day for at least six months — it's a small town in Oklahoma named Grove. Ain't shit to do but tweak, hit the casino, or go to Wal-Mart! So I know all the people who work there. I know dude in loss prevention. Either way I don't shoplift ever — it's the easiest way for someone on parole to get sent back to prison, especially when you look like me: long hair and tatted everywhere, people automatically thing you gonna steal some shit!

I pick my wallets up, I start to go down the aisle. I see two cops coming in. They stop me and ask do I have any stolen shit in my pockets.

I say "No I don't."

They pat me down and don't find nothing. They still don't let me leave.

Then one of the cops says, "What's in your pocket?"

I say, "My prescription from Wal-Mart."

It really is a prescription I filled at Wal-Mart a week back for antibiotics, at least the bottle was. They then take the pill bottle out of my pocket, open it, and see all the shiny crystals.

They ask what it is and I say, "It's what the pharmacy gave me!"

They search me again and find my two wallets in both back pockets. They ask why I have so much money on me and how much it is.

I say, "I can't get an ID to open a bank account and my spot keeps getting broken into, so I carry all my cash on my person, — and I think it's about 10 grand.

They cuff me.

I get to the jail and in booking they got to do my property and shit. Well one cop is on the counter with stacks of 100's and he's all counting my money, then a cute ass female cop named Star — I'll tell you more about her later — comes in and sees all the money and she says, "Boy that's a lot of ones!"

I look back at the cop counting the money. He looks up at me. Then we both look at her and I say, "Nah baby girl, if you find a single one in the whole stack I'll give it all to you, on my mama!"

She picks up a stack and fans through it and sees all the big faces, then looks at me and I see hearts shooting at me from her eyes, just like a cartoon!

Like I said, it's a small town, even smaller jail, so I'm standing out super bad — not the regular type to be in this town or jail. In the end the total amount I had on me was $22,000.

The cops say, "Why so much money?"

I say, "I was in Wal-Mart 'bout to buy some shit then I was gonna hit Lowe's!"

The dope only weighs out to 22.6 grams, a simple possession, no scales, no baggies, but the part about small towns you don't realize is they make their own laws, especially in rural Oklahoma. Believe it or not, in some stores and places they still got "No Colored" signs posted and they stand on it too. To them I was "Colored". It's crazy cuz I'm Native and Oklahoma is called "Native America". Tell that to the white confederates who run the whole county called Delaware County. The whole county sits and runs along the Grand Lake, the largest man-made lake in the USA. So a lot of old white money, and a lot of animosity between the Natives who break the laws and the white who enforce their version of them.

I knew it was all bad when two days later I get arraigned and the judge says my bail is $100,000. I'm like, *What the fuck, $100,000!* I don't know what to think, I've never been in this situation before.

It's crazy cuz up until this point about a year of straight nickel, dime pushing, serving no less than 100 people a day from quarter papers which are twenties (0.2) to eightballs (3.5 grams) and making more than $6,000 an ounce, 28 grams, I'd get more than 200 a gram if you do the math I'd get 50 ounces, three pounds two ounces for $10,000 in California and I was killing it. Plus the dope was pure.

Like I was saying, up to this point they never even heard of me! Crazy right? Here I am in this super small rich white town selling meth to everyone and they never heard nothing!

The judge is Judge Alicia Littlefield, the most notorious crooked judge in the whole state. She also manages the 'drug court' program. She hates drugs and drug users. And especially drug dealers. She'll give you 40 years quick and not even blink. The entire jail is max capacity: 100 inmates. The male pod is ten cells: two ten man cells, two eight man cells, two six man cells, two five man cells, and two four man cells. The woman pod is only like six five man cells. The court house sits on top of the cells.

I finally get done with the booking and find a cell. I'm coming down super bad since I literally ain't slept in over a month, so as soon as I hit my cell, I'm out.

The next time I wake up is for my arraignment. I sleepwalk through all of that too.

A couple days later I wake up and some white fool is all, "Man I know you!"

I sit up and I'm all like, "From where?"

He says, "Oh shit, you're the one who did this" and he shows me a cut across his throat still with the stitches in it! *What the fuck?*

I jump off my bed. I'm in a six man cell and it's five white boys and me.

I tell dude — 'cause now I know exactly who he is — "So what, you tripping?"

He's all, "Naw, hell naw this scar makes me look gangster!"

I wasn't tapping into none of his shit.

I tell him, "Naw it means you was a victim!"

I'm pissed 'cause the whole reason I stabbed him was he burned me. I went to holla at him at his spot — my mom's 60 year old friend drove me out there — and when I get there like eight fools run out. One hits the windshield with a bat, cracking it, I jump out the ride and it's a stand off. Then dude swings the bat at me. I guess I dodged it, and I sliced his throat.

All I remember saying was, "Dude you need to go get checked your shit is leaking."

I jump in the ride and we leave. That's the last I heard of it until now.

Like I said, I was pissed since this fool burned me so I tell him, "I'll give you two minutes to get out this cell!"

Right then on the speaker in my cell the cop says, "Thunderburk, get ready for a bail interview!"

I'm thinking, *What?*

"Okay."

So they come get me and they take me upstairs to an office. It's O.S.B.I. or the Oklahoma Special Bureau of Investigations.

The lead detective says they tested my meth and it was 98.6% pure meth. Who was I and where did I get the meth, all that. Like I said, a real small town so it's a real big deal.

I know they're mad. Then they start to get like they been on me for months, but they already showed their hand.

I ask them what they want.

They say, "Help us catch some people and we'll let you out."

Like I said, I've never been in this situation before and I literally had no one to tell on, besides my Cali plugs and no way in hell would I ever do that.

I tell them to fuck off, I'm not playing any games, take me back to my cell. I didn't have time to contemplate any of the events that transpired because as soon as I hit my bed I was out.

Two days later, I'm woken up and told to pack my stuff, I made bond. I guess one of my crazy millionaire clients posted my bond anonymously — I never found out who.

Standing on the corner by the jail I head, "Baby!"

I look up and it's Misty turning the corner in some car. I jump in and I tell Misty all the events that transpired that led up to my arrest and about what the O.S.B.I. offered me.

She says, "Oh shit, now you're a rat, huh?" "How else could you get out?"

I tell her about the dude who posted my bail. Then

I say, "Shit your bitch ass up before I slap your ass."

One of the things I was worried about was the drug testing as a condition of my bond. And that means no more meth.

It's crazy 'cause now I don't got shit — no dope, no money — and my little dope whore doesn't go anywhere. She stays right by my side. Everyone said she'd bounce — even I thought she would.

I'm at a low point.

I can't sell no more dope 'cause they are on me. Eventually I go back to what I know. Fuck it, I need to live too.

I'm pushing out of my white homie's house now. Misty still being Misty tryna play Houdini, I catch her tryna run on me but this time with my wallet so I snatch her ass up and fuck her up. Well, her little homegirl calls the cops.

When they pull up, Misty is in the bath. They immediately cuff me up.

When the cops pull Misty out of the bath, she is hissing and yelling, "What the fuck do you want?"

They tell her, "Your friend said she saw him hit you, did he?"

She says, "No bitch, leave me alone."

She's still pissed at me from her ass beating so the cop says, "So what did he do?"

She says, "He won't let me leave, he pulled me back into the house."

The cop sees some redness on her neck.

They take me to the county jail booked on a fucking "Kidnapping" charge. 50 thousand bond! I am sick as fuck. Now I for sure am stuck in jail 'cause I was already out on "OR" and I just caught another case, plus now Misty is gonna be out there alone. She is up for grabs.

I call Misty on my one phone call and she is still pissed. She says the detective said I should be calling her.

The next day she comes to the jail to get my property so I sign it out to her: my phone and credit cards so she has some money. I didn't know at the time she was a witness for the state against me.

I go crazy in that small ass corrupt jail. I manipulate the cops into giving me a free phone call saying I need to call my mom. I call Misty. They record the phone call.

Misty says, "I went to talk to the DA to tell him I wouldn't press charges. He said the state would press charges. What do I do babe?"

I say, "Just don't come to court."

She says, "I won't, I'll hide."

A week later I get a new charge: "Attempting to prevent a witness from giving testimony".

Shit. I'm just racking up the felonies. It's my third: the dope case, the kidnapping, and now this one. Not to mention three misdemeanors for assault for fighting in the jail.

I wind up signing for 5 in and 15 suspended. I'm sent to prison again, this time in Oklahoma. I first go to Lexington — it's called A&R. It's a reception/classification prison. Well they make all inmates shave their hair off, face and all. I got long hair and I'm not trying to cut it so they got two black dudes buzzing everyone's hair.

When the black fool goes to cut my hair I tell him, "Let me cut it myself."

So he hands me the machine. As soon as I have a good grip I swing it and crack the black fool in the face. All the police rush me. It's not like Cali so they ain't got no pepper spray but they are big mean fuckers so I get an ass beating then I am placed in the hole...but at least I still got all my hair.

Two weeks go by and I know they can't keep me here forever so I figure I made it out with my hair. *Shit.* I was wrong.

My door opens. I'm slammed on the floor and held down and my hair is cut. They even leave me all full of patches. *Damn.* But you can't say I didn't give it the best effort I could.

I'm sent to Cimarron, also called Cushing. It's one of the worst prisons in Oklahoma. I get there in September on the 15th, 2015. That very same day I'm in the day room when all hell breaks loose.

I see a microwave thrown into a white fool's head and everywhere white fools is running around stabbing each other. Well the end result is four people dead. Lockdown for three months. My introduction to Oklahoma corrections. All them white fools fighting were Irish Mob and UABs, Universal Aryan Brotherhood.

Oklahoma ain't shit like Cali, it's mostly all drug addicts and the politics are way different. The respect level is also very low. A lot of gay shit too. I try to keep my head down and wind up going to a low called Jackie Branon. I only last a couple weeks. It's all dorm living and I don't do very well in dorms. My neighbor is some fool named T. Loc, a hoover, very disrespectful. So one day I have enough of his mouth so I smash him out. I get told on and sent to the hole, then back up in Security and right back to Cushing.

While in Cushing I get into a fight with my celly. He is way bigger so I stab him. We get caught and he tells. I go back to the hole to be shipped.

I land in Crab Tree, it's pretty laid back.

I'm finally released and I'm on 15 years suspended probation. I bet you can't guess where I'm living? I know, I'm nuts, but I got no other choice. My mom's is the only place I can go. So here I go again...

It's cool for a couple weeks then, "Want a line, Kenny?"

I already know I shouldn't but fuck, I'm weak, so I say, "Yes!"

This ain't gonna end well...

The first argument, "I'm calling your PO and telling her you been getting high!"

I fucking knew it. Every fucking time...

If I go back, it's for 15 years this time, but she don't give no fucks. I'm desperate.

"Please Mom, no!"

I won't lie, I even contemplated killing the bitch. Don't judge me until you know all the details first...

One morning she just jumps up and says, "I want you out."

I tell her, "I ain't got nowhere to go."

She says, "Ok."

She leaves in her truck and I fall back asleep. Next thing I know she's waking me up.

"Kenny the cops are here. I don't know why."

I open my eyes to see two Sheriffs above me.

Oh shit.

"Son you need to get your shit and be out of the house. Your mom just got a restraining order on you."

Wasn't shit I could say, I'm out on the street walking to my grandparents' house.

When I get there I knock on the door. My grandma yells, "Go away Kenny or we're calling the police!"

I find out later my mom called them and told them I was on my way there to come rob them. *This crazy bitch.*

My grandma is crazy too, but she ain't evil. Like I said, she breeds dogs so she has at least forty little dogs running around her double-wide. Literally all day. My grandparents are old and they can't clean very well, so the whole trailer smells like dog piss. It's hard to breathe in there. Somehow I convince them to let me in.

My grandpa is suffering from Alzheimer's so he is pretty sporadic, but I love them both dearly. My grandpa has died since the start of my book. May his soul rest in eternal peace. My grandma has been taken care of by my mom since his death. And as far as I know she's doing a good job. I know, right? I told you my mom has a gift for helping elderly people. I guess it's just her male children she hates.

So here I am staying at my grandparents' house. I do all the cleaning and yard work, so my grandparents appreciate me. My mom literally calls every day trying to scare my grandparents into kicking me out. I also get a good job on the marina at "South-winds Marina" doing general maintenance and taking care of and detailing all the boats and yachts at the marina. I love it. I am making $2,000 a week and killing it.

Well, one day I am walking home from work — which is almost literally across the street. The local sheriff stops me, cuffs me and says, "You're a suspect in a burglary."

What the fuck?

It's about 8pm. They keep me sitting in the cop car until about 12am then all kinds of other law enforcement vehicles pull up.

We pull up to my grandparents' house. They raid my elderly grandparents' house at 12:30am, leaving them in the front yard with all the puppies all over the place. The fucked up part is that the two local sheriffs named Travis and Burly know both my grandparents, but they are all gung-ho on busting me. I didn't do shit.

They conclude their search — nothing stolen was found but I am still arrested for "Possession of Methamphetamine". Ain't no way — never once have I taken any meth in this house. I know they must have set me up. I'm thinking my mom had something to do with this. Like I said, I got 15 years suspended — my next case, it's all over for me...

I'm dead inside. It's over, I know it.

I get to the county, that same small jail. I get my one phone call — it's to a bondsman. I ask the jailer what my bond is. He says, "$800 cash bond." I am confused.

"Huh, $800?"

I don't get it, possession in this county is $5,000.

I ask, "What's my charge?"

He tells me, "Possession of paraphernalia."

I'm even more confused.

"What's the paraphernalia?"

He says, "It doesn't say."

It's a Tuesday night, well, now actually early Wednesday. They don't even book me in, they take me to a cell and that's it.

I wake up later that day raising hell, no one can tell me shit. Ain't no way I can stay in jail and not be booked in or given a charge or bond. I know something fucked up is going on.

Thursday passes.

It's now Friday and it's around 5pm. The jailer comes and gets me.

He says, "You're free. Get dressed."

My phone is dead, all my money is stuck in the jail 'cause the lady who puts the money from your books onto the debit cards won't be in 'til Monday. So now I'm stranded in the middle of nowhere. I'm raising hell. I make them go get the jail administrator to see if I could get a ride but I really want to know why I was jailed.

He comes out and says, "Look Kenneth, your mom called and said you were selling dope out of your grandparents' house and that your grandparents are scared of you and wanted you out."

That evil ass bitch!

He gives me a ride to Tomcat Corner filling station. I find a ride back onto the island to my grandparents' house.

Once I get inside my grandma runs up to me and hugs me.

She says, "I found out what your mom did, I'm so sorry honey. She called me and told me that she called the cops on you 'cause she don't want you here. It's our house and you are always welcome here!"

As for the burglary, I guess a lady that lived around the corner left her purse on her kitchen table before jumping in the car to go to church and she and her husband left together. But <u>I guess her husband noticed her purse on the table and picked it up and tossed it in the back seat.</u> He had to leave during church and took the car. The lady got a ride home and noticed her purse was gone and called the cops and when you look like me, you very easily become the most likely suspect. The crazy part is that the husband wound up returning as they raided my grandparents' house and told his wife that he had her purse. I know all this because my grandparents' neighbor is a volunteer officer and he told me. Either way, all my probation officer is gonna see is that one, I'm in jail, two, I was a burglary suspect, and three, I was booked on a paraphernalia case! All probation violations.

A part of a suspended sentence is that you have already been sentenced on that case and you've already pled guilty — they don't need any other reason to revoke the suspended case but now they got three good ones. Usually they only need an accusation.

My PO wants me in her office Monday at 8an sharp.

Even worse, I go to my job to tell them I'm out end it was all a bullshit case.

The boss says, "Son, thanks to your mom we can't hire you back."

He shows me the company's Facebook wall page:

"I just want you to know that you hired a violent criminal who now won't ever be getting out 'cause he's in jail for drugs and burglary. You need to find a new employee, this is his mother!"

I get my last check. The boss who is the owner says, "You're a great worker kid. I wish we could keep you bet you see all the negative comments. It's bad for my business!"

I tell him, "I understand sir. Thank you for the opportunity, it's been a pleasure."

Having a job would've been at least one positive I had going for me. Now I ain't got shit and Monday is one day away...I'm hit.

Monday morning I'm sitting in the lobby with my 85 year old grandmother waiting on my agent to call me.

I tell my grandma, "I love you grandma, thank vou for all you done for me. If I go to prison I probably won't see you no more. I just need you to know that I love you and I really tried."

She cries and says, "I love you Kenneth."

I know my grandma is crazy as fuck but she has never acted like anything but a lady. I've never seen her display any of the traits my mother swears she has. They are two entirely different people. Now that granny is getting old and so is my mom, in my heart I will always go back to my mom. I hope her having to take care of my grandma puts things in perspective as to why she is alone. Hopefully now that she's not alone the company is seeing her in all aspects of her being. I just want her to shed all her demons so I can shed mine too. I can't ever let my guard down until I see moms is happy.

"Thunderburk," my agent says, "You've got fifteen minutes to get into a rehab center or I'm locking you up!" She tells me, "You got three choices: 'The Howell Foundation' which is four hours away in Oklahoma City, 'Noca' which is in Jay, or — " I cut her off. Jay is about 45 minutes from my mom's house so I tell her I choose that one. I got to be there the next day, which is Tuesday.

My PO — her name is Nora — says, "Get your ass there!" The meeting is over.

I walk back out to my grandma in the waiting room. She don't even say shit, we walk out to the car and she drives us back home. So I tell her what the deal is and she says, "I will take you there tomorrow."

She looks at me and smiles and she says, "It's good to be seeing you right now Kenneth."

This lady is almost ninety — thats a lot of living and wisdom in that statement. I love you grandma. Thank you for loving me unconditionally and with no limits.

The whole time my mom is telling my grandma not to give me that ride. She even goes as far as faking an ambulance trip to the hospital so my grandma has to stay with her. All that just to try to fuck my life up. She knows that if I don't make it to this place I'm hit, but I already noticed the way things were headed and I know how petty and spiteful this woman is. She is up to something.

So I borrow fifty dollars from Grandpa the day I get home from seeing my PO and tell him exactly what my intentions are with the money and he agrees.

My mom is super pissed that one, I am back out of jail and two, that it didn't work to turn my grandparents against me. As soon as I heard about it, I already knew. The crazy thing is she is the one who posted it on her Facebook: "On my way via ambulance!" Like, who does that? *Crazy ass bitch!*

So here I go the next day, I jump off the old ass minivan these two tweakers own. I give them thirty dollars in gas money to make sure I get to this rehab center, and off we go.

We make it there that afternoon and I go inside to sign all the forms. Drug test. I'm clean except for weed. I find a room and check the place out. It ain't bad. I'm here, I'm safe and I can make it.

I am there two days before I hear, "Kenneth! They need you in the front."

I pull up in front and they tell me, "Sit down. Ok, look. We can't have you here. You have a prior violent case. It's against our policy. We need you out today."

What the fuck?

Man, I sure have been saying that a whole bunch lately. It's been just one thing after another, I can't win.

I'm thinking, *I ain't got no ride, I've got twenty dollars in cash and all my clothes and shit, out in the middle of nowhere. Not to mention now I'm in violation of my probation requirements! Fifteen years at 85% is hanging over my neck like a guillotine on a thread! My shit should have been chopped a long ass time ago just off circumstances. Fuck, fuck fuck!*

I call my grandparents.

"I'll be there asap, Kenneth."

God damn!

I know right? It can't be just that easy, but for once it is! My grandma comes to get me.

"Grandpa is pissed 'cause I'm driving in the dark, he don't like me driving at night."

I can understand why. My grandma is notorious for car crashes — all at night. Crazy lady. But neither she nor my grandpa will ever let me drive. Ornery ass old people.

We pull in at my grandparents' place and we all shuffle into the house. I see grandpa sitting in his recliner with his all-white Maltese named Snowball in his lap. He's super old so he has the same routine every day. I tell my grandma I'm gonna use her computer so I can google rehab centers I can get into.

All night I google spot after spot, take numbers down so I can call. Most of them want some type of insurance or if the state is mandating you to take it, the state will fund it, but since I'm not court ordered I get no funding plus my violent past kills more than 50% of these rehabs. After calling the questionable ones, some want a deposit. I don't have no money and neither do my grandparents. That's another 25%, so now I have a 25% chance left of making it into one of these last four places on my list.

I call 'Ray's Place'. By this time I'm getting desperate and I know he can hear it in my voice. I lay it all out to him. He tells me to come on down.

I say, "Look bro, my grandparents are old, if I show up, I need to be in and stay in."

He says, "Ok, come on down."

It's in Muskogee, Oklahoma which is three and a half hours away. This time, along for the trip is my mom. She's breaking her own restraining order. Her reasoning for riding along is she don't want her mom driving back alone.

Omce again, I'm 100% helpless. I can't say or do shit, even if I contest it's gonna fuck me. The whole trip my mom is taking pictures of us and tagging me too:

"Me Kenny and Grandma, taking Kenny to rehab."

I'm not tripping until later, you'll see — that evil bitch got me again. This time it's almost lights out. I swear I don't need to be tormented by demons, I'm smothered by my own pain...this bitch is nuts, you'll see why in a minute.

We pull up to this compound, seated on a grassy area with a lake on it and a church. It's 'Ray's Place', Ray being some old ex-drug dealer from the area who got a full pardon and been helping the community with rehabilitation and a church. Yeah, this fool be on some shit too, hence my introduction into a whole different type of Evil.

Ray is an older white fool. I swear this first look I got at him I can see the snake in him. He takes me into the office that's located in the church where I sign all the paperwork and then he tells me, "You got to cut your long hair."

I almost flip out on him 'cause I asked him on the phone if anything would prevent me from being able to come into the program and he repeatedly said for me to "Just come down."

My mom and grandma already been gone for over an hour so ain't no way they coming back. I tell Ray, "Naw, you never said shit about having to cut my hair, I asked you several times before I even came what the rules of the program are."

I guess he seen the seriousness of the situation and he let me keep my hair.

I'm told to walk down the road to where all the men live. I pass by three double wide trailers where the women sleep. The mens sleeping quarters is like an old building with bunk beds — it's pretty ghetto. Right next to it is a really nice house with two new trucks. I guess that's Ray's house.

The next day we all wake up at 5am. All total it was about fifteen men. Everyone either works at jobs where Ray has pull — 10- or 12-hour work days with all the pay going directly to Ray — or they stay at home and do odd jobs like cutting wood or mowing the lawns.

The women also got jobs — mostly at the chicken plant — or they stick around and clean the church. Breakfast is always the same dry ass oatmeal, no milk ever. It's crazy 'cause all fifteen men and the women are taken to the general relief office and made to apply for food stamps so you figure 30 times $200 is $6,000 in food a month and he don't feed us shit. Not to mention we work all day. So right there I get my first glimpse that something is up with the money, not to mention the brand new trucks, the new house and new church, his new clothes and everything to do with us in the program — ain't shit new, it's all donated... No less than twenty people all working 10 or 12 hours a day at no less than $10 an hour, 6 days a week and they never see one cent. This fool is making mad money off us.

After the first day of staying at the compound and working, Ray asks me what I do for work so I say pretty much anything.

He says, "Do you weld?"

I tell him *yeah* and the next day I'm working at Mercer Metals 12 hours a day. I should have said I didn't know how to do shit, 'cause now here I am fucking up my eyes welding 12 hours a day for free!

The program overall ain't shit — work all day, then three days a week you do a bible study for two hours in the church. On Sunday you go to church service. It's literally a work/slave program but hey, it beats prison.

So I been doing this shit for around two and a half months and my probation officer says something about no less than six months. Well the night after the bible study at about 10pm everyone gets up to leave and Ray tells me, "Kenny, I need you to stay back."

Now that everyone is gone back to their quarters Ray says, "I done some investigating on you. I know all about you — fifteen years hanging over your head. I also see you have a lot of money. So look, it'd be a shame if your PO got a call saying you'd been removed from the program, if you get my drift."

This bitch ass mother fucker just put my life in his hands, trying to extort me. *Fuck this shit.* I stand up and look across the church to the exit doors then turn back to Ray.

I say, "It's just us two in here right now, so this is what's gonna happen you piece of shit. You're gonna give me your phone, 'cause as I see it my life is now over with that threat and so is yours!"

He tries to stand up but I stop him.

"I'll say this one time. I will slice your fucking throat and cut your fucking head off right here right now." I pull out my work knife.

Then I tell him, "And after I do that I will walk down to your house and knock on your door and when your wife opens the door I'll go inside and tell her what you just tried to do. Then I'll tell her where your head is, or better yet, I'll just take her your head. Then I'll torture your wife, take your keys and drive away and ain't no one gonna know shit for hours."

I act like I'm gonna stab him and he cowers and starts to beg for his life.

"Shut the fuck up. We gonna both walk to the sleeping quarters and when we get inside, you're gonna go sit the fuck down and if I hear you say one word or try to communicate with anyone as I pack my shit, I'll kill you, and your wife is right next door."

As we walk to the mens sleeping quarters I call my homegirl and tell her I need her to meet me in a dark rural area on Country Creek road in Muskogee and wait for me there. She says, "Ok."

I'm packing all my shit. The entire time Ray is just sitting there with his head down. I can tell all the other men are trippin' 'cause they know something is going on, they just don't know what.

I say, "Let's go," and we jump in his truck and drive for about an hour out to the middle of nowhere. I see homegirl pulled off on the side of the road and I tell Ray to pull over. I tell him to get out of the truck and he starts to beg.

I say, "How does it feel to know you're literally seconds away from meeting your Jesus? You should be happy. Where is that all-conquering faith now, Ray?"

He tells me, "You don't got to do this" and I laugh.

I say, "I know I don't, I want to! Now get the fuck on your knees and tell me who's your God!"

Ray starts to cry.

I roll up his truck windows then lock the doors. He's still on his knees.

"Ray, I'm gonna show you a real life miracle. I'm gonna let you live. But if I catch any smoke over any of this I will come get you and your wife. I will know where you are 'cause you got that cash cow rehab and I know you're too greedy to leave it but as for me, you won't know where I'm at, understand? Don't say a word, 'cause I want the last sound I hear from you to be that sniveling you're doing right now. I forgive you, Ray."

I walk to my homegirl's car and jump in. We take off.

I won't lie, I was supercharged with raw energy. I finally felt I got one over on someone who tried to hurt me. It felt incredible. It took all my self control to not have my homegirl turn back around so I could kill his scandalous ass — not just for what he did, but for what everyone has done to me — but it's way better that he knows I'm still out there so he has to relive it over and over again in his head. I tell my homegirl to get a room and fuck the shit out of her all night.

To this day I still haven't caught any heat from that, nor do I fear any. Last I heard, Ray was indicted on all kinds of federal tax evasion charges and sexual assaults on several women in his rehab, and he is in prison now, so instead of giving him mercy and ending his life, I left him alive to die 1,000 different deaths.

I still have a huge dilemma — if I don't find a rehab and get into it asap I'll end up doing fifteen years. My homegirl says she knows a place called 'FBTCC' (Faith Based Therapeutic Community Corporation) run by Mark Seabolt in Fort Gibson. I soon find out he's just another Ray, but that's later.

The next day, I go to see his spot — it's on an old exotic animal ranch so it's way back in the trees. It's another work/slave camp but I guess they all are and why not exploit men who are forced to be in these programs and make free money? Any issues and all they got to do is tell you to leave and wait on the next fool to take your spot — and trust me, there ain't no limit to the fools waiting to take your spot.

I'm accepted into the program. It's the same as Ray's Place. All the church shit is superficial and it's all an act to gain even more community assistance and donations, 'cause the more donations they get, the less money they need to use on us...

All the men in the rehab are eating rations, taking cold showers with no medical coverage while the director's family is living in plush, fully furnished houses, with new cars, medical care, food, all that. It's so blatant, I don't know why nobody says shit but they don't.

So here I am once again. I call my PO and tell her it didn't work out at Ray's but I'm here now.

She says, "OK, but I need you to stay at this one."

Mind you the whole reason I'm even doing all this is to avoid going back to prison on my fifteen year suspended sentence.

A couple weeks later on a whim, I check out the OSCN — which is the Oklahoma Supreme Court News — that has all the statuses of any and all of your court cases and I'm shocked to see all my cases are in red which means they have turned into active felony warrants.

What the fuck?

I call my PO and ask her why it says 'Motion to Revoke' on my fifteen year suspended case.

She says, "'Cause I put in a violation report" which means my suspended case is in the process of being revoked. A part of going to rehab in Muskogee is I had to transfer my probation to that county which also means I need to do an office visit which means with active warrants they must arrest me, which means now I must be held until I'm extradited back to Delaware County, which means I will have to sit in jail for months until extradition, then once I'm in Delaware County I got to go back to court which means I'm in front of the judge who sentenced me to the fifteen years trying to convince him why I shouldn't have my fifteen years revoked and that means I'm almost 100% hit!

That fucking bitch double-crossed me!

If I would have known all this, I would have ran from the gate and not sat in some rehab center where they know my location and can just come get my ass. Which they sure the fuck did...that same fucking night.

Now I'm in Muskogee jail — oh yeah, here it comes — I also got a new charge! I bet you a million dollars right now you can't tell me what that new charge is! Well, if you're thinking about Ray, you just lost. Nope, it's "Violating a Restraining Order".

Say cheese!

My bitch ass mom sent those photos she took on the drive to Ray's Place to my probation officer, that's why my PO put that violation report in!

Mom strikes again, this time it's a fatal blow with no possible way to come back from the damage she'd done.

Two months later I'm extradited back to Delaware County Jail. I hate this small ass jail. It literally sucks all the life out of you but I was already dead. I was pretty much sleepwalking through my days. I got arraigned, nothing special, my next court date my lawyer isn't there so Kathy Baker, the other public defender, is filling in for her.

Kathy hands me my violation report and I read over it. I see my PO recommends six months county time, a year in sober living, and I see a little bit of light at the end of the tunnel. I try to talk to Mrs. Baker, she tells me to shut up! I ask her if the judge is gonna run with what my PO recommends. I'll plead out today and get out of the court's hair.

She turns and looks at me then shakes her head and tells the district attorney, "I wash my hands with him, do what you want with him" then walks out of the courtroom. *Bitch, I'm looking at fifteen years for some shit I ain't have shit to do with, what the fuck?*

Before she is out of the room I tell her, "Bitch, if you think you're just gonna railroad me, I will blow your fucking house up whether I'm in jail or not."

The bailiff runs over and grabs me, takes me downstairs back to my cell, and the end result of all that is another case for 'threatening acts of violence'. It's a misdemeanor but now none of the county public defenders can represent me due to a conflict of interest.

So now an outside county lawyer is provided. In the end I sit in jail seven months just for the DA to run with what my PO recommended in my violation report. I know, right? It all could've been resolved with one less case and five months ago when I asked just that very question.

January 25th, 2018

I'm released and my mom picks me up from the jail.

What the fuck, right?

She dropped the restraining order. When you're out of ideas and grasping for safety you can't bitch at the life preserver being thrown to you and we all see that by now, I'm a glutton for punishment.

Or insane.

Or both.

I get to my mom's house with instructions on having to get into a rehab in a week so I call Mark Seabolt. He says I can come back.

While I was in jail, after they came and got me from his place, Mark told me all my shit had been stolen by the other fools. Most came and went, so the same day I get to the FBTTC, I notice a Raiders blanket so I take it back. I guess this fool called Seabolt and when Seabolt gets there he sees me and tells me, "Mr. Thunderburk, you have fifteen minutes to be off my property or I'm calling the cops!"

What the fuck?

I ain't got no phone, no money, and I'm way out in the middle of nowhere. I don't even know what I did, plus it's the end of January in Oklahoma so it's literally freezing outside. The FBTCC is on 4 Mile Road — it's literally a four mile road — and that's just to the bridge crossing over the lake out in the middle of nowhere. It takes twenty minutes just to walk all the way off his property.

It's about 10pm by the time I hit the road. I turn left and start to walk. If I would have stopped I might have frozen to death. I wasn't at all tired and my anger was fueling me. The entire time I was seeing Mark Seabolt on his knees, just how I had old Ray. These motherfuckers ain't shit, just some pathetic ass greedy, two-faced heartless schemers!

I'll admit I'm at times pretty heartless, but never would I exploit and harm people like these so-called pillars of the community do. How people don't see this shit is amazing to me. I think they do see it but it's just easier to act like they don't. Either way, the outcome is still what it is and I wonder how many other people before me have been fucked over this way...

It's funny 'cause, the same as with Ray, Mark Seabolt was finally exposed. First, the church turned its back on him, saying they didn't want any association with him, then someone tried to burn him and his family up. His whole house burned down, his family barely made it out, then he caught all kinds of heat for 'food stamp fraud'. And on his old exotic animal farm he bred goars — well someone poisoned all his goats. I guess all his evil spread out to affect the ones close to him, but keeping it real his kids were just like him so they all got what they deserved. Last I heard his rehab was no more.

Anyways, after literally walking all night I get into the City of Muskogee once again. I see a bunch of people all standing outside this big ass church so I pull up on them and they tell me it's the homeless shelter. It's about to do breakfast. So I wait with them and when it opens I go in to eat some oatmeal and drink some milk with hot coffee.

I walk around the church, looking for anything I could steal to sell for some money 'cause I need to find a ride anywhere I was familiar with. I wind up stealing a microphone.

Down the street is a pawn shop.

I sell the microphone for ten dollars.

I wind up bumming a ride from some skinny ass Mexican fool right away and see he ain't shit. He says we need gas so we pull up to the gas station and I tell him I only have two dollars, so he takes it and leaves the keys in the ignition. He leaves his phone too.

I jump into the driver seat and take off!

The only thing I regret about the whole situation is giving him two dollars. I should've only given him one. I needed every dollar.

I use his phone to GPS my mom's place — it's an hour and a half away. I make it with almost no gas to spare.

My mom is tripping, "You can't be here Kenny."

This bitch literally lives out in the woods on the lake with hardly any neighbors and she's acting like we're in the hood.

I tell her what happened. She's actually sympathetic.

I stay at her place almost two weeks. Amazingly we don't fight or argue a single time. She cooks me breakfast, lunch and dinner every single day. The only neighbor she has moved in a few weeks back — Ashley and Brad, with their kids, Mercedes, Kamber and Jordan. They were Ashley's kids, Brad is their stepdad. My mom introduces us. It turns out that Ashley hates her husband Brad so we start chilling. She's a 25 year old sexy ass little Indian girl, so it's just a matter of days before I start hitting that shit. At first my mom is cool with it, then she flips and tells Brad.

Brad calls the police, but they can't do shit. They say he can file harassment charges if I call his phone again and I guess her phone was in his name. I'm still in that same dilemma with fifteen years hanging over my head if I'm not in a rehab.

I wait until Friday then call my PO. She says, "I want your ass in my office Monday at 10am sharp."

"What am I gonna do, Mom?"

Mom says, "Son you better find something!"

I literally stress over it all weekend, search the entire web for rehab centers that will take me but with my circumstances, ain't shit cracking for me. Aside from the two big cities — Tulsa and OKC — Oklahoma is pretty rural. Even in those two big cities, the resources are pretty limited. Plus it's the weekend. I feel the countdown to my incarceration literally minute by minute.

It's Sunday at 2am and I receive a Facebook message. It's from this chick Crystal Beamer. I don't know her.

The message says:

Osi, yo.

I'm like, *OK.*

Osi yo is Cherokee for "How are you?"

I reply that I'm not too good.

She asks, "Why, what's wrong?"

It's like she knows me, so I say, "It's a long story."

She says, "Call me, we'll talk" and I do, just because I kinda need someone to take my focus off my impending doom.

I call her and tell her the whole story I've just told you. The whole rehab situation.

She says, "Well Kenneth, it's your lucky day. I'm the founder of Soldiers for Christ and it's exactly what you're in need of. I specialize in helping people in your situation. Give me your PO's number and by the time you get to her office tomorrow I will have everything taken care of, I promise you. You're not going back to prison."

I hang up. For reals, I'm not putting much stock by what this lady had to say, but at the same time I'm hoping it's legit. I don't even want to fall asleep and possibly sleep away my last hours of freedom.

At 8am my mom cooks and I can't eat. I shower and dress, call Crystal with no answer, and say to myself, *I knew it. You're on your own, fool.*

While my mom is driving me to my PO's office, I tell her, "I love you, Mom."

She says, "You're gonna be OK, Kenny."

I've heard that my whole life and I've never been okay!

Head down, heart in my stomach, I'm sitting in the PO office lobby.

My PO comes out, "Here, piss in this," so I take the cup and walk to the little restroom. I say to myself, *I may be OK. If they were gonna lock me up they wouldn't need no drug test.*

I test clean.

The supervisor says, "Why do I keep hearing your name, Kenneth?"

I go to respond and she says, "I don't want to hear it. You got fifteen minutes to find a sober living house or I'm locking you up."

She slides me a pamphlet with about fifteen or twenty different places on it and yeah, I done already called every single one of them with the exception of one called 'The Oxford House' in Tulsa. I figured that if I couldn't have gotten into any of the other ones — which were all pretty low budget — what were the odds of my getting into this one that looks super fancy and expensive? This is the type of place only rich white people can get into, with all their high coverage insurance. It's literally the only one I haven't tried you so I dial the number, same as I did the last time from my PO's desk with both her and the supervisor breathing down my neck.

"Oxford House?" a man says when he picks up the phone.

"Yeah, I'm in need of a sober living spot. Is there any way I can get in there?" I ask.

He says, "We're all full up in this house, but give me your name and I'll call you back in a couple days."

I tell him, "I don't have a couple of days homie, I literally got minutes."

He asks me, "What's your name?"

So I tell him.

He says, "Oh shit, I been waiting on you to call, my homegirl Crystal told me all about you. It's why I said we had no more room in my house, 'cause I was waiting on you. Yeah, come on down fool, we got you. I'm Frank Thompson. I'll see you when you get here."

Hence my introduction into God's mysterious ways.

I tell my PO. It's the same as before — I got to be there the same day. She says this is my last chance. My mom takes me to Tulsa and dtops me off at this mansion-looking house.

"Bye son."

I tell her, "I love you, Mom," and she's gone.

In this last remaining part of the book I'm about to write, I experience all types of manifestations from God. My introduction to the spiritual.

February 27th, 2018

I step into the house and see that it's really nice. It's in Broken Arrow/Tulsa, Oklahoma. I see six other men all sitting on a huge ass couch in the front room.

"Hey Kenneth, this is the interview. It takes an 85% house vote to vote you into the house."

They ask me why I'm in need of sober living, what drugs I do, how would I respond to certain circumstances, how will I pay my deposit, if I got a job and all that. After my responses they say, "Can you please step outside so we can take a house vote?"

I step out and I know I'm 100% getting in.

They open the door and tell me, "Come in, Kenneth."

I step inside.

"Welcome to the Oxford House."

I shake everyone's hand and then Frank Thompson shows me to my room. He says he has a job opening for janitor.

I tell him, "I'll take it," and he tells me that he's gonna take me tomorrow and put in a good word for me but the rest is on me.

"OK, thanks homie."

I don't really have shit, just a couple shirts and pairs of pants. I put it all in a drawer and fall asleep.

I'm woken up at 8am by Frank Thompson.

"We need to leave at 9am so be ready."

That's easy since I'm already dressed. I wash up and go sit in the living room. We take off and eventually pull up to a company called Dapro Rubber. I fill out the application and they give me an interview the same day. An hour later I'm being told that I start at $17 and hour tomorrow and to show up at 5am. My trainer will be a guy named Miguel.

The company is only about three miles from the house so I speed walk all the way home. I'm super excited. My main concern was if I would be able to find a job in a reasonable period of time and now that I have and that stress is off me, I feel that ain't shit gonna stop me. I'm in a beautiful house, I have a job, and I'm all good. How can I fail? I can't...

Frank says I can ride with Jim to and from work, we have the same hours.

I love this job. I been working and doing the Oxford House smooth for about three months now and my mom says, "Come see me for Memorial Day weekend, the lake will be packed. I'll give you a ride back," so I say, "OK!"

I get a ride from Frank the two hours to my mom's house.

"Look fool, you need to be home for the house meeting by Tuesday. If you miss it, they will vote you out of the house!"

I say, "Don't worry, my mom is gonna bring me back, I'll be there!"

One thing besides a dirty drug test they won't accept for almost any reason is missing the once a week house meeting.

Here I am and I'm at my mom's. I won't lie, I drank some beer, which is also against the house rules, but they won't ever know I did.

So the whole weekend passes and it's now Monday. I tell my mom I need to be in Tulsa before 6pm on Tuesday and she tells me, "Well Kenny, I don't have no gas and no gas money so how am I gonn do that?"

Just like that, this bitch hits another drastic blow to my spirit. It's almost impossible to find a ride off the island, let alone all the way to Tulsa. I'm hit.

Tuesday, Wednesday, Thursday...

"Come on Kenny, I got gas. Let's go."

I already know I'm gonna get kicked out of the house but I'm just hoping I can convince them to give me a chance...

Naw, I'm kicked out.

I have a little bit of stuff now since I been working and I need to find another house 'cause I want to keep my job, so I hit up this one fool I was in prison with named Eric. I don't even want to mention his name 'cause he don't deserve a line in my million dollar story, but this is pivotal.

He says, "I know a spot for you, I'll come pick you up and help you move to the new spot."

This is my only option, so he picks me up and I put all my stuff in the back of his truck. He's all tweaked out. He wants gas money so I put forty dollars in his truck. He says he needs to do a few errands before he can take me to this place.

He's literally driving all over Tulsa, from Wal-Mart to Wal-Mart trying to return some stolen shit for cash so he can use the money to buy dope...also wasting my forty dollars in gas.

Almost four hours later I say, "Damn fool, you ain't got no more gas, how you expect to get me to this spot?"

He says, "Don't trip, we'll get there."

We drive about 45 minutes and now he's on 'E'. He stops at a QuikTrip gas station and says, "Damn bro, we almost there but I need gas." I'm thinking, *Fuck it, I'm almost there.*

I jump out the truck and my phone is on the charger inside the vehicle, and in the truck he also has a baby pit bull and it looks thirsty so I'm inside and I buy two sodas, two packs of smokes and two waters. The water is for his dog, the soda and smokes are for us. I also put another forty dollars in gas.

I guess he was pumping the gas as I was exiting the store but I go back in to get his dog something to drink out of. When I come back outside I look at the gas pump and it's empty. So I look around the rest of the gas station and the parking lot. I even walk out back. *This motherfucker is gone!*

Oh my God, you don't even know what I felt in that moment. I can try to describe it but the couple times I've told this story to some of my celly's I simply describe it by saying that my heart turned cold. I felt the demon come out. I was literally seeing red.

Literally every single worldly possession I owned just left in that truck. I was so mad I literally couldn't see straight.

It brought me all the way back to my childhood, hearing my mom yell, "You got me so mad I can't see straight!"

Shit, now I see she wasn't playing, but I honestly can't think of anything I even done to her to make her feel this bad. I guess I kinda zoned out 'cause all the noise and reality itself came flooding back to me.

I was still standing at the QuikTrip.

I see this white girl outside smoking. I ask to use her phone. She looks at me all cautious-like. I tell her, "I'm not gonna run with your phone, you can hold my wallet. It has my ID and debit cards in it."

She says she saw the truck I got out of leave a few minutes ago and asks me what happened. I type my info into her phone to log into my Facebook Messenger account so I can try to call this fool but I see he's already blocked me! This girl is asking me how she can help me — if she can give me a ride somewhere. I 100% don't have a single place to go. I've only been in Tulsa a couple of months. I only know the area by my workplace and the old Oxford House. I have no friends in Tulsa either.

Then I remember my homie Tan Tan has a girl in Tulsa so I hit her up on Facebook.

She replies, "What's good?"

I tell her I need a place to post up for a while and she says to come on.

The white girl gives me an old phone to help me out then drops me off at Viola's house, Tan Tan's lady friend. It's super dirty in the front room and she has her fat ass son, about 16 or 17, playing on his XBOX in the back room.

She gots a super fat daughter too, who literally has a mattress in the closet and she's on a laptop. I tell her to friend this fool Eric, so she does.

She says, "He won't accept."

I tell her that if she helps me I will break her off some money. I also put an alert on my FB wall:

"WANTED: REWARD, ANY INFO!"

Then I put his name and picture.

I also ask Viola where I can buy some dope 'cause I wasn't doing no sleeping until I found this fool. All I know is he lives somewhere in Tulsa.

We pull up to this older lady's house named Tori. We talk for a while and I buy a half ounce for $500. She hits me over the head with the price but fuck it.

I have Viola shoot me up.

Now I'm lit.

All focus and energy is directed toward finding this fool. The law of attraction!

"He accepted me!" yells Viola's daughter.

I tell her, "Say exactly what I tell you 'cause I know this fool is gonna be real cautious 'cause he knows I ain't gonna let this shit ride."

I tell her to write dude and say:

"Hey, what's up, me and my homegirl looking to chill."

He says:

"Cool, where you at?"

I then tell him the street she lives on and he says:

"Oh shit, you're close."

Viola's daughter writes:

"Let's meet right now."

But I didn't tell her to text that 'cause I didn't want him to catch on that it was me. Right away he says:

"Hey Thunder!"

I snap on old girl, "I told you, now you fucked it all up!"

I take her laptop and start to type:

"Thunder? Huh? What's that? Look if you ain't
tryna chill I'm cool, I don't know what Thunder is."

And he writes back:

"Let's meet but you come to me."

I text back:

"Dude I got my own spot, plus it's late at night and I'm a girl.
I don't even know you and you just want me to meet you in some
strange place, you know what I'm cool. Bye."

That last message has the exact effect I intended it to have. He says:

"OK. I'm sorry let's meet at the McDonald's on Archer Street."

Viola says, "That's right down the street!"

I'm thinking, *I got this muthafucka* so I say:

"It's gonna take me 10 minutes, I'll be with my homegirl."

He says:

"It will be just me and my baby pit, see you soon."

I say:

"OK, I'm leaving now."

Viola runs and asks her black friend named Nene to give us a ride.

We pull up to the McDonald's and park on the side of the drive-thru. Now I'm in the back seat ducked down.

Viola says, "Here he comes!"

I can't run real fast and I ain't tryna let this fool get away so I literally wait until he is two feet away from the driver side door then I jump out with my knife, "Bitch ass fool, I want my shit!"

He starts to backpedal and his dog is pulling on the leash. He starts to run and I slice the dog's leash and it runs and jumps into the back seat of the car. This fool is behind a car in the drive-thru so I need to make a decision: either risk getting him and maybe get arrested or live to fight another day? But now I got a hostage: his dog.

So I run and jump in the car. We take off and now he's running after the car, "My dog, my dog!"

I laugh, *You want this bitch back? It for sure won't be alive, 100% this dog is dead!*

I notice when I get into Viola's house that I have several new messages, plus Viola's daughter is tripping now too, 'cause Eric is texting her all talking about:

"You set me up!"

I tell her to block him and toss her $500. She complies.

I check my messages:

"Kenny, please don't hurt my dog, I got all your stuff."

then:

"Fuck you and that dog."

I simply reply:

"Don't trip fool, I'm gonna find you."

I know he's close.

A few hours later I get a message:

"What's up with you and Eric?"

I tell dude that unless he gots info on his whereabouts miss me with all that.

He asks me:

"How much you got on it?"

I say:

"I got a quarter ounce."

He says:

"I'll show you. I'm on my way."

I give him my general location and when he pulls up I jump in the car.

He's saying, "I'm not exactly sure..." but before he has a chance to even finish his statement I pull out the dope.

"How sure are you now?"

His eyes light up. Now he's 100% certain.

He stops in front of an old apartment complex and says, "It's the second door."

I tell him to hold up. I know he ain't going anywhere 'cause I still got the dope. I'm super amped knowing I'm just a few more seconds away from having this fool's head. Ain't shit gonna stop me from having it. I run as fast as I can, every step I just get angrier and angrier until my anxiety won't let me come off the blood lust.

It feels weird when you know 100% you're about to kill someone.

Facts...it's like nothing else matters and it shouldn't 'cause you're about to take a life.

But to me, to say it was a premeditated act isn't accurate 'cause all I had in my mind was sitting all day in this fool's truck with that dog, the generosity I extended to Eric, my patience, then for me to get stolen from then stranded, and then mocked. I was finally gonna get to get someone who hurt me and I won't lie, it was gonna be a pleasure.

"Revenge is like the sweetest joy next to gettin' pussy..."

-2Pac, "Hail Mary"

When you experience this all-consuming beast you'll see the ecstasy in it. All I could say was I was gonna like this. Finally!

I kicked the door, *BOOM! BOOM! BOOM!* but with three sound kicks it didn't even budge!

"Ahh! I'm calling the cops!"

Again: *BOOM! BOOM! BOOM!* but still it wouldn't budge. *Fuck.*

I run to the back. On my way around I pick up a cinder block and sprint full speed to the backyard. I see the back window to the second apartment, and I slam the block into the window. I don't throw it, I literally smash it into the window to where it crumbles in my hands. The window shatters and glass explodes into the apartment and I see that he is bleeding so I know a lot of that glass hit him.

But that's not why I slammed the cinder block into the window. I wanted in! Like a rabid dog with its victim in its sights. *This motherfucker is mines.*

After all the glass breaks I get a perfect view of him. He's like a deer in the headlights. I rush to immediately jump through the window like right after the glass. I slam up against something and I think I misjudged my jump, but naw, the window is fucking enforced with security bars. I see him clear as day as I'm' getting up but these fucking bars are in my way. If I would've had superhuman powers those bars would have been nothing. *Lucky ass fool.*

He's on the phone so, *fuck.*

I run back to the car. As I'm getting in I see the neighbor walk out and yell, "I'm calling the cops!"

Now it's fight or flight.

I know where he's at, so I'll keep him in sight. I know he can only leave out that front door because ain't no other way out. So I tell dude, "Let's spin the block."

We spin it a couple more times. No cops. I tell him to pull back up but this time I'm gonna go tell the neighbor to mind her own business and that this fool got to go — he's bad for the atmosphere.

I walk up to her front door, knock, and she don't answer. I go to walk off her porch and a cop in an SUV pulls up right in front of dude's ride and as I walk to the car the cop looks at me and tips his hat.

"Hello sir," I reply. "What's good?"

He keeps walking and enters the gate to Eric's bando apt and I jump in the car and tell dude to hit the block. He's on the phone all sketched out driving. I tell him to pay attention 'cause if you see one cop that means more are on the way. He ignores me and pulls past the corner and stops, literally, in the middle of the street looking down at his phone. I look up to the left and see two or three cop cars all in the street with their sirens on. This fool don't even see it, his head is down looking at that fucking phone. I open the passenger door and crack this fool in the side of the head, pissed 'cause I really wanted to stab his ass but I must have put my knife away. *Lucky ass fool...*

It really was like this fool was trying to set me up. He just stopped in the middle of the street, full on.

I jumped out of the car and hit some backyards. I was gone.

I pull back up to Viola's.

"What you gonna do with this dog?" she asks.

No matter what, this dog ain't gonna survive any of this! I'm still holding it 'cause it still may bring me some leverage.

"I'm gonna keep it," I tell her.

Viola says, "You better not hit it no more."

I laugh and say, "Yes bitch."

She don't even know.

I have her shoot me up with more meth. She's grossed out by the way I do my shots. I onlt really do about one good shot every three or four days. I don't like shooting up 'cause I'm scared to miss the vein, and if you do, it hurts and can cause severe abscesses. It's all bad.

Well I just crush up all the dope and throw it in the back part of the syringe, like, I take the plunger out and throw the crushed up dope into the part where your dope goes. Then I put the plunger back in, stick the needle in my vein and then I register which is allowing the blood to draw into the syringe, then I let the hot blood dissolve all the meth and shoot it into my arm. It takes a little minute just 'cause you got to let the blood melt the dope but after that it's take-off time!

I wanna go back and get this fool.

The dope chills me out, only 'cause it took everything in me to keep in control of myself. That last shot super-charged me. It's been about three days and I haven't ate no food, nor have I drank any liquids. It's all been hate, anger, murder, dope, more anger. It was to the point that I was kinda glad I lost my mind from that last shot 'cause now it's nighttime again.

I don't know where the missing hours went, but now my phone is ringing.

"Hello?"

Right away I hear it, it sounds like, "It's me, Tori," the lady I paid $500 for that dope. And she's crying hysterically. *What the fuck?*

"Black guys," she says. "They raped me, please help me!" Then more hysterical crying.

So I tell Viola, "Let's go see what's up with Tori."

We leave and I take the dog. He's still on his half-leash.

We pull up to Tori's place. She's still crying, she ushers us inside. She also has a pit bull, he's real old. His back legs don't work no more.

Tori says, "You can let that little dog go, mine won't bother it." So I do.

She says that someone drugged her and afterward a bunch of black guys raped her. She asks me what she should do. For real I don't even know this bitch, I really don't give no fucks, but it's way better being in her house than in Viola's dirty ass trap. So I'm tryna act like I give a fuck.

She says, "I'll wait 'til the morning then go get a rape kit then."

OK, that's on her.

So we chill and they smoke some dope.

It's not about 6am and it starts to thunder real loud. Eric's little dog starts to get nervous and then again the thunder gets even louder. The little pit turns and attacks the old pit bull. Tori jumps in to stop the little one 'cause it's fucking the older one up and it bites her.

She pulls back and shouts, "My thumb!"

I look and her thumb is just hanging there. *What the fuck?*

I also try to break it up but I get bitten too, right in my right hand, dead center.

"Bitch ass dog!"

I grab a metal candle holder and split the little dog's head open. It's still alive but it let go and it's also pretty fucked up. Tori is screaming. She's trying to open a pill bottle but she can't grip the lid to turn it 'cause she's minus one thumb. She somehow manages to get the top off and spills all the pills. She tosses a handful of pills back so I pick some up off the floor and eat a mouthful. It turns out these are Percocet 10s!

I run into the bathroom to find an Ace bandage, run out, and, as gently as I can, I wrap her hand using my plastic hair tie to keep it snug, but not too tight.

She turns and says, "I need to take a shit before I shit myself."

She's easily in her mid-50's so I guess she's lost some control, so I help her to the bathroom. She takes a shit, but says she can't wipe her ass.

I say, "Fuck it, then just pull up your shit."

She's having trouble pulling up her pants so I help her. She says she needs to get to the hospital. *Shit.*

I don't know the way, so Viola drives. I sit in the passenger seat and Tori lays down with her hand held in the air. We leave a while later and then we pull into the hospital's emergency lane. The entire ride, Tori is in the back sobbing. Viola stops the car.

I tell Tori, "We are here."

Viola runs up to the back door with a wheelchair. Tori gets out and into the wheelchair and then through the sliding doors they go. I'm still sitting in the car, so I jump into the driver seat and take off. I don't even know where I'm going. I guess the Percs, dope, lack of sleep and water is starting to get to me.

The next thing I know, I'm parked in the lot at the Days Inn, in the valet parking area. I jump out of the car and walk past the motel lady like I'm some rich fool in a resort and my room is all ready.

The motel lady sees me, "Hey, you! Where you going?"

I stop and say, "I got a room."

Why I thought that, I don't know but I was certain I had a room there. She tells me to leave, so I go outside and jump back in the car, put the key in and the car won't start. How the valet was supposed to move it, I don't know, 'cause I still had the keys.

Anyway, it won't start. It's 100% dead.

I jump out thinking, *it's the battery.* It's an older Cadillac and I know the battery is under the back seat, so I tear out the back seat. I put the seat outside the car on the floor. The battery looks okay. I ask a couple people if they got any jumper cables. No one says shit. I dread to think what I look like, hand all swollen and bleeding, looking like I been through some shit. Plus, I'm super tatted up...I got the back seat literally thrown on the ground.

Someone says, "Maybe it's out of gas."

So I look for a gas station.

I notice one all the way across the highway, so I start looking for a gas can. I tear the inside of the car up some more. I must have been in a rage, just tearing shit up in a pill fog. I take an empty two liter thinking, *fuck it, I'll just put the gas in there.*

With a bitten-up hand I somehow manage to jump two fences across eight lanes of highway to the gas station. I pay $15 and go to the gas pump. The nozzle won't fit in the two liter, so I cut the top off and pump the gas, spilling more than I got in the bottle all over my shoes, my pants and my hands. It's also super hot and humid out.

I fill the two liter up, and when I put the pump back and shoot across the highway, somehow I manage to jump the two fences again and still make it to the car with a little less than half the two liter full of gas.

I jump in the car and turn the key.

Nothing.

I feel my body literally shutting down, like that was my last chance. I am totally defeated.

Somehow I manage to get out of the car and stumble into the motel lobby. The clerk yells at me to get out. I turn and all of a sudden I spew vomit all over the lobby, and I keep spewing all over again, and again. The next thing I know, I'm in an ambulance and the paramedics are telling me I need to go to the hospital. I go, leaving the car to just be towed with my phone in it. I had heat stroke, it turns out.

They pump me full of fluids and the next day I get discharged.

Standing out in front of the hospital, I don't even remember why I was there.

I hitch a ride to Viola's.

I knock on the door and hear, "Go away, Thunder, the cops are look for you for rape and for stealing Tori's car! I'm calling the police!"

What the fuck?

I run around the other side of the apartment unit. I see that girl Nene and I go inside her small ass apartment. I take a pillow and go lay in her closet and crash out.

Three days later I wake up.

I don't even remember where I am. I see my hand is also bandaged, then it all starts to come back to me. I don't have any idea how I am gonna bounce back from this...

Nothing ever amounts to all the bullshit Viola said.

Somehow I find myself back in another Oxford House.

My PO is happy with my conduct.

I'm doing the whole sober shit: work, meetings, then one day I go out with my homegirl and we go to a strip club. We have some drinks and she's bisexual so we leave the club with some bad little skinny girl named Ariel.

We get a room, fuck around all night, and in the morning my homegirl needs to leave so she does, leaving just me and Ariel. When she gets she pulls out some meth and asks if I want some.

I'm like, *Naw fool, fuck that,* but that was all in my head. I hear myself say, "Shoot it," once again. This ain't gonna end well.

The next day I get a surprise drug test at my Oxford House. I'm dirty. *Just my luck, right?* So I'm kicked out.

I start to stay at a Studio Six with Ariel and I'm selling dope now. I'm doing pretty good too, then one day someone spikes my drink with some Xanax. The end result is I'm woken up by some cops, cuffed and ushered out of the apartment complex. Then they uncuff me and tell me to stay out of those apartments. The first thing I notice is that my wallet is gone, then my phone, but I got a big bag in my right pocket! I pull it out and it's about 4 ounces of meth. I'm literally on the sidewalk, the cops just left. I walk across the street to a Fast-Trip.

I'm out front just standing there when a car pulls up.

"Aye, you Thunder?"

It's some crazy-looking Indian all blasted up with tattoos on his face.

I say, "Why?"

He tells me, "Jump in."

I'm looking all sketeched-out and I'm about to say 'I'm good' when he says, "Don't be a bitch fool just get in!"

I ain't got too many options so I get in.

He has a chick in the front driver seat.

"So you're Thunder, huh?"

I tell her, "Yeah, who are y'all two?"

The dude says, "I'm Shendoa. IBH. I been hearing a lot about you. I hear you hustle hard. I need someone like you."

IBH is the Indian Brotherhood. It's an Oklahoma Indian prison gang. I've also heard about this fool Shendoa — he's a real nutcase.

He says, "It looks like you been through some shit."

I haven't even had time to register all that just happened to me.

I tell him, "Something happened..."

He says, "I fuck around in those apartments and I heard they hit you with some Xanax then robbed you."

I guess that clears it up for me.

"So what's up homie, can I use your phone?"

He shoots me a phone, "You can have this one. And here is some cash. We 'bout to pull up to my spot. You can shower and get some clothes, sleep and eat. All that. When you ready let me know and I'll tell you what's up."

We pull up to his spot and I take full advantage of all his generosity. I even fall asleep.

When I wake up, he tells me, "Okay look, I'm gonna sell these fools some dope and right after they leave you gonna run up on them and rob them."

I'm thinking, *Naw, fuck that!* I ain't scared, but that ain't my type of hustle. Plus, if I hit a lick I keep it all, I ain't gonna nust no lick and give up a piece of it.

So I say, "Here fool." I shoot him back the phone and money then I tell him, I appreciate you fool, but I'm good. That ain't me!"

He gives me back the money and phone and says, "Okay, I respect that. I got another lick for you."

He takes me to a trap and gives me a pound and says, "I want three thousand, the rest is yours."

At $400 an ounce I could easily make over $6,400, not to mention what I'd get if I nickle and dime it. So I sit in his trap and collect all this free money. He always gets everything he asks for — no excuses — plus they are all his people. He just needed someone he could trust.

Shendoa's trap that he serves at is a couple blocks over.

One day it is early morning and I notice the ghetto bird is hovering outside, all kinds of cops is shooting by so I get kinda flipped out thinking, *they coming for me!* but real quick I see that ain't the case.

They rushing a couple streets over so I walk to see the source. It turns out they went to serve a warrant to Shendoa. I guess they thought he pulled a gun and the police shot him dead! A lot of controversy follows all this 'cause no gun was found, and he had a tattoo on his right hand: the thumb and pointer finger was a gun...

I go back to the trap and pack my shit and get into another Oxford House!

About a month after struggling in the Oxford House I just get tired of it all. I want to just do me so I leave again.

I get a cool lick selling a pound of meth to these John Brown University students in Siloam Springs, Arkansas. I sell them the pound for $20 thousand and they sell it, grams at a time, to all the different fraternities at like 400 bucks a gram, so each pound is literally making them over $60 thousand.

They are buying two pounds a week! They don't use it either — all money in.

At the same time, I am doing a lot of moves for the UABs that are in the pen.

One day I have to go to Home Depot to get a trailer loaded with $200,000 worth of lumber so I pull up, get the receipt, hitch the trailer to my borrowed truck and pull off. Now I got to find a buyer for all this wood. It don't take very long.

I pull into a fresh construction site and talk to the foreman. He shoots me a check for $100,000. He keeps the wood plus I give him the trailer.

I call up the fools who set all this up and they tell me how to distribute the money so I do it. They also tell me to keep $40 thousand to use out here.

So one day I'm chilling with these four girls and they all bragging how ain't none of them every been in trouble. I see a commercial on TV about how the Oklahoma Department of Corrections needs workers. I see a cool plan.

So I ask these ladies, "Ain't none of you got no jobs, if I pay for your apartment and buy y'all a car, would you relocate and apply for jobs at this prison??"

I can't say the prison 'cause I don't want to incriminate myself, but three of them say yes!

I find a three bedroom apartment in the town of the prison, pay the deposit, buy all three girls a car, and off they go, all three to apply to work at the prison. Only two get an interview. Next thing we know, they're training. They're in.

I call the UAB big homie and ask him how they got in this prison. All these fools got cell phones in the pen inside their cells so it don't take long 'til he can tell me. I tell my two ladies all they have to do is take cell phones and tobacco inside. I even make the packages and put them inside the females' coochies every day myself. Cell phone and tobacco make the most money in prison, plus if they happen to get caught smuggling it in, it ain't a felony, they just get fired.

I say, "Every time you take a pack in I will give you $1,500 cash the same day, plus you get to keep the car and I keep paying your rent. All of your paycheck is yours too." They can't lose. I say to them, "No matter what, you don't fuck with none of any of those fools in there for any reason. You will know when to drop the pack." I also tell them to keep the pack in their coochie until the last second.

They do a cell search, close the door and put the window block up, then take the pack out in the cell and stash it in the assigned person's locker. If they don't work that unit, they keep the package in all day and when they get home, I watch them take it out — all this is a security measure. As soon as the pack is dropped off, they get a confirmation on it. If no confirmation comes, she has to have the pack inside her when she gets home — no exceptions.

If they were to divert from any of these measures, I would have not given them any more packs or money — the whole jig would be up. They were making a lot of easy money so they were more than willing to comply.

Man, for about three months everything is cool. I done drilled it into their heads that they were never to fuck with no one else — especially an inmate.

One day I jump into one of these girls' car — let's call her "girl *** 2" — and I notice some electrical tape all shriveled up and tossed in the cup holder. I automatically think, *Why she got balled-up tape, did she open one of the packs I sent in?* I'd wrap the packs in plastic then in black electrical tape.

I ask her about it and she says it was her homegirl's and changes the subject. I let it slide but I keep thinking on it. I decide to cut her off — no more packs for her. I am getting around to telling her she gots to go when girl *** 1 calls me pissed as hell. She tells me that girl

*** 2 got caught bringing in dope and she told on her, girl *** 1. They didn't have shit on the first girl but they still put her on suspension for an investigation to be made. It was over that quick. I didn't know the feds were involved and my name was already in it. Well, actually my Facebook name, "Thunder". None of these females knew my government.

So now my main play is in Siloam Springs serving those University girls a pound for two racks, plus I'm still curb serving in Tulsa with nickels and dimes. My casino addiction fucks me all the way up. I was banned until 2032 from any Cherokee Nation gaming commissions 'cause in early 2015 I ran into a white boy named Kristen Rozell. Before I went to prison in Oklahoma I was looking for him — he not only stole from me, he also fucked Misty while I was busted so I was salty.

Well, one day I see him in the Cherokee Casino so I walk up to him and say, "So you didn't never think I would catch up to you huh?" He doesn't say shit. I hit his cashout ticket and take it — a quick $1,200. He just turns and walks out the casino. I follow him out. He jumps in his car and leaves, so I cash out his ticket and take the money then I leave.

A couple weeks later I'm back in the casino playing when security asks me to come to the back with them. I have no choice, so I do. Once we get to the back they ask me if I robbed someone in the casino.

I tell them, "Hell naw!" and they say, "We got a call saying that you did. We checked the camera footage and saw you hit a gentleman's cash-out button and take his ticket."

I say, "He owed me money so he said I could have it," but it don't matter.

"Sir, it's against casino rules to hit a button on another player's machine."

The end result is I'm banned until 2032. Good thing no criminal charges were filed.

So now here it is in 2018, I been in this Hard Rock Casino literally every day for six months, not in the main casino but the smoke shop which sells all the tobacco and has slots in it. I stayed in there 'cause they didn't fuck with me. I know I'm banned so I don't want to be in the main casino 'cause the security in there is nosey and they like to pull up on people who look like me...people who look like drug dealers. Meaning people who in the casino at all hours spending thousands of dollars, and they know it.

So, my casino addiction is growing with the more money I get. I don't have a house aside from the traps I pull up on and sell dope out of but I have nowhere I can sleep safely so I just don't sleep.

All the UAB's people they fucked with before me were all bitter 'cause the main UAB fools stopped fucking with them, since now they had me. Well one day I take this Indian girl named Rhonda with me to my older homie's spot in Oaks, Oklahoma. She's coming down off meth and heroin. She leaves her sister who was locked up's kid with some tweakers back in Tulsa. Well, we get to the spot and she says she don't want to go back to Tulsa and she crawls in the homie's bed and falls asleep. It's a come down sleep so she pretty much crashed and burned out.

The next day I need to leave and she won't wake up, so I leave her. Back in Tulsa, Rhonda's sister gets out of jail and that day she finds out her baby was in the hands of some tweakers. She is pissed.

I pull up to that same house to let Rhonda's people know she is safe and where she is. Like I said, all these fools are already pissed at me for, as they see it, stepping on their toes, so they're just looking for any reason to blow on me.

Right away: "What you do to my homegirl, she ain't picking up her phone!" and "You sick fuck, if we find out you hurt her..." all types of shit.

"I left her at the homie's place, she crashed and burned plus she didn't want to come back!"

This white girl named Trisha says, "You hurt her," so I just go to my car and leave.

I do all my business in Tulsa and now I'm coming down off the dope and I'm on the interstate driving back to Oaks to go pick Rhonda up. It's three in the morning and I'm using my phone's GPS to navigate my trip.

I fall asleep.

I'm jarred awake by the whole car shaking. *What the fuck?*

It's the warning track on the highway that is meant for exactly this purpose — when drivers fall asleep it is meant to wake them up. Damn good thing it woke me because I was out.

I look at the GPS and it says 4.9 miles to my destination. I'm doing like 80, so next thing I know I'm jarred awake again. The car is just about to go air-born. It's all in slow motion but the car is about to flip in the air. I close my eyes and cross my arms over my chest. *BAM!*

The car lands on the passenger side wheels, flips again, and again and again — this last time it flips but stands on the passenger side wheels then falls back on all fours. I see fire in the hood. I literally pretty much live in my car so all my worldly shit is in there.

I grab baggies and my phone and take off on the interstate. *I can't get caught.*

I ain't got no license and the car was stolen, plus I got all this hot ass shit on me. I just want to make it to the homie's. It's also a week before Thanksgiving so it's freezing cold.

I eventually make it to the homie's. He lives in a super small town in rural Oklahoma.

Once I walk in Rhonda sees me and says, "Why did you leave me?"

I tell her, "I didn't, bitch. I'm here now, right? What, I'm supposed to watch you sleep?"

She tells me, "I need to get back."

I tell her that her sister got out and got her kid and that she's pissed.

"You need to call all your people 'cause they thinking I killed you or some shit. By the way I crashed on my way here, too. So I ain't got no wheels."

I fall asleep for a little while, but something wakes me up...

"Let me get some money so I can walk down to the little store at the gas station and buy some food."

I look at me phone and it's 12 noon. I give her $20 and fall back asleep. Out in this area I don't get no data so no Facebook or Messenger. Hell, barely any phone coverage at all. I'm using an Obama phone.

When I wake up again it's 4pm. She ain't in the house. I do some dope and decide to walk down to the little store to see if Rhonda is there. She ain't.

So I ask the cashier about her and she tells me, "My grandparents gave her a ride to Tulsa."

I say, "Okay."

Then the cashier tells me, "At first she was all cool then all of a sudden she says she'd been kidnapped and left in an abandoned house and she needed to get to her baby!"

I'm like, *What the fuck?* So I tell the cashier, "That bitch was tweaked the fuck out, she's trippin'."

She says, "Yeah, it kinda looked like it. But she said she had a baby so I had to help her."

I tell her, "It was her sister's kid, she left it at some tweak house."

I walk back to my friend's house. I need a ride back to Tulsa. It takes all day but I convince some fool I'll give him $100 once he gets me to Tulsa so he agrees.

Once I get to Tulsa, I jump out of his car and leave him just sitting there in a Wal-Mart parking lot. I take off to a client's house down the street. In my head I'm laughing at that fool. Keeping it real, if he wouldn't have been so greedy I would've paid him at least $50 for the 45 minute ride, but he wanted to capitalize on my predicament so I taught him a lesson.

Once I'm at the client's house I have data again. My phone is blowing up with all the Messenger alerts I got while out of service:

"Fucking rapist!"

"We gonna kill you!"

"You sick ass muthafucker!"

"I told you if you hurt our homegirl you are dead!"

Holy shit, what the fuck is going on?

I hit up Trisha. She says Rhonda told them I took her to the sticks and raped her and left her in a bando. *Naw, hell naw.* But it seems they all believed that stupid ass bitch. They ain't even open to any type of reason. Like I said, they were already salty over the whole UAB business, they were just looking for a reason to salt me up to them fools to kill my business with them in the hopes of getting it back for themselves. Keep in mind, every one of these fools is tweaked out to the max! All bad.

I say, *Fuck it,* but now I really need to be careful who I sell to, or where to go, 'cause I got fools looking to kill me now over all this shit and the streets of Tulsa, Oklahoma are awfully small.

I move cautiously for about five days with a couple close calls, but it seems most of these fools wasn't 'bout shit. This dope sack supercedes any other feelings they may be feeling in the end.

On Thanksgiving Eve I get a message from Trisha. She says,

"Look fool, fuck Rhonda. We need some dope. We got two racks. What's up?"

I'm feeling like, *I know I never touched that weird ass bitch so I ain't got nothing to really trip on...*so I tell her:

"I'll pull up soon."

She says:

"OK."

I ask a white boy client of mine to give me a ride and tell my Native homie Savage to roll with me.

We pull up to the spot. It's a back shed, behind the main house in Oakhurst on the west side of Tulsa so it's kinda rural. We stop.

I know in that back shed they got a camera monitor that shows the front area of this six foot high fence where I'm parked so I sit in the car a minute waiting to see if they all run out. I got my gun — it's on my right hip in the holster.

No one comes out, so I tell the fools with me, "I'll be back, keep the car running just in case. Savage, if I need you, be ready," to which Savage says, "I got you big dog!"

I jump out the ride, walk into the backyard and up the three steps to knock on the door.

I knock and no one answers.

I go to knock again and just then the door swings open violently.

A machete is swinging in a downward motion toward my head. I raise my right hand to block it and the machete cuts right through the thumb and down the middle of my hand.

I throw an elbow and hit the dude in the face.

He falls and I get hit in the back of the head and neck with a sledgehammer. I fall down and I'm bracing my right hand on my chest so I only have my left hand to stop my fall. I hit the ground and roll over.

Whack!

They hit my right shin with that sledgehammer, then my left ankle. I sit up and I'm just trying to find some type of bearing. I know I'm in shock 'cause I don't feel no pain, just a desperation to find a way out. I get on one knee.

I see dude swing the machete again and I raise my right arm to cover my face and feel the machete hit my back arm, slicing it open.

I look up and see about eight people. The only two I recognize are Trisha and Rhonda. I'm on one knee looking up at these fools. I see Trisha hand Rhonda the sledgehammer.

"Get his ass, girl. He hurt you"

Rhonda looks almost as scared as I am.

She says, "No, no, leave him alone!"

Just then the fool with the machete stabs me right in the center of my chest. I hear an internal *pop!* and feel a shortness of breath.

"Hit him bitch!" says Trisha.

Rhonda drops the sledgehammer and runs towards the shack. I see her actions have instantly revealed the truth to all these fools about to kill me, and that was that. Rhonda was full of shit. But still I'm here on my knees with my hand cut off, my legs smashed in, with two stab wounds plus I can't breathe too well.

I get a sudden burst of energy and I jump up and run. I'm literally feeling these fools right behind me about to hit me with the finishing blow so I turn to look behind me. I wind up falling down. The whole time I'm protecting my hand. I won't lie, as soon as I see how bad my hand is I think, *Ain't no way they can fix this.* It's literally cut in half!

I'm face down. As I'm getting up I'm tensing up and just waiting for the machete to slice me across my back. Finally I'm up and I somehow manage to jump that six foot fence.

I look back and see all them people just standing there, looking at me.

My gun is on my right hip so I use my left hand to reach across my body and grab the gun. I unload all ten rounds. I don't know if I hit anyone. I also realize I need medical attention, I have a gun and dope on me too, so I look at the ride with Savage and that white boy in it. It's backing up so I go towards the car and it speeds up and leaves me.

What the fuck?

I start to walk to the next-door neighbor's house but first I see a plant in a pot. I take the plant out and put the gun and the dope in the pot and put the plant back on top of it. I bleed all over my left hand purposefully to hide any gunshot residue.

I stumble to the neighbor's house. I see it's a door with square windows. It has blinds on it but I can see people are in the house. I bang on the door then sit on the porch swing and pass out.

The next time I wake up, I'm in the emergency room.

"Sir, we need you to stay awake. What's your name? Stay with us, sir."

I just want to sleep, I'm so comfortable, I'm starting to get pissed. They keep waking me up!

"Sir, you're gonna feel a little warmth in your feet. It's okay but you need to stay awake, we're gonna put you in here for a couple of minutes," 'here' being a big circular machine. I find out later that the warmth in my feet was a dye they put in my veins, the circular machine was an MRI. I guess they were checking for internal bleeding.

The end result is that I got a blood transfusion, I had a punctured lung, a broken right shin bone, a reattached severed thumb and several staples to the back of my right arm. My chest wound took four staples. The police come in to interview me.

I say, "I was jumping a fence."

I guess they aren't gonna waste no more time on me, so they leave.

The next day is Thanksgiving Day and they discharge me.

I won't like, the first thing on my mind is, *I want to show these fools I'm still ticking.* The second is revenge. The third is I want to get my gun and dope out of that pot.

I send a Facebook post to all them fools showing my hand. It says:

"Happy Thanksgiving!"

I was using my reattached hand to flip them off.

I get a message from Trisha:

"Holy shit, I didn't know we cut you, it was dark and we couldn't see shit."

Damn, what do you think a machete does?

My homegirl picks me up and we shoot to that neighbor's house to get my gun and dope. I see the shack and it looks empty. *I guess they all cleared out.*

I get my stuff and my homegirl takes me out to the country to lick my wounds. I actually have a nice Thanksgiving dinner too. Her older friends cooked it for us. *How nice.*

I only stay a couple days 'cause I want to get back to Tulsa to see what the word is.

It's like nothing even happened.

About a week later or so, about December 10th — it's been about two weeks since the incident — I'm jumping out my car about to go into a liquor store and some pretty little white girl runs up to my car and says, "Can you give me a ride?"

She looks to be in a panic so I say, "Yeah, get in. I'ma go buy some smokes," and she jumps in.

I'm on my way out the store about to jump in my car with the driver side door open and a car pulls up and some black fools jump out.

"Aye man, why you got my bitch in your car?"

I got to say something but I see the fool about to go into his car like he's gonna get a gun so I pull mines out and shoot his car up, jump in my car and take off. I literally just go tight around the corner and pull into a garage, jump out, close the garage door and tell old girl, "Come on."

She's just looking at me like, *What the fuck did I just get myself into?*

I go into the house. It's a two story house and I know it's a tweaker spot 'cause I've sold dope here before.

I see a couple black fools. They say, "What's good?"

I take a sack of dope out and toss it on the counter, that's all they need to hear.

I walk up the stairs, the cute white girl just follows me.

Once we get upstairs I see another white girl I know — she's a hooker.

She sees me and says, "I thought you was dead."

I say, "Naw, not yet."

I'm only wearing a tank top and she sees my chest ans says, "Baby you need to take those out, your skin is starting to grow over them."

She's talking about the four staples in my chest, so I show her the ones on the back of my arm and she says, "Those too."

I ask her if she can do it.

She says, "Let me go get the tweezers."

She comes back out with the tweezers and goes to work. But she's trying to finesse them out. It takes forever just to get one out, plus it's bleeding. As she leaves to get some towels, I say, *Fuck this,* and I pick up the tweezers. I put the flat part under the staples and yank those shits right out of my chest then I do the back of my arm.

When she comes out she's all like, "What the fuck?"

I say, "Shit, I just had to get it done."

Cute little white girl is just staring at me like I'm a mad man.

I leave, drop cutie off, then I go to the casino.

I meet these two white people — a couple — and I give them a ride to their motel room. I wind up falling asleep.

I wake up on December 12th.

I run them all over town, helping them do all their errands. It's the least I can do after they let me sleep in safety.

Now it's 3am on December 13th. I leave and go to Riverside Casino. I put $100 in a slot machine. I start to play — oh, while I was with the couple in their room I did two 25mg Roxy pills — so now I'm here in the casino nodding off at the machine. I'm really not even paying attention to my machine but I guess I was hitting on it 'cause it says I'm up $12,000.

A cute little black girl sits down next to me and says, "Honey, they gonna kick you out if they see you sleeping."

I look at her and say, "If you keep me up I'll take care of you."

So she stays, plus she's also playing my machine.

I'm there all day.

It's about 4pm, I got $15,000 racked up on my machine. I cash out and tell black girl, "Roll with me."

I give her $500 cash and buy her a motel room for two weeks.

I chill with her for a few hours.

I go buy some more dope with the money I won and decide to go to the Hard Rock Casino — it's a Cherokee Nation establishment. I got a lot of cash on me so I go into the main casino. I usually sell dope at the casino too, so all the tweakers know if they see me I got it on me.

I sit and start to play. *Shit.*

I been in about an hour losing, already lost two racks. I see one of the cocktail waitresses — I know her, she's super sexy too — wearing those short casino uniform skirts.

She sees me, "Hey Thunder!"

I say, "Oh shit, what's up Maya?"

She says, "You want a beer?"

I tell her, "No, I want you!"

She laughs.

I say, "Sit on my lap real quick, just for luck!"

So she does. I got my arm around her waist and she's asking me if I want to chill with her when she gets off in a couple hours. It's now about 1am, December 14th.

I say, "Sure, I'll be here."

She says, "I better go, look at all the security. They all be on my line but I won't give them no play so I know they gonna hate on you, be careful."

I look and sure enough they all grouped up and lookin' at me like they got the sun all in their faces. Once she leaves, I see them tell her something. She just keeps walking, ignoring them. But now I see them on their way over to me.

"Sir, do you have an ID on you?"

It's an easy way to ask you to leave the casino 'cause by law you need an ID to be inside. I acutally have my ID but I tell them "No," 'cause I don't want them to run it and see I'm banned.

So they say, "Well sir, we gonna need you to leave," so I cash out, leave the main casino, but they follow me all the way out, even to my car. I jump in and just then some white girl I been trying to fuck with sees me and says, "You doing any good?" which means, "Do you got any dope?"

I say, "Hell yeah."

She says she wants an ounce and I say, "I want $500."

She says, "Okay, let me go cash my ticket in the smoke shop and I got you," so I pull out the parking lot of the casino and into the lot of the moke shop. It's still on the Hard Rock property and I see the security is still watching me. Now I'm sitting out front waiting on this white chick. It's been about ten minutes so I already know she stuck inside playing a machine so I get out my car and go inside.

I see her. Just as I said, she's in there playing so I put a hundred in a slot just so I can play until she's ready.

Next thing I know I hear, "Mr. Thunderburk." I look up and it's five Catoosa police officers and I'm at gunpoint. The first thing I think is, *I'm hit. Plus I got a pocket full of dope.*

The fucking facial recognition got my ass.

I'm handcuffed and taken out the smoke shop, they say I'm under arrest for trespassing. They search me and find all the meth and money on me — 48 grams and $13,000 cash.

I'm taken to Rogers county jail, booked on trafficking charges and a trespassing charge. All my money is seized as dope money.

I sleep my first few days, then reality hits me — I still got that 15 year suspended and now a worse case over my head (it's also aggravated, making it a 100% charge in the worst county possible in Oklahoma.

My life is now over.

LIFE!

Ain't no way out. I still have the stitches in my right hand too.

December 14th, 2018

My life is officially over.

I am dead inside. I stop caring. I literally hate the world.

I fight every day in the county jail, not just with people but internally — I killed myself in my head all day every day. No money on my books, no one to call, no visits, starving, angry and lonely — not to mention defeated. I couldn't come to grips with never getting out of prison again.

My first court date, the DA said, "Our first and only offer is 28 years day-for-day. If you don't want it, well, go to trial and we'll just give you life."

I got back to the pod, I was defeated. I just couldn't shake all the fucked up thoughts in my head. No one in the pod even liked me either 'cause I was so negative. No one would help me with a phone call, not that I even had anyone to call though. I was the most fucked up I'd even been.

February 12th, 2019, 2am

I been in jail almost two months. I am up talking to my neighbor in the dorm when this 70 year old man that runs the prayer circle gets out of bed and walks up to me and says, "Don't you ever shut up?" then storms off. If he wouldn't have been so old I would have beat the shit out of him. I just thought, *Fuck that fool.*

The next day I'm playing chess and that same old man walks up to me and says, "I apologize to you. When you find the time, will you stop by my bed area. I got some things God wants me to tell you — he's been talking to me about you."

I laugh and go, "Oh yeah? What's he saying?"

He says, "Stop by and I'll tell you." Then he walks off.

I'm left thinking, *I wonder what he gots to say?* I'm super anxious by nature so I kinda want to know what he gots to say. I lose my chess game and tell homie, "I'm good."

I speed up to old dude's bed area about to pull up on him but as I get to his bed area, I keep walking. I feel a weird feeling. I don't know what it is, but I actually take a couple laps before I find myself stopping at his bed.

To be honest, I wasn't putting too much stock into what this old man was gonna tell me, but I thought, *What the hell?*

I say, "What's up."

He says, "Have a seat. Do you mind if I pray with you first?"

I say, "Okay." So he prays.

He says, "Lord, bless me with the right words to say to Kenny, to relay the message you want me to get across to him, in your name, Amen."

Then he says he has a couple verses God asked him to share with me:

"The Lord knows your every fiber, He knows all you are feeling, He knows your heart. He has gifts he wants to give you, but first you need to repent and ask forgiveness."

So I say, "What, you want me to ask God to forgive me right now in front of you?"

He says, "No, I can help you pray but this you need to do on your own. God just wants me to tell you that."

Then he shares with me the story in Chronicles about when Hezekiah became king — the first thing he did was rebuild the church, enforce the doors, and let the Levites in. He asked me what I thought that meant.

I knew exactly what it meant. I don't know how, but I did.

I said, "I take it to mean I'm the church and once I'm forgiven, I've rebuilt the church — my heart is the doors. I enforce what comes in. And the Levites are God's words."

He smiles and says, "Amen, that's what God asked me to share with you, Kenny."

I went and sat on my bed.

Later that night, I prayed this exact prayer:

I said, "Look fool, I don't know how any of this works but I ask you to forgive me all I've done wrong. I don't ask you to help me with my case or to free me. All I ask is that you take away these feelings I have. Amen."

The next day I hear the prayer circle call and I say, *What the hell,* I attend. I keep attending every day.

I don't even realize it but it's been weeks. I got a little money on my books, I'm not so hungry no more, I'm not so angry, I don't feel so fucked up no more.

This old man says, "God's gonna show you a miracle, he told me he was, you'll see..."

I'm in the gang pod, it's full of UABs — the exact people whose homies cut my hand off.

One day, a UAB fool says, "Surround that fool Thunder, he hurt Rhonda on the streets. It's why they cut him," so they all surround me.

I say, "Naw, I never touched her homie."

He says, "Well we gonna give her a call and if she says you did, you're dying today."

All these fools got knives, ain't no way out, so I sit on my bed and I'm so scared but I turn and get on my knees and recite my favorite Psalm, the third:

O Lord
I have so many enemies
So many are against me
So many are saying,
'God will never rescue him!'
But you O Lord are a shield around me
You are my glory
The one who holds my head high
I cried out to the Lord
And he answered me from his holy mountain
I lay down and slept
Yet I woke up in safety
For the Lord was watching over me
I am not afraid of ten thousand enemies
Who surround me on every side
Arise O Lord
Rescue me my God!
Slap my enemies in the face
Shatter the teeth of the wicked
Victory comes from you, O Lord
May you bless your peoples
Amen

This passage couldn't be more literal as I was actually, <u>physically</u> surrounded by enemies.

I get back up and see dude talking on the phone. He hangs up and says, "Thunder, come out to the rec yard with me," so I get up and go outside. He starts to say something but I say, "Look fool, if you're gonna do it just do it. I can't take it any more..."

He shakes his head and says, "She said you didn't do it. She lied."

As soon as he says this, I see the demon leave him and he stands up straight and shakes my hand.

I'm thinking, *Only God could have put it in her heart, 'cause no matter what, she would have never had no consequences if she lied.*

My first miracle. I should have been dead that day. But God saved me from my enemies.

The old man tells me, "God has a miracle he's gonna show you," and I tell him, "He already did."

He says, "Naw, be ready to go home," and I'm thinking, *Yeah right, me go home, ain't no way!*

March 6th, 2019

I am served a federal indictment for 'intent to distribute' 'cause getting caught with dope on casino property is a federal crime.

The same day at 10am the Marshalls come to take me but first they make the state DA dismiss all my cases.

They do.

11am: Tulsa Federal Detention Center

12pm: I go to see my lawyer. He tells me, "Today is your detention hearing, we gonna try to get you out on a PR bond.

1pm: I see a Federal probation officer. He asks me all kinds of questions, "Do you got a place to live?" "Do you have a job?" I tell him, "No," "No," and he leaves.

3pm: I go to court.

The judge tells me, "Mr. Thunderburk, it seems you're running out of chances. I suggest you utilize this opportunity to straighten out your life."

I'm thinking, *What?* and my lawyer tells me, "You'll be released after court."

Wait, what the fuck just happened?

I'm taken back downstairs. I sign some papers and the next thing I know, I'm outside on the street as a free man to fight my case. This all literally happened in just a few hours. I also have the federal government paying for my Oxford House while I am out fighting my case. I get a job working at a steel factory.

I know my case isn't just gonna go away. I also know I am still gonna go back to prison. Don't forget that 15 years state I got too. It is evident that God is playing a major role in my life since, on my indictment, it doesn't have an amount of meth I got caught with and I don't have a mandatory minimum on my sentence — it is zero to twenty years.

The fact that my dope was 99.6% pure put me at a category 5, plus my extensive criminal history moved it to a category 6. This means that on the guidelines, I get way more time.

The first offer is 120 to 160 months. I can't get any less time than that due to the guidelines. I am upset but if it was state, I'd be doing 28 years.

So I sign all the papers and am about to let my lawyer turn it all over to the Federal judge to determine how much I get from the 120 to 160 months.

But I ask, "What about the money?"

My lawyer says, "What about it?"

I tell him, "It wasn't drug money, I won it at the casino."

He says, "Do you have proof?"

And I tell him, "It's on my casino gamer card."

He says, "Well the only evidence against you is the amount of money and meth you had on you. If we can prove you won the money we may be able to get a lesser charge, but we go to trial. Are you sure about the money?"

I say, "I'm 100% positive about the money. Fuck it, let's go to trial."

My next court is supposed to be my change of plea — where I plea guilty — but my lawyer says, "We have a change of plans. My client has decided to take it to trial."

I'm taken into custody that day.

I'm held in David L. Moss Detention Center, or Tulsa County Jail. This time I'm healthy, I have a little bit of money, so I'm not as bad off as I was last time.

While in jail, I meet this dude named Rick French. His mom and dad are pastors. I meet them on the video messages. They speak to me every day and encourage me to start holding Bible studies. I've never done no Bible study but I make an announcement to the pod that I would be doing one every day in cell 10 at 7pm, and everyone is welcome. That night I sit and prepare my very first Bible study. It's crazy 'cause fools actually show up, and they keep showing up every day. I felt blessed to have people ask me to pray for them. I'd tell them, "I'll pray with you!"

The district attorney gets upset that I decided to take my case to trial, so he supersedes my case, making it a more serious offense. It goes from an 841.a at zero to twenty, to an 841.b with a five year mandatory minimum — 40 years max.

I tell my lawyer, "I'll take the mandatory minimum of five years and get out of the court's hair. The DA agrees. It's like, by making my case worse, it did me a favor 'cause it took away the sentencing guidelines and the 120 to 160 months. I literally got half of that. Another blessing! I could feel God's power being shown to me in all types of different ways.

The state drops my case, killing the 28 years. I am suddenly released, and now there has been a drastic cut in the time I am gonna have to do!

April 2019

I sign for 60 months federal.

A week later I am in the federal transfer center.

Two weeks after that I land in Fairton, New Jersey FCI (Federal Correctional Instutution). It's a medium security prison.

I lost my sight 'cause it was easy now — I can honestly say I took all that God did for me for granted. It wasn't on purpose but it happened. I guess I felt I could handle it now on my own...

One day some fool tries to hit me as I am laying down in my cell. He has a lock on him, so I take it and beat his head in with it. We get told on, so now I'm in the SHU. They get me for an assault using a weapon. Now I'm to be shipped to a USP — a high security prison. While still in the SHU, I act out every day.

I "took the team" six times, which means I refused to cuff up and made the cops have to put on full body armor, throw tear gas canisters into my cell, shoot pepper spray, shoot me with the pepper ball gun, use the battering ram, then open my cell and rush into it using a big plastic shield, and slam me on the floor, dog pile me, handcuff me, then beat the shit out of me.

Once they get you out of the cell, the "fun" starts — it's "wall-to-wall therapy" meaning they literally slam you into every single wall on the way to the hard cell. Once in the hard cell you're slammed face-down and uncuffed. They cuff you in front, pull your arms up above your head and stretch you out then handcuff you to little metal rings on the metal bunk. They do the same to your feet. It's called 'four point restraint' 'cause you're cuffed at all four points.

Your whole body is on fire from the pepper spray, not to mention all the being slammed and beat up. It's literally the worst experience ever. It's 100% torture. They make you shit and piss yourself. Those cuffs ain't coming off for nothing. They literally put them on as tight as possible. I passed out from the pain several times. I don't know how I kept from going nuts but I survived it — six times!

I also took out hits for people: I'd refuse my cellys until the person with the money on his head lands in my cell, then I'd jump on him right when he comes into my cell while he is still handcuffed.

I got stuck in the SHU ten months 'cause COVID hit.

The feds shut down all transfers until further notice. I didn't pray or even think about God the whole time...

I get sent to USP Coleman 1 in Sumterville, Florida.

I'm an ex-Sureño, but that's in the state, they don't know all that in the Feds. I tell the Sureños I'm a Sureño. I'm there a couple months and I'm not feeling all the politics — that's why I pulled out in the state. I thought I was over all that but here I am once again...

I go talk to the Natives and tell them I want to be on Indian Time. I don't want to be on gang time no more.

They say, "You need to go clear that up with the Sureños first, then holla at us."

I see one Native leave the area and watch him go straight to the Sureños. I already know he's telling them I don't want to be a Sureño no more. I also know if I don't act now I'm a dead man. I can see all the way across the yard the Sureños are looking at me but they can't make a move until the Black Hand says so.

The first Sureño that approaches me, I start to stab. The cops break it up. Back to the SHU for a 224 assault.

SIS (Special Investigative Supervisors) pulls me out and asks me what happened so I tell them I'm done with gang time.

I leave Coleman 1 and I'm sent to the Oklahoma Transit Center.

September 2020

My sister Jessica tells me she needs to go get some tests done 'cause she found a lump on her breast.

November 24th, 2020

I'm in the RDAP program. I get my first introduction into K2. It's a drug that's sent via mail or in visits. It's usually sprayed on paper and when you smoke it, it fucks you up. Some is a good, intense weed high for about 45 minutes, but other types can make you have an episode and start convulsing and doing "The Exorcist."

I love it. I'm hooked. But it's expensive. I don't really got no money so I'm always having to hustle.

I get kicked out of RDAP and sent to the other side of the compound.

I get my $600 and $1,400 stimulus checks and literally smoke it all in less than three months.

One day, I'm in my cell and I smoke a piece. I don't have a celly. I start to have these crazy visions and in my head I see all the way back to my birthday in 2015, when I died.

I see myself taken out of my body. I see my face all black, the foam coming out of my mouth, my sister beating on my chest, my mom frozen by the door with the phone.

Then I am with God.

He says, "This is your life so far, all the bad you've done," and instantly every single thing I've ever done wrong is shown to me. All of the ripple effects my wrongs have created. I've done so much wrong, I've affected literally millions of people. I also know everyone — if I were to ever see one of the people from my vision today, I would know their names instantly, even if I never met them before.

God says, "This is all the good you've done," and it's the same as with the wrong I've done and just as numerous. He even show me how my good has rippled to 'cause more good. I'm amazed at the number of good deeds I've done.

He says, "I'm going to show you how special you are to me," and he puts me in the body of Jesus as Jesus to feel and see and experience all that Jesus felt during his time on earth. I feel all the pain Jesus felt to be mocked, ridiculed, betrayed and finally crucified. The emotion he felt when Judas sold him out, how it felt to be denied three times by one of his most devout followers. How even Jesus had doubts and felt forsaken and all alone, even though he knew who his Father was.

When I/Jesus was placed on the cross as the nails were driven into me physically it was torture, as they placed that crown of thorns on my head it killed me, when they gave me vinegar was the worst. But at the same time those stakes being driven into me were pure ecstasy, the crown was the softest feathers, the vinegar was the most nourishing water, when they pierced my side I said, *Finally!*

I looked at God, he knew my every thought.

He said, "He knows it's over. He's coming to the promised land to be with his Father, Kenny."

Instantly I knew! God showed me how much he loved me to watch his own son suffer for me — not only that he showed me I'm exactly like his son, no different, he said we are all Jesus.

He then walked me to the throne room and I saw Jesus sitting in his throne and God said, "Sit Kenny." There were only two thrones: God's, and the one Jesus was in. Instantly, Jesus was standing up and ushering me to the throne he was sitting in. He then got onto his knees and began washing my feet. I didn't have to voice my thought, God said, "You are my son, the same as Jesus, Kenny."

I'm in my cell. I think I may be in a drug-induced vision, but now I'm fully sober and the visions continue. I understand all this I just mentioned could be me tripping, but this next vision is hard truth:

While in Heaven, God shows me all my children. I tell God I never had no kids.

He says, "Any time you conceive a life, no matter how small, it's still a child in my eyes."

Let me remind you, all these visions are being shown to me five years after I died that day on my birthday in 2015.

I see a pretty little girl, I ask God, "How can that big one be mines?"

He says, "She's five and she has a name — it's Mya."

I say, "I never had no children that were actually born."

He says, "No Kenny, you had a child, but her mother chose to abort her."

In 2010, when Shorty suddenly disappeared on me and hid out at her mom's house, I felt she had to be hiding something. You don't just leave someone you live with and have been with for over ten years. I really didn't put too much thought into it though. Especially since I went back to prison and had my mind occupied with the shit I was facing in there. But deep inside, I knew something drastic had made her do me how she did me.

Sitting in my cell, having just revealed this, I'm shocked to the core. I don't know what to think. I'm wide awake.

God touches my head and says, "Kenny, keep me in your heart. All I ask of you is to preach my Gospel, and you don't have an option; you will fight for me."

The vision is over. I'm in my cell all alone. I'm in awe. The unbeliever in me immediately the next day has my people contact Shorty and ask her if I could have her number. It's been ten years. Last I heard, she'd married and had some babies.

The next day I call my people back and they give me her number, which is a miracle in and of itself.

So I call Shorty.

She picks up on the first ring.

"What do you want, Kenny?"

I hear the annoyance and anger in her voice.

I say, "I only got one question."

She says, "What?"

I ask her, "Did you abort my child?"

Instantly she breaks down in hysterics.

"Did you follow me? Did the doctor tell you? Were you stalking me?" All sorts of questions of that nature. She's also sobbing hysterically. I was with this female over ten years and never once did I see her this uncomposed.

I tell her what God showed me and then she says, "I never told a soul, Kenny. It's been eating me up for ten years. I'm so sorry but I couldn't have your child, Kenny."

I told her, "It's okay. She's in heaven and she's beautiful. I forgive you."

Then I hang up the phone and go into my cell and cry and ask God to forgive me. He tells me she needed to get it out too, and now we can both heal.

Everything else could have been speculation but the revelation I just told you about is all facts. Undeniable truth...

I never told any of my family that last story. Actually, the only person that knows any of it is my celly.

You would have figured that after all I've been show by God, I'd be different, but I keep neglecting his blessing. It's like jewels being handed to a child. I still continue to avoid His calling and I once again find myself back in the SHU in Coleman 2.

Then I find out my sister has full blown stage 3 breast cancer. I don't even know how to take it.

My grandmother dies as well, then so does my uncle George. I don't even cry. They both lived full, happy lives. My only sadness is knowing my dad was taking care of them both in the same house and he is real old school so I know their deaths affected him profoundly.

But the possibility of losing my sister, it cauterized all my emotions, leaving me with no feeling except anger. And my anger is only a one person — God.

I feel He knows He can do anything to me personally and I'll maintain, I'll suffer, I'll endure pain. But now it seems this fool ain't playing fair. I feel he's affecting my loved ones just to get at me! It's personal now.

I know I can't win. My sister has never been anything but a source of love, protection and comfort. Never done no drugs, raising three great children, been a loyal and loving wife. What did she ever do to deserve this, besides having a stubborn-ass brother who keeps rebuking God?

How could God allow this to happen? Why would He allow this to happen? He knows me 100%, he knows it's only gonna push me away — my faith was solid but it was now in jeopardy. I'm just a man, I survive off of instinct.

I'm in a living Hell. It's not looking good at all.

I fight my next two cellies, wind up pissing off the officer and getting all my stuff taken and moved to the very back cell in the unit, then losing my third celly who I actually liked. He himself was battling his own demons and was trying to get back in the good graces of his baby mama so he could speak to his daughter, and besides not being able to talk to his child, he had to deal with just being convicted of a crime that ostracized him from most of his people, not to mention the 30 years he was sentenced to at 85%. I guess watching him do all it took to talk to his child gave me something to root for. Watching him deal with it also gave me something to focus on.

So I just left all that my sister was dealing with in God's hands.

Like it says in the Bible, "Ask and be assured."

In Matthew 7:7, in God's own words, "Ask and you shall receive."

So I asked in accordance with this verse and didn't dwell on it anymore. I guess in that action I finally displayed my faith, even if it was just a mustard seed.

I focused on finishing my book and waiting until November for my phone sanction to fall off.

My celly winds up getting the officer to move him with me into the back of the unit. We both do music and write so in that, we bond. My celly looks out just 'cause by nature he's a good fool.

He tells me, "I don't look out for you 'cause you're my celly, Kenny. I do it because it's you."

This is my dude. I can say, aside from one of my other cellys, I have zero friends. I'm cool with that 'cause these fools is family. I don't need friends when I got family.

My celly and I are talking, he shares with me some stuff that happened to his mom. He says it killed him inside and he ain't been able to shed no tears for what happened to her or ever since. That fucks me up 'cause he's like me, a real deep dude. He been through some shit too. So we also bond through our ordeals and the struggles we've survived.

My celly knows all about my sister and her cancer 'cause I've told him over and over that I need to finish this book, because it is for her and it's crazy how shit comes together 'cause the writing of my book is the easy part — I still need to type it out to make it truly readable. What do you know, my celly types like a beast and has literally typed out every word since page 62 of my book. Add to that, he can read all my writing.

I tell him, "I need to finish this book 'cause my sister may not be around much longer and I want her to read it."

He understands and works on it every day and gives me insight on it. He not only hears it after I write it, he then types it and hears it after one more time when I read to him what he's just typed. He's literally heard every word in my story no less than three times.

He been talking to his baby mom every day, so the first month he can't spare too many of the 500 minutes they allow us for phone time every month, nor do I want to ask him to sacrifice some for me, but he still does, and he offers — I don't even have to ask.

I call my baby sister Amanda a couple of times. My uncle just passed in June and the family took it well, and she tells me that Jessica is still being strong and just taking things day-to-day.

My celly runs out of minutes. I see him every day of the two weeks he needs to wait to revalidate, and he's going through it, stressing. He wants to sleep all day. He even says, "I just want to get to the 16th so I can call babymama and keep moving forward so I can finally talk to my daughter."

The two weeks finally pass. He jumps on the phone.

Later in the cell I ask about the phone call and he says, "Babymama got a job. I can only call after 6pm or on the weekend," and I know it fucks him up 'cause it fucked me up. Then to top it all off, he calls on the weekend and she tells him the same thing. I guess she gots a new boyfriend. It fucks him up but I guess he feels, *What can I do?* At any rate, he has a lot of free phone time, which is good for me.

One random Thursday on August 4th, 2022, I call my sister Jessica.

To be honest, I am a little glad that I lost my phone privileges because I can't take calling every day just to hear her suffering. I can hear it in her voice, and to hear someone who's always been the strong one talk and say things unbecoming of her nature is very depressing.

But my celly asks me, "You want to make a call?" and I say, "Yes."

So I call Jessica, and before that, the few times I've tried to call, she didn't pick up. My baby sister said it's 'cause she was in a bad place. But today, on August 4th, she answers on the first ring.

"Hey you!"

I can hear it in her voice. It's 11:30 in the morning. I'm on the phone with her waiting for them to call us out to lunch.

I say, "Hey, what's up?"

She says, "Nothing, just home. How are you?"

And I tell her, I'm good."

I wasn't even gonna bring up the cancer but then she says, "Oh, I'm cancer free!"

Hearing my sister tell me that she's cancer free, I'm almost at a loss for words. It's like everything came full circle, all the bullshit, all the blessings, all the chances I've been given, it's showing me how powerful I am to have all His personal attention, how special I am to Him. I know I can't take this blessing for granted.

This entire book is meant to be, since the very beginning, everything has been provided to me from the first moment I decided to write it. I was provided all the paper I needed as well as an unlimited supply of sharpened pencils to the point where I never had to sharpen a single pencil. I got the time and the peace and quiet I needed to focus on my writing, I had numerous cellys that heard and proofread my manuscript. I was even able to get my hands on a typing wheel in a facility that doesn't sell nor provide them, the countless ink ribbons I needed to actually produce this type-out body of work, to once again, the free paper.

At first I was typing out my book, and then another blessing — I get a celly who's a typist! Not to mention in here it's $7.50 per 50 copies and I've been able to make a copy of each page of my 250 page book, and on top of all this, I'm indigent. Another blessing, I'm on phone restriction but I was provided free phone calls by my celly. It's all meant to be.

I look out for my celly all the way to the dining hall but can't find him, and we don't sit together at lunch. I finally find him when we get back from chow, and I tell him to come talk to me in the cell. I can't wait to tell him how God had blessed my family, and I can tell that he doesn't know what I want to talk to him about.

I sit back on my rack and he stands in front of me and asks me what the deal is.

I tell him, "I just got off the phone with my sister before we went to chow," and I pause, caught up in the rising tide of my emotion. "She just told me she's cancer free."

My vision blurs as my eyes fill with tears.

"What?" my celly shouts. "That's amazing bro are you serious?" and as I recount to him just what my sister told me on the phone, I see fresh tears in his eyes.

He told me he hadn't been able to shed a tear in longer than he could remember, but today we are crying together, moved by the awesome power of God.

At first I say, "I need to finish my book so my sister can get it before anything happens to her," but now I say, "I want to finish my book so my sister can read it."

It may sound simple to you, but the significance of that statement is enormous. I won't like, I didn't have an ending to my book for a long time, but I always wanted it to be my testimony, however unconventional it may be. At the end of my testimony, you won't find me on top of the world or even living a blessed life. I'm still in the same place, writing these words at the desk in my cell in a Federal prison, but my spirit has been shifted, my heart has been touched, my faith has been reinforced. I truly feel that being a man of faith is all about the way you react to the circumstances you face. I feel like the dedication to get my book finished manifested the blessings and overall lessons God had in store for me.

I think the lesson is that "God loves us as we are." He has tests for us just like he has gifts and blessings for us — if you're blessed enough to be tested by God, well it speaks for itself.

Just look at Job. The restoration of my sister's health is not a miracle, it's not even a blessing, it was simply God's will! I 100% know and believe all God showed me in my vision.

I know why he told me to preach his gospel. It's because I'm a very talkative individual. I have a way with words so he wanted me to utilize the gifts he gave to me. This book is my greatest accomplishment to date, and it's also my testimony. That means that my greatest accomplishment is God-inspired. The greatest news I've ever heard was, "I'm cancer free," and it was also God-inspired. So if I could sum this whole book up, I'd say the message in it is that, in the words of Barbara Brown Taylor in her book, 'An Altar in the World':

"What if the gravel of a parking lot looks as promising to God as the floorboards of a church? What if a lost soul strikes God as infinitely more reachable than a lifelong believer? What if God can drop a ladder absolutely anywhere, with no regard for the religious standards developed by those who have made it their business to know the way to God?"

I know I'm exactly that lifelong lost soul and that the ladder God dropped was this book, because every chapter written to completion was another rung I climbed in order to reach Heaven and see the full glory of God.

I'm not nowhere near perfect. I know if you're reading my book you may think, *How can he say this or talk the way he does if this is a testimony?* Well the Bible says come as you are!

I can say that my future is still in limbo, but I can also say that I still have a future that includes my freedom! Amen.

I've always wanted to be a rapper, but why not a minister? It's not always the messenger, but the message being delivered. I see myself continuing to preach God's gospel, either with my book or verbally, whatever God expects of me. I know I will never take another blessing for granted, and I only hope that in time, I will grow to be a better person.

I also encourage and invite any help and constructive criticism from anyone with something positive to say to me. All prayers are greatly appreciated and I will gladly listen to any and all forms of advice either on spiritual matters, worldly concerns, or artistic expression.

Also, anyone who has any questions pertaining to the text are freely welcomed to ask and may be thoroughly assured that I will receive you warmly and will give you an honest and sincere response.

Keep in mind that the writing of my book all took place in my cell. It was all written with a heavy heart and a mind full of chaos, with no outside help, no editor, no one to aid and assist me on how to write such a book, aside from the other books I've read in my life. It was not written to be a source of entertainment, it's always been my intention to give my family an idea of what happened with me, where I went, and who I am. It was only later that through receiving my blessings it turned out to be my testimony.

All glory be to God, even though, as a man accomplishing my greatest feat, I want to take the credit for having done the work to complete my task. But in truth, none of this would be at all possible without God. All my talents are God-given, all the emotion in my words are only because I always kept the spirit of God within even at my darkest. God didn't bless us with the spirit of fear.

A perfect love casts out fear.

End

Made in the USA
Las Vegas, NV
24 November 2024

11682692R00070